Gendered Choices

Lifelong Learning Book Series

VOLUME 15

Aims & Scope
"Lifelong Learning" has become a central theme in education and community development. Both international and national agencies, governments and educational institutions have adopted the idea of lifelong learning as a major theme in the coming years. They realize that it is only by getting people committed to the idea of education both life-wide and lifelong that the goals of economic advancement, social emancipation and personal growth will be attained.

The *Lifelong Learning Book Series* aims to keep scholars and professionals informed about and abreast of current developments and to advance research and scholarship in the domain of Lifelong Learning. It further aims to provide learning and teaching materials, serve as a forum for scholarly and professional debate and offer a rich fund of resources for researchers, policy-makers, scholars, professionals and practitioners in the field.

The volumes in this international Series are multi-disciplinary in orientation, polymathic in origin, range and reach, and variegated in range and complexity. They are written by researchers, professionals and practitioners working widely across the international arena in lifelong learning and are orientated towards policy improvement and educational betterment throughout the life cycle.

For further volumes:
http://www.springer.com/series/6227

Sue Jackson • Irene Malcolm • Kate Thomas
Editors

Gendered Choices

Learning, Work, Identities in Lifelong Learning

 Springer

Editors
Dr. Sue Jackson
Birkbeck Institute for Lifelong Learning
Birkbeck University of London
26 Russell Square
WC1B 5DQ London, UK
s.jackson@bbk.ac.uk

Kate Thomas
Schools and Colleges Partnership Service
University of the West of England
Frenchay Campus, Coldharbour Lane
BS16 1QD Bristol, UK
kate2.thomas@uwe.ac.uk

Dr. Irene Malcolm
School of Education, Social Work
and Community Education
University of Dundee, Nethergate
Dundee, DD1 4HN, UK
i.z.malcolm@dundee.ac.uk

ISBN 978-94-007-0646-0   e-ISBN 978-94-007-0647-7
DOI 10.1007/978-94-007-0647-7
Springer Dordrecht Heidelberg London New York

Library of Congress Control Number: 2011921330

Cover design: eStudio Calamar S.L.

Printed on acid-free paper

Springer is part of Springer Science+Business Media (www.springer.com)

Editorial by Series Editors

This volume is a further production in the *Lifelong Learning Book Series* published by Springer. In previous volumes we have followed a set of agenda for future research and development, analysis and expansion, strategies and guidelines in the field. It is still widely accepted that the domain of lifelong learning offers a rich and fertile ground for setting out and summarising, comparing and criticising the heterogeneous scope and remit of policies and proposals in its different constitutive parts. Certainly the scholars, researchers and education policy-makers with whom we have discussed this matter seem to agree with us that each of the themes to be found and identified in the Lifelong Learning domain merit a separate volume on its own – to say nothing of the other possibilities that a more extended analysis of the field might further generate and develop.

This volume is an outcome of the work of our colleagues Sue Jackson, Irene Malcolm and Kate Thomas. They examine the impulse towards and agenda of lifelong learning from a feminist point of view and the perspective of "non-traditional learners". The authors are concerned to alert their readers to the point that lifelong learning policies, structures and activities can become a forum for "academic" women in "the academy" to work alongside women participants in the workplace and in educational institutions and social associations to press forward a feminism that promotes all women's interests. Their argument is that feminism has a responsibility to offer useful solutions that take into account the realities of all women, maintaining coherence between theory and practice.

They lead us in this direction by demonstrating, through concrete examples, the importance of taking note of the point that many of the choices that are open to women in developing their desire to engage in lifelong learning activities are largely silent on the importance of addressing the issues of gender and to that extent tend to militate against the emancipation which might otherwise be promised and made available through such activities. The arguments advanced in this volume are directed towards the end of arguing for and demonstrating how the experiences expressed in the "voices" of women and non-traditional learners may throw light upon ways in which all lifelong learners can enjoy equal emancipation and benefit from their enmeshment with the work and insights of women in the academy in an interactive, participatory dialogue, where both can undertake and achieve a deep educational emancipation. The present work presents arguments to show why and how this might be brought about; it does so by concentrating on and distilling lessons from the experiences of individuals with such emancipatory interests, working together in dialogic interchange in ways that can function to promote and expand resistance to the hegemony claimed by many of such writers to be found in most current policies of lifelong learning, particularly in its globalised form.

Gendered Choices: Learning, Work and Identities in Lifelong Learning brings together insights and narratives of a group of women scholars, who address issues of feminism and social inclusion within the framework of adult education and learning throughout life. The authors discuss the experiences and insights of feminists in adult education, among them them many non-academic women, who, they argue, have been historically silenced from the feminist mainstream discourse and are now claiming their voice. The work is particularly concerned to emphasize the following:

- That the field of gender studies is currently under-represented in lifelong learning literature
- The role of gender as a shaper of participation in and experience of lifelong learning
- The importance of gendered choices across the lifespan and personal and professional identities
- The need for gender(ed) perspectives on work-based/work-related learning and the labour market
- The importance of developing international comparisons and the significance of globalisation in the text.

This volume assumes the standpoint of feminist epistemology and ontology and seeks to provide a rigorous theoretical analysis of feminist thought and real women's lives. It seeks to draw a connection between the lack of gendered choices and marginalised women's workplace location, social participation, dialogically oriented adult education and solidarity. These the authors see as key elements in the creation of personal meaning and social transformation in situations in which their workplace and life choices can be given value and significance. Grounded in a dialogic educational perspective, the authors' insightful work and the voices of the women with whom they have worked is based upon the realisation that the "personal is the political" and that praxis will serve to call into question and resist many of the 'taken-for-granted' assumptions with which globalised lifelong learning policies, practices and institutions have been hitherto normalised. The style, tenor and purpose of the arguments contained and set out in it this volume make for a unique, engaging, accessible reading experience. This book will prove to be of great value to professors, researchers, graduate students, teachers and teacher trainers with a strong interest in Adult Education, Lifelong Learning and Gender Studies. Above all it is a work that should be defined as required reading for all those engaged in promoting and providing lifelong learning activities in workplace, home and society.

Sue, Irene and Kate have done all of us a signal service in their writing of this book. They have shown us the experiences and contributions of women making choices and decisions about the valued elements in their lives and how these may contribute to de- and re-constructing educational and social practices and theories. These, and the policies emanating from them, should in future embody lessons arising from and validated through women's experiences of learning, working and developing a sense of identity in all aspects of learning throughout and across the lifespan. Their work shows how women may in future make better and more informed decisions on the pathways and explorations of their own future learning by articulating their own voices for themselves and pursuing their own interests and needs for growth. These authors tell us that it is vital to listen to women's voices in explaining and exploring their problems of choice; for they have much to teach us.

It also shows us how institutions must take the interests of such learners seriously and seek to open up and ameliorate their learning options offered to all learners indifferently in all the structures and lifelong learning activities they provide by incorporating their own contributions of thought and language into more traditional approaches and, by effective dialogue and learning activities, seeking to change both for the better. Finally their analysis locates all these arguments and explorations in a thoroughly informed, complex and sophisticated set of theoretical considerations bearing upon, underpinning and implicitly or explicitly shaping all such initiatives and undertakings. This is where the experience of the authors, their gifts and abilities with interests and concerns of the "non-formal" students with whom they conducted their research are so fruitful for and helpful to the counter-hegemonic and wider emancipatory agenda of lifelong learning.

We are pleased and excited that this highly important work helps carry forward the agenda of the Springer Series on Lifelong Learning. We trust that its readers will find it as stimulating, thought-provoking and controversial as we have found it and we commend it with great confidence to all those working in this field. We are sure that this further volume in the Springer Series will provide the wide range of constituencies working in the domain of lifelong learning with a rich range of new material for their consideration and further investigation. We believe that it will encourage their continuing critical thinking, research and development, academic and scholarly production and individual, institutional and professional progress.

November 2010   David Aspin and Judith Chapman

Contents

About the Editors

Prof. Sue Jackson Sue left school at 15, and began her educational journey with an 'A' level at her local further education college, soon after the birth of her first child. With the birth of her second child, she made the step into higher education as a mature student with the Open University, and went on to take a master's in women's studies, and then a PhD in women and education. She began her academic career teaching 'fresh start', access and new opportunities for women courses at adult education centres and further education colleges before developing her career in higher education. Sue has been working at Birkbeck, University of London, since 2001, when she was appointed to a lectureship. She is now professor of lifelong learning and gender, pro-vice-master for learning and teaching, and director of Birkbeck Institute for Lifelong Learning. She has been a convenor of the Women in Lifelong Learning Network of the Universities Association for Lifelong Learning (UALL). This publication is therefore born out of Sue's personal as well as her professional experiences.

Dr. Irene Malcolm Irene is a lecturer in education at the University of Dundee where she teaches on the masters programme in applied professional studies and undertakes doctoral supervision. She has spent her career teaching in post-compulsory education, in further education and in higher education. She has also worked as a field researcher on a research project funded by the Economic and Social Research Council (ESRC) which studied the learning biographies of adults. Through this project and through her doctoral studies of women in the new economy she developed her interest in women's learning at home and in work.

Kate Thomas Kate worked in book publishing and broadcasting before finding her way into higher education through temporary work. She moved from organising other people's courses at the University of Manchester, to become programme manager of a European Science Foundation (ESF) project at the University of Bristol, training adults to become support workers for disabled people. During this period she gained a postgraduate certificate in teaching in lifelong learning from Birkbeck, University of London. For the past four years she has been based at the University of the West of England as a Progression co-ordinator for the

Western Vocational Lifelong Learning Network, focusing on project work and research into vocational progression to higher education and the experiences of Foundation degree learners and staff. Kate recently completed an MA in education with the Open University and is currently Convenor of the UALL (Universities Association of Lifelong Learning) Women in Lifelong Learning Network.

About the Authors

Penny Burke Penny's first career was as a classical ballet dancer. After the birth of her first son, she longed for intellectual engagement and discovered an access to higher education course. Penny went on to study sociology and developed a passionate commitment to women's access to higher education. She explored issues of women's access further through an MA in women's studies, and then went on to gain her PhD in 2001. Penny started a lectureship at the Institute of Education in 2002, just after the publication of her first book *Accessing Education: Effectively Widening Participation*. Her interest in masculinity and educational participation grew out of her experiences of mothering three sons and wanting to talk back to discourses that oversimplified gender and access to higher education. In 2008, Penny received the Higher Education Academy's prestigious National Teaching Fellowship Award. She is the Access and Widening Participation Network Leader for the Society for Research in Higher Education. Penny is now professor of education at Roehampton University.

Carrie Cable Carrie began her teaching career in Nigeria in 1974 and then taught in London schools in the 1980s and 1990s. Her specialist field is English as an additional language (EAL) and she led a team of peripatetic teachers and bilingual assistants and was involved in advisory work before deciding on a career change in 1998. She is now a senior lecturer in education at the Open University involved in developing courses for teachers, teaching assistants and early years practitioners and researching the impact of study on practice. She has contributed to national training and development initiatives in the field of EAL and has authored and edited papers and books on EAL, bilingual practitioners, supporting children's learning and professionalism. She is currently director of a research project funded by the Department for Children, Schools and Families (DCSF) examining the learning and teaching of languages in primary schools.

Leona M. English Leona is a professor of adult education and chair of the Department of Adult Education at St. Francis Xavier University in Antigonish, Nova Scotia, Canada. She pursued a traditional route through higher education, going straight from high school to earn a BA and BEd from Memorial University. Having taught high school, she earned a master's degree from the University of Toronto. This was followed by an EdD from Columbia University, NYC, after she spent several years in curriculum and professional development work. Leona is past president of the Canadian Association for the Study of Adult Education and editor of the International Encyclopedia of Adult Education. Her main research area is gender and learning especially with women in the nonprofit sector. Her website on gender is located at www.stfx.ca/people/lenglish.

Jan Etienne Jan Etienne is a graduate of the School for Policy Studies, University of Bristol and teaches Sociology in the School of Social Sciences, History and Philosophy at Birkbeck, University of London. She is co-author of 'Beyond the home: informal learning and community practice for older women' and has a particular interest in lifelong learning and first generation African Caribbean women. She is the 2008 recipient of the Michael Stephens Award for her research into women learning later and is a former local elected member in the London Borough of Brent. She stood for Parliament in the 2005 UK General Election.

Rosalind Foskett Ros Foskett started her career teaching geography in schools and further education followed by a period of self-employment as a curriculum consultant. She has worked in higher education (HE) since 1990, firstly in a college of HE (variously as lecturer, programme manager and dean), and then at the University of Southampton where she held several senior roles including associate dean for enterprise and innovation in the Faculty of Law, Arts and Social Sciences. She is currently deputy vice chancellor and professor of HE at the University of Worcester. Her teaching specialism is in post-compulsory education and training. She has also been involved in a number of research projects at Southampton and Worcester. These have included participation in higher education, partnerships between universities and business, career and education decision-making, and leadership and management capacity building in African universities.

Alison Fuller Prior to joining the School of Education at the University of Southampton in 2004, Alison Fuller held research and academic posts at the Universities of Lancaster and Leicester. Alison is now head of the Lifelong and Work-Related Learning Research Centre at Southampton. Her main research and publishing interests are in the fields of education—work transitions; vocational education and apprenticeship; workplace learning; lifelong learning and changing patterns of adult participation in education. Alison's most recent book (co-authored with Alan Felstead, Lorna Unwin and Nick Jewson), *Improving Working as Learning*, was published by Routledge in 2009.

Gill Goodliff Gill originally qualified as a residential social worker and until the birth of her first child, worked in family centres in London run by the National Children's Home. She began teaching adults—parents and childminders—in community-based education in inner London Boroughs, and when her youngest child started school in 1990, she returned to study at the University of London, Institute of Education. Whilst working as a lecturer in early years in a college of further education in Hertfordshire, she completed her master's in education. Gill has been working at the Open University since 2004 developing courses for early years practitioners and re-searching the impact of study on practice and professional identity. She is now a senior lecturer and head of Awards for Early Years and completing doctoral studies exploring young children's spirituality.

Clem Herman Clem Herman is a senior lecturer in the Department of Communication and Systems at the Open University in the UK. She has worked for over 25 years as an educator, practi-tioner and researcher to support women in ICT and other science, engineering and technology sectors. Before joining the Open University, she was the director of the Women's Electronic Village Hall (WEVH) in Manchester pioneering the use of ICTs to empower women and as a tool to combat social exclusion. Clem is currently running an award-winning online course for women returners and her most recent research has been about the impact of career breaks for women in European science, engineering and technology (SET) companies.

Barbara Hodgson Barbara is senior lecturer in ducational technology at the Open University (OU) with a particular interest in teaching and learning in distance higher education. She currently directs the postgraduate teaching programme in online and distance education, and works with colleagues on the development of their practice through a postgraduate certificate in academic practice. She has worked on the development of a wide range of science, science education, women's studies and educational technology courses at the OU. Throughout her career she has had a research and implementation/intervention interest in gender and science at all levels of education. Most recently her research has been concerned with women's careers in science, engineering and technology (SET) and, as a partner in the UK Resource Centre for Women in SET, she has been working to help women return after career breaks.

Suzanne Hyde Suzanne began her paid working life as a youth worker before moving into adult and community education, and has now spent over 20 years working across the community and voluntary sector, adult education, further and higher education sectors. She currently works between the universities of Brighton and Sussex as a lecturer and researcher. Areas of interest include narrative and life history approaches and participatory action research methodologies. The focus of her research has included workplace learning and employer engagement, widening participation into higher education, mature student experience and issues affecting young people labelled as NEET (not in employment, education or training).

Brenda Johnston Brenda Johnston is a senior research fellow in the School of Education at the University of Southampton. Her particular areas of interest and expertise lie in the fields of higher education pedagogy, especially criticality, academic writing and assessment. She is also interested in issues of widening participation and graduate employment.

Gill Kirkup Dr. Gill Kirkup is a senior lecturer in educational technology at the Institute of Educational Technology, Open University, UK. Between 2008 and 2011 she is seconded part-time as head of research, data and policy to the UK Resources Centre for Women in Science Engineering. She is a fellow of the Higher Education Academy and a member of the Association of Learning Technologies and the Fawcett Society. She would classify herself as a feminist educator and researcher. Her main research interests lie in the complex relationship between gender and technology, and learning technologies in particular, and she has published widely in these areas.

Narjes Mehdizadeh Narjes developed her interest in higher education and lifelong learning through her involvement in a research project in the Centre for Research in Lifelong Learning (CRLL) in the Glasgow Caledonian University as well as her master's and doctoral studies. Her current area of research interest is an exploration of the significance of welfare for women's experience of citizenship and the impact of contested values in one area of welfare—childcare—in Iran. Publications include journal articles about adjustment problems of international students as well as reconciliation of work and family in the international journals, in addition to a number of conference papers in the UK. She is currently a member of the research team in the research project of the Economic and Social Research Council (ESRC) entitled 'Social Policy and Religion in the Middle East: Beyond the Rentier State, Toward a New Ethic of Welfare'.

Linda Miller Dr. Linda Miller is a senior research fellow at the Institute for Employment Studies. She undertook two of the studies that contributed to the general formal investigation of the Equal Opportunities Commission (EOC) into occupational gender segregation and she has examined factors affecting women's and men's choice of vocational and academic qualifications and careers, in particular focusing on the factors that affect women's decisions to enter science, engineering and technology (SET). In 2007–2008 she was an advisor to the EU project analysing the impact of national policies on the entry of women into SET, and in 2002 contributed to Baroness Greenfield's review of women in SET. Her more recent work has examined the position of women in London's economy and the role of coaching in helping women move into board-level positions.

Ursula Murray Ursula Murray joined Birkbeck just over 10 years ago. She tutors courses on public sector management and local government, voluntary sector studies, gender and management, and lifelong learning. Previously she has worked in both the voluntary sector undertaking action research projects around local economic change and women's employment and subsequently as a senior manager in local government co-ordinating policy and commissioning roles. She has an MSc in group relations, organisations and society from the University of the West of England (UWE), Bristol (2001) and completed her PhD at the Complexity and Management Centre, University of Hertfordshire Business School in 2006. Her research using narrative and psychosocial methodologies explored the meaning of the public sector and a public service ethos in the context of current restructuring and change.

Esther Oliver Esther is 'Ramon y Cajal' Researcher at the Department of Sociological Theory, University of Barcelona where she completed her doctorate in sociology in 2003. From 2006 to 2008 she was a postdoctoral fellow (visiting academic) at the University of Warwick in the UK. Esther's research interests are focused on gender issues and social and educational inequalities. She is member of CREA (Centre of Research on Social and Educational Inequalities) research centre at the University of Barcelona where she is now the main researcher of the RTD (Research and Technology Development) project: 'The Mirage of Upward Social Mobility and the Socialization of Gender Violence' funded by the Spanish Ministry of Science. Esther's work is published in international journals, and she has recently completed another work in English language: 'Opening Schools to All Women: Efforts to Overcome Gender Violence in Spain', published in the *British Journal of Sociology of Education* (E. Oliver, M. Soler & R. Flecha, 2009).

Karen Paton Karen Paton was the research associate on the project: 'Non-participation in Higher Education: Decision-Making as an Embedded Social Practice', funded by the Economic and Social Research Council (ESRC), conducted at the University of Southampton. Prior to working at Southampton, she was a researcher at the University of Bristol.

Gill Scott Gill Scott is emeritus professor of social policy at Glasgow Caledonian University. She was director of the University's Scottish Poverty Information Unit, a policy and research unit, for 10 years before retiring in 2007. She acted as external adviser in 2003–2006 to the development of the anti-poverty strategy of the Scottish Government's Cabinet and to the UK Parliament's Work and Pensions Committee Inquiry on Child Poverty 2007–2008. She is currently specialist expert on women, enterprise and economic development to the European Commission's URBACT programme. Relevant publications include *Exploring Social Policy in Scotland* (co-editor, 2004, Policy Press), *Women in Local Partnerships* (2000, Scottish Executive) and 'Gender, Poverty and Wealth' in T. Ridge and S. Wright (eds.) *Understanding Inequality, Poverty and Wealth* (2008, Policy Press).

Anita Walsh Anita is a senior lecturer in work-based learning and an expert in designing academic programmes which are based on people's professional activities in the workplace. She took her first degree as a mature student when her younger daughter started school, and her studies in the social sciences awakened her interest in gender. Her subsequent PhD focused on the British Women's Liberation Movement and the politics of experience. Anita has been interested in the relationship between experience and learning since the early 1990s, and her current work considers experiential learning outside the university. She defines herself as a practitioner-researcher and draws on her life and work experience to inform both her practice and her research. Anita's longstanding interest in gender has been integrated with her active interest in the role of experience in both learning and the development of professional expertise.

Elizabeth Whitelegg Elizabeth Whitelegg is a senior lecturer at the Open University. She is an experienced researcher in science education and science communication and was co-principle investigator on the Invisible Witnesses project (www.open.ac.uk/invisible-witnesses) which examined gendered representation of girls and women in science, technology, engineering and mathematics (STEM) on UK television. She is an expert in the participation of girls in physics, and co-authored a major report on this commissioned by the Institute of Physics. She is the inaugural director of the OU's science short course programme; leads the master's course in science teaching and learning; and is an author on the master's course in science communication.

Chapter 1
Introduction

Sue Jackson, Irene Malcolm and Kate Thomas

> Building a world in which women are not subordinated requires
> the development of a world view in which this is possible.
> (Aaron and Walby 1991, p. 1)
>
> Being oppressed means the absence of choices.
> (hooks 2000, p. 5)

This book is about choices: the choices we are able to make, whether or not in situations of our own choosing, and the choices we are not. It is about the gendered choices that affect our engagement with lifelong learning, including learning at work, and what that means for our identities. It has become difficult to write about 'choice' in recent times, with discussions of individual choice located in the neo-liberal discourses of market forces. The current language of policy is based within an individualised notion of personal choice, which is constructed as rational and equally available to all. However, whilst 'choice' has been a mantra in education policy, the issue of the gendering of choice has been relatively neglected, although 'choices' continue to be gendered (and classed, racialised and sexualised). Nevertheless, discussions of apparently neutral and rational choices have become embedded in discourses, ideologies and policy developments of lifelong learning. This book aims to deconstruct such discussions and develop a different world view. The book reflects a variety of approaches to gender sensitive research in a range of contexts. It captures the voices of women as authors, researchers and practitioners as well as subjects in the contemporary field of lifelong learning.

The late twentieth/early twenty-first century has been heralded as a new age in lifelong learning. Lifelong learning policies have risen to prominence in recent years, and are high on the educational, economic and social agendas of many governments (including in Europe, Japan and other Asian countries, North America and Australia) as well as of international organisations such as the OECD, UNESCO

S. Jackson (✉)
Birkbeck Institute for Lifelong Learning, Birkbeck University of London,
26 Russell Square, WC1B 5DQ London, UK
e-mail: s.jackson@bbk.ac.uk

S. Jackson et al. (eds.), *Gendered Choices,* Lifelong Learning Book Series 15,
DOI 10.1007/978-94-007-0647-7_1, © Springer Science+Business Media B.V. 2011

and the World Bank. Although 'lifelong learning' is considered to be a compara-
tively new concept, it has existed in different guises and been differently named
across a century and more, including as recurrent, popular, continuing, liberal and
lifelong education (Jackson 2010).

Towards the end of the twentieth century, lifelong learning became a catchphrase
for many governments across the developed world. For example, both Canada
(OECD 2002) and Australia (Australian National Training Authority 1998) were
engaged throughout the 1990s in developing adult education and training within a
lifelong learning agenda with a strong focus on skills; whilst in Japan, an act to promote lifelong learning was passed in 1990, providing the systematic encouragement
of active participation of all people in lifelong learning (Fuwa 2009). In Europe,
1996 was declared as a year of lifelong learning and in 2000 a 10-year Mission
was set for Europe to develop lifelong learning to become the most competitive
and dynamic knowledge-based economy in the world (European Council 2000). In
Britain, the first Minister for Lifelong Learning was appointed in 1997. Although
the UK Government's early policy papers (see, e.g. DfEE 1988) argued that learning has a wide contribution, including enabling people to engage in community
participation, one of its prime benefits was seen as economic, with an emphasis on
the links between education, employment and economic prosperity.

Lifelong learning has been seen as a solution to a host of local and global problems (Jackson 2009). It is claimed that lifelong learning enhances social capital and
promotes active citizenship and social cohesion (see, e.g. Schuller 2001), thus increasing community participation and developing opportunities for disadvantaged
groups and individuals. However, such individuals are also expected to make the
most of the policy developments which have led to a growth in vocational education and training, to benefit themselves, their nation states and the global economy.

Current discourses and policies show major and sometimes conflicting messages. Lifelong learning is seen as a key to self-improvement (including economic
improvement), as a means for national prosperity, and as contributing to social
good. Yet for most countries in the developed world, the lifelong learning and widening participation agenda is one that has been primarily concerned with skills-
based vocational learning. There is an assumption that the more training, skills and
qualifications people have, the more likely they are to be in work, with little or no
discussion of the ways in which the workplace is gendered, classed and racialised.
Despite the European Union's pursuit and subsequent adoption from 1993 of 'gender mainstreaming', within the policies of lifelong learning there is little consideration of the relationship between gender and the knowledge-economy and even
less concern regarding social class, race and ethnicity (Webb et al. 2006). Although
rarely explicit, "policies and practices of lifelong learning, in very different contexts
and with different groups of learners, are gendered in their construction and effects"
(Leathwood and Francis 2006, p. 2).

This publication addresses issues of gendered learning in different contexts across
the (adult) life span during the first decade of the twenty-first century. In doing so, it
fills a major gap in the literature. There is currently little work on gendered learning
which considers a range of learning contexts, including not only formal and informal

learning but also work-based learning, which is central to current policy regarding lifelong learning. In addition, for women the public/private spaces of work and home are often conflated, an issue frequently ignored in texts exploring lifelong and work-based learning. This book explores some of these critical issues through the multiple and fractured identities which constitute gendered lives. It brings together key aspects of adult learning from a gender perspective, including widening participation, work-place learning and informal pathways. It goes beyond conventional settings for adult learning to consider the way learning is gendered in the workplace and in voluntary and community sector organisations. Adult learning sits within a shifting landscape of educational policy which is cross-cut by the skills agenda, funding policies, new qualifications and the widening participation debate. Gender is central to these developments and shapes participation in and experiences of lifelong learning.

The book addresses issues of gender within in the growing skills-based approach to lifelong learning, career decisions, professional identities and informal networks. In this introductory chapter we focus on some of the key themes, returning to others in the concluding chapter: the themes, although presented separately should be read not as discrete sub-sections but rather as indications of some of the complexities of the issues and debates which inter/weave their way through the book.

Neo-liberalism

At the level of macro analysis, a significant theme throughout the book is the inter-action of lifelong learning policies with broader policy discourses, including those informed by neo-liberalism. Critique of such discourses and a consideration of miti-gating measures are essential, not just to address limitations placed on women, but to overcome false gender divisions that affect identity possibilities for women and men. While the chapters reflect diverse learning cultures, they also reveal the ways in which learning experiences are embedded in, and interact with broader political, economic and social circumstances. The present volume brings fresh insights to issues of gender and lifelong learning by positioning neo-liberalism in a way that shows it to be complex and differentiated. For example, in Chap. 4 we see how the interviewees' discourses of aspiration draw on neo-liberal notions, such as respon-sibility for one's own learning. However, the research is set in a multicultural con-text, where neo-liberal ideas interact with cultural influences from countries such as Pakistan and Iraq in the experiences described by the interviewees.

Part of the paradox of neo-liberalism is that it presents itself as a non-political and common sense world view, and part of its ideology is to convince us that it is not ideological (Eagleton 1991). In the light of this influence there is a danger that critiques are narrowed as some educationalists confine themselves to discus-sions from a western-dominated perspective. Recent feminist analyses in the field of gender and education have begun to critique the western and Anglophone domi-nation of academic discourses, highlighting "a preoccupation with Western femi-nist concerns and a relative lack of interest in other parts of the world" (Öhrn and

Weiner 2009, p. 427). By bringing together, in the present volume, research related to women's gendered experiences in countries beyond Anglophone regions we seek to move away from a purely western-dominated response to neo-liberalism as it relates to gendered choices in lifelong learning.

In some cases, neo-liberalism interacts with political philosophies and religions which predominate outside the west. This is highlighted in the present volume where, for example, the interaction of western, neo-liberal policies with local Iranian cultures and values are analysed (see Chap. 12). The coexistence of political, economic and religious ideologies influences the way these manifest themselves in women's lives (Barrett 1997). Women's learning and the position of women, both in industrialised and in less-industrialised countries, are issues that appear caught in the confluence of such philosophies, restricting choices of learning and career pathways. It seems that the constraints placed on women have made such gendered positions a barometer for the social values that prevail: in many countries these values reflect the policy imperatives of neo-liberalism and the marketisation of all areas of life (Burman 2006).

Marketisation, 'Choice' and Skills

Marketisation involves the introduction of market principles to public services, as well as the "privatization and the contracting out of state services to the independent sector" (Lewis et al. 2000, p. 44). The movement to private provision has been seen as presenting citizens with more choice, and lifelong learning has been recruited to support them in developing capacities for choice making as part of economic and social assimilation. In discourses of choice, citizens (and learners) are configured as consumers of services who are encouraged to participate in marketisation (Seddon 1997). Marketisation has affected lifelong learning choices by making the provision of adult learning subject to market demand. In the present volume, the effects of this are analysed in a lack of funding for non-accredited courses in adult education and in struggles due to competition for the funding of social initiates and informal learning.

Marketisation is identified by a number of chapter authors as narrowing conceptualisations of lifelong learning, as learning is equated with the development of skills, conceptualised as isolated and measurable. To meet the needs of industrialised economies operating in globalised markets, skills have to be developed efficiently and quickly (Billett et al. 2006), serving individual nations' or regions' economic competitiveness. One of the roles of professional practice in lifelong learning is to validate evidence of these skills that are atomised in relation to where they are required in vocational performances, rather than embedded in broader theorisations of learning (Canning 1998). In this situation, performativity and productivity take precedence over long-term approaches (Morgan Klein and Osborne 2007). While gender segregation is an unforeseen policy outcome, new possibilities are envisaged by authors in this volume, offering alternatives to the narrowing of lifelong learning choices along the lines of what is calculated to be financially viable.

As the chapter authors demonstrate, women's achievements in education are equal to, or in some areas surpass, those of men. However, the gendered nature of the hidden curriculum in vocational and post-compulsory learning interacts with market imperatives to restrict women's access and limit their choices. The gendering of work roles and work spaces makes it difficult for women to enter certain occupations, or pursue particular career pathways (Fenwick 2004), and women's access to senior positions and high salary levels still lags behind that of men. The fact that women earn less reinforces gendered choices and domestic roles (Hartman 1997). The multifaceted ways in which such faults in the landscape of post-compulsory learning affect women are in part determined by the complexities of globalisation.

Globalisation

Globalisation represents a significant theme in the chapters, influencing neo-liberal policies and marketisation that inform gendered choices. However, globalisation is difficult to pin down, its influence appears to be hidden and its expression complex and diverse. Our approach to understanding its impact has been through its articulation with the other themes that we have explored. One of the challenges of writing about globalisation and its implications for gendered learning is that it appears to resist such articulation. Conventional representations of globalisation are narrowly economistic, and neglect the question as to the specific ways in which women and men are (differently) affected, and what this means for learning choices (Malcolm 2009). Feminist critique of configurations of globalisation as an indeterminate force insists on specificity and the importance of its political implications through a focus on interrelations (Massey 2005). Global spaces are interpenetrated by local concerns and vice versa. Specifically, the discussion in Chap. 12 highlights the way that the global and local become part of one another as questions of women's employment are subject to global influences through, for example, the International Labour Organisation (ILO). The discussion in the chapters that follow challenges assumptions about the effect of globalisation, and highlights a neglected paradox of the phenomenon. This consists in the tension between discourses of high-level knowledge work and the reality that women are frequently excluded from such work. This is exacerbated by lifelong learning policies that are driven by a narrow emphasis on atomised skills.

Discourses of global competition construct the development of a knowledge society as an essential aim of lifelong learning. While, this places a focus on the need for work-based skills, the authors in the present volume emphasise the absence of a gender analysis in such policies. As a number of authors show, the policy emphasis on vocational skills has entrenched the gendering of work roles and women's predominance at the low-skill/low-paid end of the economy at hidden sites of globalisation. Choices in post-compulsory learning and in vocational areas of specialisation are highly gendered in many countries. The effect of globalisation, through its drive of competition and its links with the skills agenda has been to reinforce women's low-paid status.

Gender, Power and Resistances

This book is about gendered choices in lifelong learning, and the ways in which power and resistances are played out through the choices that are (able to be) made. Resistances take place in different places and in different contexts, including in the learning pathways with which we engage (see Part I of this book); in the workplace (Part II) and through identities that are constructed and de/re/constructed (Part III). Resistances are counter-hegemonic practices that challenge or subvert hegemonic ways of being and knowing, and are attached to deeply embedded structural inequalities (Burke and Jackson 2007). They can occur at an emotional level, and/or within the micro levels of everyday experiences, and through engagement with policy. We demonstrate ways in which policy can be resisted through, for example, new pedagogies of transformation which make resistance possible.

Chapter authors argue for the importance of feminist or woman-centred networks in order to resist hegemonic ways of being and to discover new ways of knowing, so opening up possibilities for choice. At times, this seems like an impossible task. For example, in her consideration of ways in which women's choices can be shattered through violence on campuses (or of course anywhere else), Esther Oliver calls for changes in attitudes and values as well as in behaviours and policies. However, she also shows how solidarity amongst women can lead to attempts to repair the shattered choices she described. Other authors emphasise the importance of feminist networks to support women's choices in male-dominated areas. They argue that innovative approaches to learning that have their roots in feminist principles and pedagogies can support women to resist gendered identity constructions while engaging with learning and work.

New Knowledges—New Ways of Knowing

The book aims to highlight ways in which 'knowledge' about learning, learners and 'choice' are framed within gendered and classed hegemonic discourses, outlining ways in which new knowledges, and new ways of knowing can be created. Burke and Jackson (2007, p. 27) argue that there are

> particular ways of thinking about lifelong learning that have gained hegemony and these have a profound effect on the policy and practice of lifelong learning and yet these are largely uninformed by the complex, contradictory and multifaceted experiences of learning. This is largely due to the processes and politics of knowledge validation and the ways that these operate around shifting and complex inequalities.

Some knowledges and ways of knowing are privileged, whilst others are marginalised or even made invisible. For example, Suzanne Hyde (Chap. 10) shows that a word search of the Leitch report on skills in the UK (HM Treasury 2006) reveals that gender is mentioned only once. As Foucault (1974) demonstrated, knowledge is always related to power: indeed he chose to refer to power/knowledge to indicate the impossibility of separation. However, power can be resisted and feminist approaches enable gender to be explored through relational perspectives, bringing different, and valued, ways of knowing. We argue that this can mitigate against the assumption that valid knowledge is only created in the academy by those with the power and influence to do so. Nevertheless, normative expectations sometimes make new knowledges difficult to come into being. One way in which new ways of knowing can be developed is through reflection in action which can enable us to develop and value the knowledges that have been developed at a range of sites where women live and work, and that can be applied to new understandings of learning work and identity.

The development of new knowledges remains central to this book, with chapter authors drawing on feminist epistemology in a range of theoretical and methodological approaches that emerge at different sites, from universities to community learning in three different continents. The range of methodologies that underpins the discussion is considerable and reflects the complexity and sophistication of feminist scholarship. The chapters draw on postmodern feminism and complexity science; discourse analysis; action research; life history; policy research and Foucauldian feminism. Conceptual and methodological innovation is reflected in many of the chapters. In this way, the volume expresses the diversity of feminism(s) and the range of possibilities offered by feminist epistemology.

Organisation of the Book

The book is organised in three sections. The first section examines gendered learning pathways, discussing the interaction between learning and gendered choices, and examining how policies and current methodological approaches frame both women's and men's learning. The second section is concerned with setting an agenda for gender in work-based learning, exploring gendered choices at different stages of the employment cycle and in different employment and learning contexts. Like the other sections in this book, section two has an interest in the interaction of policy and experience and the way these interactions are crosscut by gender, class and race. The final section of the book explores gendered identities, considering the ways in which our gendered identities impact onto 'choice', which itself is gendered. This publication arises from a conference hosted jointly by the Women in Lifelong Learning Network of the Universities' Association for Lifelong Learning in the UK, and the Birkbeck Institute for Lifelong Learning (University of London), which attracted contributions from practitioners, policy makers and academics. This resulting collection therefore represents a broad range of perspectives on adult learning in practice, in the early twenty-first century. The contributors to the publication are adult learning practitioners and academics who share a commitment to adult learning and an interest in exploring the ways in which gender informs their practice, wider policies and the experiences of individual learners. A range of theoretical perspectives is represented within this collection, grounded in empirical research and practice.

The collection is entirely authored by women and advances feminist understandings of lifelong learning, with the authors placing the social construction of gender and women's experiences (intersected with 'race', social class and age) at the centre of their work. In her consideration of *Gendered Education,* Sandra Acker considers six core assumptions in feminist research, one of which is to show that the personal is political (Acker 1994). In addition, feminist research, she says, aims to show an awareness of women's injustices; to improve women's lives; to highlight the centrality of women; to replace existing knowledges; and to consider the position of the researcher and the researched. In their different ways, the authors of the chapters in this book cumulatively fulfil all these aims, making this a feminist engagement with choice and lifelong learning. Perhaps one of the most central components of a feminist methodology is the engagement with research as praxis, bringing about change in women's lives. Feminist research can be a radical and liberatory force for both researched and researcher (see, e.g. Jackson 2004), and the calls for change in developing a different worldview about gender, choice and lifelong learning is apparent throughout the book.

This book is written at a transitional moment in women's lives, represented by the first decade of the twenty-first century, through an international context that embraces perspectives from the UK, continental Europe, Canada and Iran, extending knowledge, understandings and critiques of gendered choices (and constraints) within lifelong learning. The book addresses the complexities of gender issues which are in danger of becoming obscured in contemporary widening participation and lifelong learning debates.

References

Aaron, J., & Walby, S. (Eds.). (1991). *Out of the margins: Women's studies in the nineties.* London: Falmer.

Acker, S. (1994). *Gendered education.* Bucks: Oxford University Press.

Australian National Training Authority. (1998). *A bridge to the future: Australia's national strategy for occupational education and training 1998–2003.* Brisbane: ANTA.

Barrett, M. (1997). Capitalism and women's liberation. In L. Nicholson (Ed.), *The second wave reader: A reader in feminism* (pp. 123–130). London: Routledge.

Billett, S., Fenwick, T., & Somerville, M. (2006). *Work, subjectivity and learning. Understanding learning through working life.* Dordrecht: Springer.

Burke, P., & Jackson, S. (2007). *Reconceptualising lifelong learning: Feminist interventions.* London: Routledge.

Burman, E. (2006). Emotions and reflexivity in feminised education action research. *Educational Action Research, 14,* 315–332.

Canning, R. (1998). The Failure of Competence-based qualifications: an analysis of work-based vocational education policy in Scotland. *Journal of Education Policy, 13*(5), 625–639.

DfEE. (1988). *The learning age: A renaissance for new Britain.* London: HMSO.

Eagleton, T. (1991). *Ideology.* London: Verso.

European Council. (2000). Lisbon, March 2000. (http://www.europarl.europa.eu/summits/lis1_en. htm. Accessed July 23 2009)

Fenwick, T. (2004). What happens to the girls? Gender, work and learning in Canada's "new economy". *Gender and Education. 16*(2), 169–185.

Foucault, M. (1974). *The archaeology of knowledge.* London: Tavistock.

Fuwa, K. (2009). Is the expansion of higher education in Japan for young students only or for all? A critical analysis from a lifelong learning perspective. *International Journal of Lifelong Education, 28*(4), 459–472.

Hartman, H. (1997). The unhappy marriage of Marxism and feminism: Towards a more progressive union. In L. Nicholson (Ed.), *The second wave: A reader in feminism* (pp. 97–122). London: Routledge.

HM Treasury. (2006). *Prosperity for all in the Global Economy: World Class Skills: Final report (Leitch review of skills).* London: HMSO.

hooks, b. (2000). *Feminist theory: From margin to center.* Boston: South End.

Jackson, S. (2004). *Differently academic? Developing lifelong learning for women in higher education.* Dordrecht: Kluwer.

Jackson, S. (2009). *Lifelong learning and older women: Localising the global. Local problems, global solutions?* Asian Conference on Education, Osaka.

Jackson, S. (2010). Learning through social spaces: Migrant women and lifelong learning in post-colonial London. *International Journal of Lifelong Education, 29* (2), 237–254. (Special issue: Lifelong Education in the Age of Transnational Migration.)

Leathwood, C., & Francis, B. (Eds.). (2006). *Gender and lifelong learning: Critical feminist engagements.* London: Routledge.

Lewis, G., Gewirtz, S., & Clarke, J. (2000). *Rethinking social policy.* London: Sage.

Malcolm, I. (2009). *Globalisation, technology and identity: A feminist study of work cultures in the localisation industry.* Unpublished EdD thesis, University of Stirling, Stirling, Scotland.

Massey, D. (2005). *For space.* London: Sage.

Morgan, K. B., & Osborne, M. (2007) *The Concepts and Practice of Lifelong Learning,* London: Routledge.

OECD. (2002). Thematic review of adult education, background report—Canada. http://www.eric. ed.gov/ERICDocs/data/ericdocs2sql/content_storage_01/0000019b/80/1a/7f/2a.pdf. Accessed 26 Aug 2009.

Öhrn, E., & Weiner, G. (2009). The sound of silence! Reflections on inclusion and exclusion in the field of education and gender. *Gender and Education, 21* (4), 423–430.

Schuller, Y. (2001). Tracing links between adult education and civic participation. *Journal of Adult and Continuing Education, 4,* 5–16.

Seddon, T. (1997). Markets and the English: rethinking educational restructuring as institutional design. *British Journal of Sociology of Education, 18*(2), 165–185.

Webb, S., Brine, J., & Jackson, S. (2006). Gender, Foundation degrees and the knowledge-driven economy. *Journal of Vocational Education and Training, 58* (4), 563–576.

Part I
Learning Pathways—Gendered Learning

Chapter 2
Part I: Introduction

Irene Malcolm, Sue Jackson and Kate Thomas

The chapters in this section of the book deal with gendered choices in learning. While this is the principal focus, gendered learning is interwoven with the other two themes of the volume, as learning experiences affect work and identities. Drawing on critical analyses of the field, the authors discuss the interaction of learning and gendered pathways, examining how policies and pedagogies frame both women's and men's learning. The chapters investigate lifelong learning at various sites, including in the virtual environment. While the data on which the authors draw reflect the diversity of UK society in the 21st century, discussions and analyses are of significance beyond the UK, reinforcing the book's international relevance. This is further supported, for example, with an account of research that is based on a continental European study (see Chap. 6). All of the chapters in this section draw on empirical research into learning experiences: Chaps. 4, 5 and 6 are based on sizeable research projects with research council, institutional and government funding, and Chap. 3 is a vivid and detailed analysis of learning in the author's own classroom. The authors include teachers as well as academics; they highlight the problems of gendered choices and advocate ways of overcoming them in lifelong learning.

The writers analyse the ways that current policies enhance or restrict learning, casting doubt on some policies that claim to extend equal opportunities (Thomas 2001). The notion of widening participation that is at the heart of neo-liberal thinking emphasises everyone's rights to access (Leathwood and Francis 2006). Yet, as all of the authors in this section show, complexity and disjuncture surround such policies in lifelong learning. In promoting the rights of individuals as more significant than valuing shared experience, neo-liberal economics and related education policies affect learning pathways by stimulating competition, not just among nations in globalised markets (Brine 2006), but also among the individuals and institutions in these markets. The analyses in the chapters that follow illustrate how pathways that emerge from such policies are both gendered and classed, as they derive from imperatives that promote the survival of the fittest (Davies and Saltmarsh

I. Malcolm (✉)
School of Education, Social Work and Community Education, University of Dundee, Nethergate, Dundee, DD1 4HN, UK
e-mail: i.z.malcolm@dundee.ac.uk

2007). Sometimes this has the effect of reinforcing existing hierarchies (Chap. 6): At other times, the constraining influence of neo-liberal policies appears to be in tension with contradictory discourses of enablement (Chap. 4).

An important feature of present lifelong learning policies examined in the following chapters is the skills-based approach. Curricula that promote skills and measurable outputs as the prime goals of learning are widespread among western countries and have their roots in the introduction of marketisation in education (Apple 2006). In the discussions that follow, the authors subject this approach to critical scrutiny, demonstrating how the over-concentration on measurable outputs detracts from broader aims and diverts attention from pathways that promote social and relational learning. In the first two chapters, both Ursula Murray and Penny Jane Burke draw attention to the inadequacies of approaches to lifelong learning that fail to take account of complex learning processes to engage situated and embodied learners (Boler 1999). Developing this argument further in Chap. 5, Clem Herman and her colleagues discuss the evaluation of a learning programme that offers a broad developmental base, linked to shared experience and peer support. In this chapter, as in the final chapter of the section by Esther Olivier, learning is conceptualised in relation to critical engagements that draw on life experiences which are shared as well as individual (Merrill 2007). In this way the authors offer an alternative vision to neo-liberal domination of the lifelong learning agenda.

In Chap. 3 Ursula Murray introduces the theme of gendered learning pathways by drawing on qualitative research from her own teaching. She explores the benefits that derive from attention to the learners' own experience. Against current policies and practices, Murray discusses the advantages of a relational model of learning which she reasserts as a counterbalance to an over-concentration on skills. Murray begins the chapter with a detailed overview of neo-liberal policy in UK public services. She discusses instances where academics and educational institutions are enlisted as market players (Davies 2003), compromising critical distance to the detriment of educational provider and learner. Drawing on ethnographic data from a reflective journal, Murray uses narrative analysis that is nuanced through psychosocial understanding and complexity science (Stacey and Griffin 2005). In data excerpts from her engagement with three groups of learners, including some who are studying for employer-sponsored Foundation degrees, Murray explores the importance of taking learners' experience seriously and bringing this into dialogue with theory. The author points to some of the problems entailed when learning pathways are dominated by curriculum outcomes that are driven by short-term economic goals: In response to this Murray discusses the benefits that can be gained from a critical and reflexive focus on learning processes.

In Chap. 4, Penny Jane Burke develops further the theme of gendered learning pathways. She examines widening participation frameworks in education policy through a study of learning, aspirations and complex identifications (Hall 1992). Her analyses add to the themes initiated in the previous chapter as she highlights the implications of marketisation for learning choices. Using data from an ESRC (UK Economic and Social Research Council) funded study of learning identities and masculinities, Burke examines gendered influences on goals and decision-making among men who are accessing higher education. Her research is based on language analysis, drawing on data from her engagement with policy discourses and with the discursive repertoires of interviewees. Like Murray, Burke contextualises her analysis in a critique of policies that affect lifelong learning in the UK and which are replicated, or have parallels further afield (Allen et al. 2005). Burke locates the needs of the economy and the market as strong imperatives in many lifelong learning policies. The complexity of neo-liberalism's impact on lifelong learning is captured in Burke's account of the paradoxes in policy discourses where transformation and social justice are linked to competition. At the same time, her critique underlines the problems entailed when learning that seeks to embrace social justice is aligned with technologies of self-improvement.

Burke finds that gendered identities exert a strong influence in shaping the learning experiences and subsequent ambitions of the men in her sample. Rather than focussing only on individual perspectives in decision-making and the formulation of aspirations, Burke draws on sociological insights to illuminate relational and contextual dimensions of learning. In her analysis, the aspirations of lifelong learners emerge as complex and nuanced, produced through gendered identifications and intricate social negotiations.

While the first two chapters in this part of the book deal with the policy influences of neo-liberalism, the writing of Herman, Hodgson, Kirkup and Whitelegg in Chap. 5 and Olivier in the final chapter, deal with broad cultural factors that affect women's choices and their lifelong learning (Colley 2006). Chapter 5 furthers the critique of gendered learning choices by describing a possible route through these in a learning programme designed for women. The findings in this chapter draw on the analyses of data from the authors' action research based in the UK. In an example from teaching and curriculum development, practitioners address the constraining influence of existing power hierarchies in SET (Science Engineering and Technology). They consider the rationale for and the impact of a programme of generic, personal and professional development that offers a broad range of support to women wishing to take up SET careers after career breaks. As the authors explain, women are underrepresented in SET, not just in the UK (Faulkner 2007), but across many countries on an international scale (Faulkner 2004).

On the basis of a critical review of the policy background of SET in the UK (Murphy and Whitelegg 2006), the authors highlight the benefits of certain initiatives, while drawing attention to the detrimental effect of short-term funding. The authors describe the crucial role played by a collection of women academics and activists at one institution who were able to draw on interdisciplinary strengths to access UK and EU funding. They emphasise the innovative nature of the resulting programme, where women's networking is central to its pedagogy, design and outcomes. The prominence given to reflective activities that draw on the learners' experience links the pedagogies described in this chapter to those discussed by Murray and Burke.

Despite the achievements of the programme they describe, Herman and colleagues identify continued challenges presented by structural and institutional factors that militate against women pursuing careers in SET. In addition, the authors identify a prevalent male culture in SET workplaces that makes it difficult for women with appropriate qualifications to develop their careers. In the light of the international dimension of women's underrepresentation, the authors conclude with a series of recommendations that are relevant to HE institutions in a number of countries. The theme of addressing constraints on women's learning and participation is continued in the final chapter of this part of the book.

In Chap. 6, Esther Olivier gives an account of her research into gender violence as a barrier to women's full participation in the academy. The author challenges the stereotypical notion that only certain women are affected by gender violence, while emphasising the scale and international character of this hidden problem in universities. Olivier draws on a review of international literature as well as on her own research data to analyse how the phenomenon crosses boundaries and affects women's learning and careers (Osborne 1995). Her study data are taken from interviews conducted with representatives at a number of universities, in addition to daily life stories elicited from feminist and student organisations. Using a qualitative methodology, Olivier obtains an institutional view that complements the individual perspectives captured in her data from interviews with those who deal directly with the impact of gender violence. While Olivier's data gathering is conducted at UK universities, her research originates in Catalunya and is funded by the Catalunyan government, in cooperation with the University of Barcelona. Olivier points out that unequal conceptualisations of gender relationships create the preconditions for violence (Bondurant 2001). It is this in particular that makes the academy susceptible: it is principally male-dominated, with complex hierarchical power relations that affect women's learning and career choices. By studying gender violence in the academy as a workplace, as well as a site of learning, Olivier brings together the themes of women's learning and work, preparing the ground for the discussion in the next section of the book.

References

Allen, W. R., Jayakumar, U. M., Griffen, K. A., Korn, W. S., & Hurtado, S. (2005). *Black undergraduates from Bakke to Grutter: Freshmen status, trends and prospects, 1971–2004.* Los Angeles: Higher Education Research Institute.

Apple, M. W. (2006). *Educating the "right" way: Markets, standards, God, and Inequality.* London: Routledge.

Boler, M. (1999). *Feeling power: Emotions and education.* New York: Routledge.

Bondurant, B. (2001). University women's acknowledgment of rape. Individual, situational and social factors. *Violence Against Women, 7*(3), 294–314.

Brine, J. (2006). Lifelong learning and the knowledge economy: Those that know and those that do not—the discourse of the European Union. *British Educational Research Journal, 32*(5), 649–665.

Colley, H. (2006). Learning to labour with feeling: Class, gender and emotion in childcare education and training. *Contemporary Issues in Early Childhood, 17*(1), 15–29.

Davies, B. (2003). Death to critique and dissent? The policies and practices of new managerialism and of "evidence-based practice". *Gender and Education, 15*(1), 91–103.

Davies, B., & Saltmarsh, S. (2007). Gender economies: Literacy and the gendered production of neo-liberal subjectivities. *Gender and Education, 19*(1), 1–20.

Faulkner, W. (2004). *Strategies of Inclusion: Gender and the Information Society.* European Commission, 5th Framework, Information Society Technologies (IST) Programme. Edinburgh: SIGIS.

Faulkner, W. (2007). Nuts and bolts and people. Gender-troubled engineering identities. *Social Studies of Science, 37*(3), 331–358.

Hall, S. (1992). Introduction: Identity in question. In S. Hall, D. Held, & T. McGrew (Eds.), *Modernity and its futures.* Cambridge: Polity.

Leathwood, C., & Francis, B. (Eds.). (2006). *Gender and lifelong learning: Critical feminist engagements.* London: Routledge.

Merrill, B. (2007). Recovering class and the collective. In L. West, P. Alheit, A. Bron, A. Siig Andersen, & B. Merrill (Eds.), *Using biographies and life history approaches in the study of adult and lifelong learning.* Frankfurt a. M.: Lang.

Murphy, P., & Whitelegg, E. (2006). *Girls in the physics classroom: A review of research on the participation of girls in physics.* London: The Institute of Physics.

Osborne, R. L. (1995). The continuum of violence against women in Canadian universities. Toward a new Understanding of the Chilly Campus Climate. *Women's Studies International Forum, 18*(5/6), 637–646.

Stacey, R., & Griffin, D. (2005). Experience and method: A complex responsive processes perspective on research in organisations. In R. Stacey & D. Griffin (Eds.), *A complexity perspective on researching organisations.* London: Routledge.

Thomas, L. (2001). Power, assumptions and prescriptions: A critique of widening participation policy-making. *Higher Education Policy, 14*(4), 361–376.

Chapter 3
Re-asserting a Relational Model of Teaching and Learning: A Gender Perspective

Ursula Murray

Whilst tutoring adult students online for a personal development skills course, the absence of any meaningful relationship with them prompted my own need to reflect and learn from this experience. Little attention is currently given to questions of student–teacher relatedness in considering the purpose and roles of higher education. This chapter will explore and re-assert the importance of a relational model of teaching and learning and consider the impact of gender on this approach to teaching.

I will begin by addressing the wider changes in the education of adults in the UK and particularly the impact on women. I will then place these changes in the context of the marketisation of education and public services more generally. The introduction of 'business model' ways of thinking into the educational sphere in the UK has had a major impact on current pedagogical practice, and yet alternative thinking about pedagogy from the past still resonates today. This in turn raises interesting questions as to what is knowledge which lays the basis for my understanding of the role of story as a research methodology. Using three stories from my own research, I then seek to capture the kind of interactions experienced in different teaching and learning contexts. While these are drawn from the UK, the policy development and data analyses that follow have resonance with learning developments in the broader international context. Several key themes emerge: firstly, the importance for students of being able to connect up their learning from experience with an engagement with theory; secondly, the critical role of the teacher as a 'container' of student anxieties; finally, whether and how the gender of learners impacts on this kind of interactive and experiential way of teaching. Each theme also draws attention to the under-the-surface experiences of any learning situation. They highlight the contribution that psycho-social thinking could make towards a better understanding of what takes place in the classroom, and also to rebutting the narrow, linear ways of thinking which are coming to dominate how we understand pedagogical practice.

U. Murray (✉)
Department of Social Policy, Birkbeck, University of London, London, UK
e-mail: u.murray@bbk.ac.uk

S. Jackson et al. (eds.), *Gendered Choices,* Lifelong Learning Book Series 15,
DOI 10.1007/978-94-007-0647-7_3, © Springer Science+Business Media B.V. 2011

The Gender Impact of Adult Education Changes

The past decade has witnessed the impact of education systems re-conceived as a supply side lever of the UK's long-term economic survival. Enhancing 'skills,' as advocated by the Leitch Report (Leitch 2006), has radically reshaped higher education policies in the UK. This is bringing about paradoxical changes in the education of adult learners more generally. There is an increased recognition of the role of adult learning and more resources for some parts of the system where new skills and employability training is being prioritised. However, this is paralleled by an erosion of traditional forms of access to adult education and an understanding of adult education for its own sake which, for example, played a part in bringing about social change for women.

The refocusing of attention of the education of adults on employability and on access to employment undermines a long tradition which served the interests of older people and women in particular. Kamler (2006, p. 156), for example, describes the kind of accessible, creative writing project which can challenge negative and diminishing narratives of ageing. But the funding for this kind of non-skill-based course is fast disappearing. As fees rise, subsidy is withdrawn and classes fold. Potential students find they are being encouraged to organise courses themselves which in turn is undermining an inclusive and properly supported professional service. A community librarian working with a local authority adult learning service described to me how a woman had come in looking for a course. She had told her that she now had a 9-to-5 job and did not have to work evenings, but did not want to stay at home every night with a husband who would only watch a foreign language TV channel. She wanted a course for relaxation. However, the worker had to advise her that yoga was all that was on offer to someone like herself. Yoga, this worker told me, was typical of their marketing strategy aimed at drawing in learners with a view primarily to encouraging them to then move on to work-related, skills-based courses.

The Director of the National Institute for Adult and Continuing Education (NIACE) has pointed out how this re-direction of funding has rapidly resulted in 1.4 million fewer adults in Learning and Skills Council funded courses in the further education (FE) sector (Tucket 2008). The head of education and training of the shop workers union (USDAW) has also pointed out that "closing the skill gap is opening up a social divide" (Rees 2008). His concern is that the policy shift discriminates against those who work in the lowest skilled jobs because the new subsidy is focussed on the skills needed to develop you to do your job. As opportunities for such workers to develop new skills are generally not a priority for employers in his sector they lose out. In his view, this discriminates against those in the lowest paid jobs. Inevitably, this has significant gender implications, as 81% of the lowest paid workers in the UK are women (Daly and Rake 2003, p. 82).

Marketising Education

Such changes in adult education also need to be understood as part of the wider process of marketisation of public services in the UK more generally over the past three decades. While the discussion that follows is drawn from UK policy development, the propagation of neoliberal policies in education is affecting other western and westernised societies. The neo-liberal 'modernisation' of public services has been closely associated with embedding a private sector derived 'business model'. The 'New Public Management' (Hood 1991; McLaughlin et al. 2002) and the managerialism which ensued, has brought with it an emphasis on performance measurement, targets and learning outcomes, the importance of the user as customer, the prioritisation of the role of IT and an understanding of equalities more as human resources competencies rather than as the outcome of collective social movements. In parts of the public sector such as local government, a *private* public service sector is now very well established. The parallel extension of this market thinking into higher education has been discussed more fully by Tolofari (2005) and Davies (2003).

In 2007, after a 10-year lifespan, the demise of the Learning and Skills Council (LSC) was announced. This has led to adult learning passing to a Department for Innovation, Universities and Skills (DIUS)[1]. Previously, the LSC was responsible for funding adult as well as young people's learning in FE, and the Higher Education and Funding Council for England (Hefce) for funding adult learning in higher education. The absence of a reference to education in the title of the then new DIUS signals a new blurring of education and training. In its wake there is also a major shift in thinking towards co-funding with employers through the initiative 'Train to Gain'. This enables employers to become 'gatekeepers' or commissioners of new streams of public funding for higher education. It represents the introduction of the purchaser/provider split already widely experienced in health and local authority services.

In April 2008, the DIUS announced the co-funding by employers of 30,000 new university places and the launching of ten new skill orientated universities. This consolidates a funding shift towards 'Foundation degrees' in both FE and universities as a means to encourage wider participation and access routes into full higher education degrees. The (as then) new DIUS minister, also announced a review of higher education. As an advocate of closer links with industry and widening access and encouraging innovation, the expectation in policy terms is that he may lean towards a reduced emphasis on the research role of universities, resulting in an increased separation of research and teaching only universities.

All these developments have aroused concern among some academics about merely re-branding employer-based training as higher education and the sidelining of research and academic scholarship. Debates such as that between Adrian Monk and Antony Grayling (Monk and Grayling 2008) reflected the sharply differing views about how far public money should be closely tied to promoting particu-

---

[1] DIUS was itself replaced in mid 2009.

lar employer-led courses or to entrepreneurial research spin-offs. The fundamental meaning of what a university is for has therefore become the subject of vigorous exchanges. Anthony Grayling (Monk and Grayling 2008) argues a university is a source of intellectual, economic, and social vitality, of scholarship, and a developed capacity for critical reflection on the meaning of life. This he believes spills over into an appreciation of the experience of being a citizen of the world. The concern of academics like him is that education becomes a commodity, driven increasingly by employer and student-as-consumer interests in gathering a job-related accredited skill. Ferudi (2008) also singles out a recent new Foundation degree in retail management at one university as an example of the danger, in his view, of merely re-branding what should be a company training scheme. He argues that the company itself, not public subsidy, should be paying for this.

Yet a contrary argument can also be put. Better management is precisely what the country needs to invest in, and linking this properly to appropriate subject disciplines will bring a desirable depth. The long-term competitiveness of the UK economy matters, and universities have a key role to play in this. Professional and vocational training has also always occupied a place in higher education as in, for example, medicine or architecture. But these recent changes and policy shifts towards the 'skills agenda' mark a step change. There is an interventionist strategy on the part of government towards universities in which business is being given much greater influence over the form and purpose of higher education and there can be real hazards and pitfalls in this development. The purpose of an academic course is to inculcate a capacity for critical thought and not to meet an employer's specific training needs. Clarity on this point is crucial if the role of academics is not to become very conflictual.

Business and management have been some of the most popular courses in universities over the last decade in response to employer and student demand. Yet in the wake of the 2008 global economic crisis, MBA courses have now been charged by academics such as Willmott (James 2009) and others, with teaching concepts which have contributed directly to the global economic crisis and the corporate excesses which have discredited the last decade. They argue that the behaviours and ethics which have led to the economic recession have roots in what has been taught in our business schools. In chasing their market, business-related courses have failed to retain a sufficient critical distance. It is suggested that they have identified too closely with the student job market, and compromised their professed concern for disinterested scholarship which a university course should signify.

Lifelong Learning as a Contested Space

Where does adult and lifelong learning sit within this progressively more marketised understanding and structure of higher education? Mojab (2006) has critiqued how the changing economy has underpinned the re-organisation of adult education into a training, learning, and skilling enterprise more fully responsive to the requirements of the market. Within this political and economic context 'lifelong learning' has, she argues, been deployed in two ways. Firstly, it is a central concept in the hegemonic claim that lack of skills causes unemployment which supposes that constant retraining prepares workers to be ultimately adaptable, and always ready to acquire new skills as the needs of capital dictate. Secondly, 'lifelong learning' has been deployed as an ideological distraction that shifts the burden of increasing adaptability onto the worker, and at the same time also acts as a ray of hope for a more democratic and engaged citizenship. She rightly asks why is lifelong learning being enthusiastically endorsed by some adult educators, policy makers, the business community and others; and poses the question, should we welcome it or resist it? Is it just a hollowed-out concept which merely invites a cynical response?

Winners and losers in terms of funding support and access to higher education for adult learners are both evident now. Certainly, the decision by the DIUS in early 2008 to pursue the withdrawal of subsidy funding from students wanting to take equivalent or lower level higher education qualifications (ELQs) seems a perverse interpretation of lifelong learning. It reflects a decision to privilege access for young people to university over mature students and it specifically undermines widely valued routes used by women seeking to re-skill after career breaks in caring roles. Yet at the same time, it is equally the case that the expansion of the Foundation degree route into higher education can be seen as widening access and providing a stepping stone for different groups of women to access higher education. It particularly compensates those who missed out on earlier educational opportunities. But policy may be changing again with a re-orientation towards addressing professional development programmes if account is taken anecdotal evidence from within the field of practice.

Although institutionally many faculties of lifelong learning are being mainstreamed out of existence, the ideas around 'lifelong learning' are a contested space in which debates about the policies and purpose of higher education have been argued out. There is concern about overcompliance with a work-orientated, employability 'skills agenda', which has prompted a robust defence of traditional approaches to scholarship and maintenance of academic standards. The implication is that standards are being sacrificed in a rush to develop industrialised forms of teaching in the new world of higher education as a business response that brings larger numbers and wider participation. There is a questioning of outcome-based models of learning which imply that a tutor can and should predetermine what will be achieved in any session. Cummins (2002, p. 116) describes a strategy of 'strategic compliance' in which key outcomes are delivered in order to maintain target-free zones of learning.

These concerns are valid, but does the polarisation of positions as expressed in the debate between Monk and Grayling (Monk and Grayling 2008) necessarily stand up? New approaches to teaching *are* called for in addressing the needs of access and Foundation degree students and are not to be equated with a lowering of academic standards. In the past, pedagogical practice has always been innovative and varied in the wider adult education world, whilst continuing to be shaped by the depth of an academic discipline. I would argue this alternative tradition also returns us to the central importance of the idea of education as an interaction between student and teacher. Re-asserting the importance of a relational approach draws us back to alternative roots of thinking about learning in which an understanding of power relations is integral. Holmes (2007) emphasises that power relations are always contested and constructed in any social interaction. Newman (2002, p. 89) also uses a relational understanding of power in this way in her research about the way local government workers interpret their roles. She speaks of the existence of 'unstable settlements' and draws attention to how new policy agendas get laid down on top of one another. She argues that public service workers engage in 'bending bureaucracy' (Newman 2005, p. 191). As a result older norms and ways of thinking, and practices which deviate from the prevailing performance measurement culture, continue to flourish and find some expression.

I would like to draw a parallel here with ways of thinking about the experience of teaching in higher education. In other words to turn the spotlight onto one's role as a teacher, and question how it still embodies or resists an understanding of learning as one driven by measurement, pre-set targets and learning outcomes. Using analogies with complexity ideas, Stacey (2003b) argues the present way of thinking about learning represents a 'systems' approach, which is essentially about control, whereas it is a 'free flowing conversation' that is key to creativity (2003, p. 79). Alternative and more radical discourses have always understood learning as a complex social interaction which impacts in multiple ways, and these influences continue, albeit in the shadow of the mainstream discourse about education.

Friere (1970) inspired diverse movements around adult education, extra-mural studies, and continuing education in higher education. In the UK, his thinking was also very present in the Workers Education Association (WEA), the trade union education and feminist inspired learning movements. His pedagogy emphasised "constant reflection and action upon the world to transform it" (Friere 1970, p. 33). Four decades on, Sharma (2008, p. 8) underlines Friere's continuing influence on development activists and scholars, emphasising how this pedagogy is an "active, inter-subjective process of transformation" which continues to resonate in her scholarship around gender and development theory and her work with rural women's groups in India.

Feminist informed models of teaching and learning have also long sought to explore gender through a relational perspective. Carol Gilligan (1982) spoke of a 'connected knowing' and argued for a way of learning in which knowledge does not come from detachment but from living in connection with oneself and with others and from being embedded in the conditions of life. Both Gilligan (1982) and Belenky et al. (1986), who used the phrase 'women's ways of knowing and learning', have been criticised for taking up an essentialist viewpoint in gender terms. Hatcher (2003) rightly argues against defining women as innately or naturally more open to emotional expressiveness. However, I would argue that many, if certainly not all women, *are* still strongly socialised in ways which make them, initially at least, more open to an empathic or relational awareness. As Gerhardt (2004) points out, our brains are plastic, and we very much develop as a by-product of our attachments and emotional experiences. The powerful gender differences we acquire are part and parcel of this: not innate but deeply embedded.

Different Forms of Reasoning

Gilligan's study *In a Different Voice* (1982) set out to counter research by Kohlberg (1981) whose fallacious and essentialising theory suggested that young men had a more developed moral sense of right and wrong because they more easily adopted a philosophical form of reasoning. In contrast to this, Gilligan argued that young women were caught up in situations shaped by the complexities of the human relationships in which they found themselves. As a consequence, she suggested that young women were penalised as intellectually and morally deficient rather than being understood as having been socialised into a different way of reasoning which is more involved with the complicated ambiguities and paradoxes of human relating.

All of this raises interesting and contentious questions within the traditions of social science as to how we understand 'knowledge' and the legitimacy of 'learning from experience' and from personal narratives versus 'objectivity'. Minsky (1998, p. 218) questions why academics balk at a 'tangled web' of biological, cultural, and unconscious elements which produce different ways of knowing and she concludes that academics "prefer signifiers and abstract notions of desire to desiring bodies and a notion of knowledge, truth and morality derived from personal experience" (Minsky 1998, p. 225). She goes on to suggest that 'thinking' can become a substitute for feeling and sexuality and a form of dissociation and mastery. Walzer (1987) emphasises the potential capacity for engagement alongside detachment and the ability to remain "a little bit to one side but not outside a situation" (quoted by Hoggett 2002, p. 18). Stacey and Griffin (2005, p. 9) similarly speak of "a paradox of detached involvement". Eagleton (2003, pp. 128–129) also makes a very direct connection between ethics, emotions, and politics in which he sees moral capacities such as care, selflessness, vigilance, and protectiveness as social attributes. He points out we rely on sharing our affective and communicative life with others, otherwise literally we do not become persons. For Eagleton, the moral and material are two sides of the same coin. He also argues for valuing objectivity as dispassionate judgement and bringing 'disinterestedness' (p. 169) to bear as the opposite of self-interest. As he points out, this is an arduous and emotionally taxing affair as it is about grappling with self-deception. Objectivity he suggests, "requires a passion for doing the kinds of justice which might throw open your most deep-seated prejudices to revision" (p. 134).

Finally, Worth (2005) has argued that there are two kinds of reasoning which we regularly use to make sense of our world and our experiences: discursive and narrative reasoning. She points out that discursive reasoning relies on logic, reasoned argument, inductive and deductive reasoning, and conceptualisation in an ordered string of events. Narrative reasoning, on the other hand, is abductive reasoning, which depends on a narrative to order a certain experience. It is a "form of reasoning that can find morals, reasons, explanations, description, inference, causation (on occasions but not necessarily), and all kinds of other information through the understanding of narrative, particularly well-constructed narrative" (Worth 2005, pp. 11–12). She adds that since we do not tend to think of reliable inferences as coming from anything other than discursive reasoning, we end up having an extremely limited notion of where belief and true justified belief can come from. We may not be expert storytellers, but in most, if not all, adults it is one of the primary ways we impose coherence and give meaning to our experience. Narrative then is an under-represented form of reasoning, grounded in everyday storytelling as a form of communication.

Using Story as a Research Method

What does bringing emotional and rational experiences together in teaching mean in practical terms? Does teaching with a relational focus impact differently with male and female students? In what ways does encouraging students to draw on their own experience bring about experiences of transforming ethical reflection?

To explore these questions I will draw on my own stories of teaching, using an ethnographically influenced narrative research methodology which is also integral to my own approach to teaching and learning practice. As noted above, stories capture the ambivalence and paradoxes which are the stuff of lived experience. They are the carriers of emotion and are thus about much more than information. Stiles (1995, pp. 125–126) points out that "When you've heard a story you know more than you can say". In qualitative research terms, stories are sources of rich data which can then be subjected to critical analysis.

The use of story in this way still challenges academic norms of rational, objective, knowledge, but it has specific theoretical roots. My own story-based narrative research methodology draws on a synthesis of two theoretical frameworks which emphasises an ethnographic or participant observation stance (Murray 2006). I drew firstly, on a narrative research methodology which is informed by complexity sciences and learning theory described by Stacey and Griffin (2005, p. 13). The second framework draws from a psycho-social approach to research elaborated by Cooper and Lousada (2005, p. 205). While there are certain differences between these two discourses, both emphasise the importance of interrogating one's lived experience.

Complexity theory emphasises uncertainty and the need for diversity and novelty as key elements in nurturing creativity (Stacey 2003a, b). Conversation and story are seen as metaphors for this way of thinking which radically challenges the need for control and certainty as expressed through the audit culture with its pervasive emphasis on measuring targets and outcomes. Using story and narrative as a research method, Stacey and Griffin (2005, p. 22) emphasise the need for 'taking one's experience seriously', and see this as encouraging a reflexive, ethical way of critiquing one's own experience and capturing how power relations emerge in every social interaction. Drawing on early thinking using this approach, Aram and Noble

(1999) describe experiences of classroom practice in educating managers in a way which emphasises the place of ambiguity and anxiety in their experience in the here and now of teaching. They reflexively illustrate the complex processes of relating occurrence in the classroom and, by implication, organisational life. This, they argue, is in sharp contrast to the norms in management textbooks which traditionally imply certainty and control.

Psycho-social theory brings an emotional depth to this way of thinking about narrative research. Cooper and Lousada (2005, p. 211) note that while areas of social theory have now begun to acknowledge a place for emotional life, the development of an empirical methodology and study of social life as dimensions of human relating and experience remain sparse. In setting out a research methodology, they place emphasis on direct emotional contact and registering of patterns of experience using sensibilities which are open to emotional and unconscious processes that lie below the surface. They argue that what is happening in society is coursing through us if only we can come to know what is happening to ourselves (Cooper and Lousada 2005, pp. 222–223).

The Emotional Life of Teaching and Learning

I will now take three stories from my own research that convey what the experience of a relational approach has meant in practice in differing educational contexts. These three stories are Story 1: 'A Place to Think'; Story 2: 'An Intergenerational Workshop' and Story 3: 'Learning Reviews'. Each story is an extract selected from longer stories.

Story 1: 'A Place to Think'

This first story is about teaching a social policy certificate/diploma course with a strong gender and critical management component. The course brings together a diverse student group and functions as an access course to higher education for some and as a post-degree springboard for others who continue onto masters courses.

> …After some general discussion one student raises the point that her single homeless organisation is dominated by women at the management level. I am pleased with this contribution as I want to begin to open up the differences *between* women and I steer the discussion further into what equality issues arise in women-dominated organisations. I am aware that this shift mirrors the group itself—what is happening in the here and now in the room—and could trigger strong feelings. The thought passes through my mind as to whether any conflict might arise, and I am aware of my momentary anxiety. Different views are expressed over parental leave, and the sense of discrimination single women feel is sharply articulated by several women and this becomes the focus of discussion. Beyond this, the group struggles to differentiate differences between women, ignoring or avoiding obvious differences around race and other potential equality differences. To illustrate a

dynamic interpretation of equalities thinking, I draw a hexagon (Newman and Williams 1995, p. 117) to show how multiple and shifting connections can be made between different inequalities. They then quickly identify race, gender, age, disability providing many different illustrations and examples of discrimination, elaborating a 'gender-*and*' perspective. But after raising gender, race, age and disability other categories remain latent.

Then sexuality eventually emerges dramatically in a very personal story. Catharine suddenly tells the group that she is a lesbian, but to voice this in her workplace (a Hospital Trust) would, she believes, be a career disaster. A few voice more progressive organisational situations, but this is quickly countered as particular to gay men. After this the group struggle to name the eighth category of the hexagon and I tell them eventually that it is 'class'. At this point Karen who has just joined the group speaks for the first time. She speaks powerfully about how surprised she is that she never thought of class and continues with a story. She had gone to a 'top' university in the north of England with a high intake of public school students. Coming from a working class background, she described how she had increasingly experienced this as a painful narrowing of the 'social space' she could inhabit. As she put it, "I lacked the necessary social capital and eventually this caused me to drop out of university". This story moved me as it resonated strongly in some way with my own experience of coming from the north to a similar kind of situation at a college of the University of London. I tell them how when I came south I discovered for the first time that I had a northern accent. I have enough distance now to laugh along with everyone else!

Karen then comments on how Catharine's story has prompted her to think about tackling sexuality as her term project on managing change. This would be totally new territory for her small voluntary sector organisation. The rest of the class are still digesting the fact that they individually must choose the theme of their project report on managing change and there is some anxiety around about this. Karen has only just joined the class, but has instantly found a theme. I draw attention to how a transforming idea emerged so quickly and unexpectedly out of our joint conversation...

Story 2: 'An Intergenerational Workshop'

This 'group behaviour' event (Obholzer 1994, p. 45; Stapley 2006; OPUS 2007) brought together 16–19-year-old students with 'older' students (mainly women students in their twenties and thirties on various access courses in further education). Their joint task was to explore and understand their generational differences. As one of a team of consultants to the group, I was allocated to a room in which I waited, unsure if anyone would come to make use of it.

> ...Eventually a group of ten young women noisily came into the room and launch off talking about how they felt about 'older people' and their dislike of teachers with whom they felt no sense of a relationship, particularly, they said, those who took a "this is not my business attitude". This made them feel, they say, that there was no respect, no trust, and very judged: in short that there was no confidence in them. Sitting quietly to one side of the room I take this as a warning to myself. I wonder anxiously whether at any moment they will decide to just get up and leave. But they then move on to talk animatedly about being strongly motivated by some teachers who related to them and had clear boundaries. I make a few comments on the themes which have dominated their conversation, but clearly signal it is for them to shape their conversation. They follow this with reflections about the experience of being young, black and demonised in the media. They comment on how the way they speak and dress provokes great anxiety and tensions in their parents, but they also express the desire for them "to sit us down and just talk to us".

Story 3: 'Learning Reviews'

An essential aspect of new Foundation degrees is the inclusion of employability skills. Personal development planning (PDP) was designed as a process to support this development and is described by the Higher Education Academy (HEA 2008). I initially tutored an online 'bolt on' course largely designed around a learning manual and supported by a small number of group meetings.

> …In the brief hour available I have face-to-face contact with the student group. I feel these first year students are subdued and finding it hard to share much of what they are experiencing. They are struggling with new work-life-study pressures, new subject classes and for many, the additional pressure of writing and speaking in English. The women students talk more freely, but overall this class is rather quiet. They just want me to tell them how to go about completing the PDP assignment tasks and so letting them get on with the onerous pressures of their subject course. The time allocated feels too brief to allow us to make any strong connection. Over the intervening weeks before we are scheduled to meet again, I write emails which receive very few or no responses. Overall I feel ignored, distant and disconnected from them. My previous experience of emailing students has been built on regular, direct interaction with students, and in my experience students always reply. This experience feels very disconnected and I tell myself these students too must be finding their experience of college distant and disconnected.

In the following year, the course was radically redesigned. It became a fully integrated course module around a complex weave of subject discipline, academic study skills and personal development planning. So a year later I was in a position to make comparisons with a very different experience of teaching the first module of a Foundation degree for public sector management students.

> …As the term unfolds, Damian remarks that he found the first readings "easy but also hard". He goes on to tell the group "the reading you gave us was not asking me *how* something was to be done but *why* something was happening and that feels very different from work". I feel energised by his insight and recognise that he has grasped a depth of understanding about the fundamental transition to university through his own very honest reflections about his anxious feelings. Later in the term, I ask the group to undertake a close observation of user-worker interaction in their workplaces which they will use as a basis for an essay but also an oral presentation. Solly describes how he was shocked at the impersonal way an elderly couple are treated in a council benefits office. He notes the absence of any awareness of the emotional impact of such ways of interacting. In his presentation, he connects this up to a key reading about the role of 'social defences' (Hoggett 2000, p. 151) in the workplace and how this shapes behaviours. His reading has illuminated his experience. It prompts him to discuss the experience with colleagues and his family, drawing them into thinking with him about what all of this means. As the students connect up and reflect on their rich observations of the familiar in unfamiliar ways, there is also a growing openness between them. I realise with pleasure that the class is becoming a place to think.

What Do These Stories Tell Us?

Several key themes emerge from these stories: firstly, the importance for students of being able to connect up their own experiences in a dialogue with theory; secondly, the critical role of the teacher as a 'container' of student anxieties, particularly about the legacy of past failures in education; finally, the degree to which relational and interactive ways of teaching work well across both genders.

All the stories emphasise the importance of 'taking one's own experience seriously' (Stacey and Griffin 2005, p. 22). Learning is clearly engendered through the connecting up of experiential awareness, critical thought, and ethical reflection. Story 1: 'A Place to Think', captures a flow of developing insight around the experience of inequality and power. As the conversation emerges in unforeseen ways, people contribute and risk speaking. They begin to speak more freely in ways which reveal that they feel safe enough to connect with their own specific experiences and in some cases reveal a vulnerability. Story 3: 'Learning Reviews' also emphasises how our life histories are always integral to the way we come to interpret what we mean by learning and knowledge. It underlines the importance of 'process' rather than just exposure to academic content. The students develop self awareness of what their own learning involves as they come to understand their move from a 'how' culture of work to the 'why' culture of university. They see the relevance of critical thought to their own lives coming to *know* their own experience rather than merely *knowing about* objective, social policy theory alone.

Ideally, we contain our own emotions, but under situations of stress this is often not possible. Any learning experience arouses anxiety, and it is necessary for this to be 'contained' if one is to take the risk of speaking and interacting in ways which lead to thought and new insights. In Story 1: 'A Place to Think', I am also aware of the anxiety aroused in myself, but I am able to build on the relationships formed to provide the necessary containment of student anxiety as this rises. We see in Story 2: 'The Intergenerational Workshop', how the 'older' students (in their twenties and thirties who were mainly also mothers), were quickly pushed into a parental role by the younger students, triggering acute anxiety in them and provoking an extremely authoritarian response as the event unfolded around such issues and conflicts as dress codes. In my small group session with the younger students, I was eventually made very aware of how I was experienced as someone who listened.

Story 3: 'Learning Reviews' contrasts the initial absence with the subsequent presence of a relationship which contains anxiety. The sense of disconnectedness where face-to-face contact was minimal contrasts markedly with the interactive model of teaching adopted the following year. It highlights the phantasy that online support can automatically be a substitute for a face-to-face relationship. The absence of any real inter-personal relationships induced a sense of disconnection and failure in myself. Although there is limited research into successful models of PDP implementation, the available evidence is that students benefit when it is integrated fully with other elements of their study programme. This example would substantiate this and the need for a relationship between student and teacher as an integral element of this.

Finally, what do the stories tell us about gender? Overall the stories suggest that, given a supportive environment, male students as well as female students can respond just as positively to a teaching approach which called on them to reflect on their own experiences. In Story 3:'Learning Review', the male students positively embraced it. In Story 1: 'A Place to Think', the all women group provided a textbook example of the adeptness of many women managers in the practice of 'soft skills' (Strebler 1997). However, I found that individual woman students in Story 3 'Learning Reviews' were not always at ease with such empathetic skills, underlining the danger of stereotyping gendered behaviours. Acquiring rational, cognitive skills such as target setting and time management can also be the dominant need for some women at a particular moment.

The Relevance of Psycho-Social Literature on Education

Each of these three stories illustrate the under-the-surface experience in learning situations. Thinking and learning also draws on our life histories to find meaning which can interfere with an ability to think and to relate to the cognitive logic of 'study skills'. It is the emotional basis of thinking and learning which is the key. Colley (2006) has argued that teaching and learning in FE is not primarily a technical question of developing new skills and competencies. Likewise, Youell (2006) in a commentary on schools argues the relationship of student, teacher and institution are central. Burke and Jackson (2007, p. 136) have also highlighted ways in which displays of emotion are deemed unacceptable and how people are silenced in gendered ways. Unusually in education discourses, they also specifically draw attention to their own pleasure in working on a project to re-conceptualise lifelong learning.

It is the process of containment which, crucially, allows a student to develop the capacity to think and thus to learn. Yet little attention is given to developing the emotional capacities in teaching staff compared to the emphasis on IT skills or 'setting goals' (Smith and Spurling 2001). Salzberger-Wittenberg (1973) was a key initiator of thinking about the emotional basis of teaching and learning and the problematic nature of staying open to experience. She suggests the whole process of thought is inhibited by the inability to tolerate difficult feelings. While not ignoring the very practical support which students always require, French (1997) similarly emphasises the crucial role of a teacher as a 'container of anxiety'. He also draws attention to two fundamentally opposed conceptions of learning: on the one hand learning from experience and on the other what might be called learning as skill acquisition or competence development (French 1999, p. 1125). In his view, the former is multidimensional and is not only intellectual, but also emotional, political, and spiritual, whereas the latter is a linear conceptualisation of learning, defined as a succession of competencies or skills that are pre-defined. He sees the capacity to stay at the edge of 'knowing and not knowing' as the painful requisite to any real learning (French and Simpson 2000, p. 5). Vince (1996, pp. 45–52) specifically adapts Kolb's learning cycle to take account of the notion of how anxiety prompts great uncertainty as new knowledge is faced or the risks involved in speaking in one's own voice or using critical judgement are engaged with. In his terms, if this can be managed, it leads to insight and an inner authority, but if it cannot, it leads to avoidance, diversionary activity, willed ignorance, and, as a consequence perhaps, the need to show contempt.

Menzies (1960/1988) examined what happens when people are trapped in institutions which do not respect emotional experience in this way and do not provide the necessary level of emotional containment. She defined the concept of 'social defences against anxiety' which will then arise in such workplace. Applying this concept to present day higher education, Cummins and Thomas (2006) reflect on high dropout rates, plagiarism, and dependent and self-destructive behaviour. They conclude that the problem is less about failing individuals and more about the relations going on between student and teacher and institution. In other words, the solution does not lie in more study skills support but rather in preserving and building on those aspects of current teaching which provide for a relational model. The move to impersonal industrialised learning works against a sense of connection and produces the experience of absence and unavailability. In other words, the institutional systems are not emotionally containing but impersonal. Cummins and Thomas argue for a return to a tutorial-based system so that the dependency needs of students are better met, this being the precursor to becoming an independent learner. Their analysis closely echoes the shift described in Story 3: 'Learning Reviews' with the move away from a largely impersonal, online approach for PDP courses and towards developing a successful module with a 'complex weave' around the subject discipline in which the relationship between teacher and student is once again central.

Conclusion

The dominant view in education now places great emphasis on performance, competencies, and learning as skill acquisition. The role of a 'teacher' is increasingly being interpreted as one of ensuring delivery of predefined outcomes. This 'business model' language penetrates ever more deeply across all public services and now is extending into higher education. It de-emphasises the importance of learning as a complex social interaction. There seems at best to be a growing ignorance, and at worst a contempt, for the idea of learning as an embodied, relational process. In psycho-social terms what is happening can be interpreted as the annihilation of an approach which values the place of a creative 'third space' (Shipton 2007). Yet other alternative approaches have always understood the impact of learning in multiple ways—intellectually, emotionally, politically, and spiritually, and it is from these we need to draw inspiration.

The stories in this chapter describe from a teacher's perspective how women but also male students in general responded well to an interactive, conversational approach to teaching: one which closely integrated their reflection on learning from experience with theory and critical judgement. The students as a consequence developed confidence, a sense of agency, and a greater capacity for intellectual and ethical reflection. Finally, the chapter draws attention to the way psycho-social ideas can bring a new awareness and understanding to the 'under the surface' experiences in the classroom. Such thinking can also contribute to a practical and theoretical rebuttal of the now overly dominant linear and systems-driven ways of thinking about teaching and learning.

References

Aram, E., & Noble, D. (1999). Educating prospective managers in complexity of organisational life. *Management Learning, 30*(3), 321–342.

Belenky, M., Clinchy, B., Goldberger, R., & Tarule, J. (1986). *Womens's ways of knowing*. New York: Basic Books.

Burke, P. J., & Jackson, S. (2007). *Reconceptualising lifelong learning: Feminist interventions.* Abingdon Oxon: Routledge.

Colley, H. (2006). From childcare practitioner to FE tutor: Biography, identity and lifelong learning. In C. Leathwood & B. Francis (Eds.), *Gender and lifelong learning: Critical feminist engagements.* London: RoutledgeFalmer.

Cooper, A., & Lousada, J. (2005). *Borderline welfare.* Tavistock Clinic Series. London: Karnac.

Cummins, A.-M. (2002). The road to hell is paved with good intentions: Quality assurance as a social defence against anxiety. *Organisational and Social Dynamics, 1*(1), 99–119.

Cummins, A.-M., & Thomas, J. (2006). *Relational psychoanalysis and student's learning.* Paper presented to the Organisation for Promoting Understanding of Society (OPUS) Conference, November 2006, London.

Daly, M., & Rake, K. (2003). *Gender and the welfare state.* Cambridge: Polity.

Davies, B. (2003). Death to critique and dissent? The policies and practices of new managerialism and of "evidence based practice." *Gender and Education, 15*(1), 91–103.

Eagleton, T. (2003). *After theory.* London: Penguin.

Ferudi, F. (April 22, 2008). Flat-pack degrees: Learn how to sell furniture—but not at university. *The Guardian, EducationGuardian,* p. 13.

French, R. (1997). The teacher as container of anxiety. *Journal of Management Education, 21*(4), 483–495.

French, R. (1999). The importance of capacities in psychoanalysis and the language of human development. *Journal of Psychoanalysis, 80*(6), 1215–1226.

French, R., & Simpson, P. (2000). Learning at the edges between knowing and not knowing: Translating Bion. *Organisational and Social Dynamics, 1,* 54–77.

Friere, P. (1970). *Pedagogy of the oppressed.* New York: Herder and Herder.

Gerhardt, S. (2004). *Why love matters: How affection shapes a baby's brain.* Hove: Brunner-Routledge.

Gilligan, C. (1982). *In a different voice.* Cambridge: Harvard University Press.

Hatcher, C. (2003). Refashioning a passionate manager: Gender at work. *Gender, Work and Organization, 10*(4), 391–412.

Higher Education Academy. (2008). PDP update: Policy and practice 25 March. http://www.ukcle.ac.uk/resources/pdp/varnava.html. Accessed 29 July 2010.

Hoggett, P. (2000). *Emotional life and the politics of welfare.* Basingstoke: Macmillan.

Hoggett, P. (2002). The love that thinks. *Free Associations, 9*(1), 1–23.

Holmes, M. (2007). *What is gender?* London: Sage.

Hood, C. (1991). A public management for all seasons. *Public Administration, 69*(1), 3–19 (RIPA).

James, A. (April 7, 2009). Academies of the apocalypse. *The Guardian, EducationGuardian.* http://www.guardian.co.uk/education/2009/apr/07/mba-business-schools-credit-crunch. Accessed 29 July 2010.

Kamler, B. (2006). Older women as lifelong learners. In C. Leathwood & B. Francis (Eds.), *Gender and lifelong learning: Critical feminist engagements.* London: Palgrave.

Kohlberg, L. (1981). *The philosophy of moral development.* San Francisco: Harper and Row.

Leitch, S. (2006). *Prosperity for all in the global economy—world class skills.* Norwich: HMSO.

McLaughlin, K., Osborne, S., & Ferlie, E. (Eds.). (2002). *New public management.* London: Routledge.

Menzies Lyth, I. (1960/1988). *Containing anxiety in institutions: Selected Essays, Vol. 1.* London: Free Association Books.

Minsky, R. (1998). *Psychoanalysis and culture.* Cambridge: Polity.

Mojab, S. (2006). War and Diaspora as lifelong learning contexts for immigrant women. In C. Leathwood & B. Francis (Eds.), *Gender and lifelong learning: Critical feminist engagements.* London: Palgrave.

Monk, A., & Grayling, A. (April 8, 2008). Is the Renaissance scholar dead? *The Guardian, EducationGuardian.* http://www.guardian.co.uk/education/2008/apr/08/highereducation.uk. Accessed 29 July 2010.

Murray, U. (2006). A narrative exploration of meaning in the public sector. Doctoral dissertation, University of Hertfordshire.

Newman, J. (2002). The New public management, modernisation and institutional change disruptions, disjunctures and dilemmas. In K. McLaughlin, S. Osborne, & E. Ferlie (Eds.), *New public management: Current trends and future prospects.* Routledge: London.

Newman, J. (2005). Bending bureaucracy: Leadership and multi level governance. In P. du Gay (Ed.), *The values of bureaucracy.* Oxford: Oxford University Press.

Newman, J., & Williams, F. (1995). Diversity and change. In C. Itzen & J. Newman (Eds.), *Gender, culture and organisational change.* London: Routledge.

Obholzer, A. (1994). Authority, power and leadership: Contributions from group relations training. In A. Obholzer & V. Z. Roberts (Eds.), *The unconscious at work.* London: Routledge.

OPUS. (2007). *Organisation for promoting understanding of society.* http://www.opus.org.uk. Accessed 29 July 2010.

Rees, J. (March 18, 2008). Lost opportunities: James Rees on how closing the skills gap is opening up the social divide. *The Guardian, EducationGuardian,* p. 8.

Salzberger-Wittenberg, I. (1973). *Psychoanalytic insights and relationships: A Kleinian approach.* London: Routledge.

Sharma, A. (2008). *Logics of empowerment: Development, gender and governance in neoliberal.* Minneapolis: University of Minnesota Press.

Shipton, G. (2007). The annihilation of triangular space in David Mamet's Oleanna and some implications for teacher–student relationships in the era of mass university education. *Psychodynamic Practice, 13*(2), 31.

Smith, J., & Spurling, A. (2001). *Understanding motivation for lifelong learning.* Leicester: NIACE.

Stacey, R. D. (2003a). *Complexity and group process: A radical social understanding of individuals.* Hove: Brunner-Routledge.

Stacey, R. D. (2003b). Learning as an activity of interdependent people. *Learning Organisation, 10*(6), 325.

Stacey, R., & Griffin, D. (2005). Experience and method: A complex responsive processes perspective on research in organisations. In R. Stacey & D. Griffin (Eds.), *A complexity perspective on researching organisations.* London: Routledge.

Stapley, L. (2006). *Individuals, Groups, and Organizations beneath the surface: An introduction.* London: Karnac.

Stiles, W. B. (1995). Stories tacit knowledge, and psychotherapy research. *Psychotherapy Research, 5*(2), 125–127.

Strebler, M. (1997). Soft skills and hard questions. *People Management, 2*(May), 21–24.

Tolofari, S. (2005). New public management and education. *Policy Futures in Education, 3*(1), 75–88.

Tucket, A. (January 15, 2008). Further falls. *The Guardian, EducationGuardian,* p. 8.

Vince, R. (1996). *Managing change: Reflections on equality and management learning.* Bristol: The Policy Press.

Walzer, M. (1987). *Interpretation and Social criticism.* Cambridge: Harvard University Press.
Worth, S. (2005). *Defending narrativity against Strawson.* Paper presented to the Royal Institute of Philosophy Conference Narrative and Understanding Persons Conference, 12–14 July, University of Hertfordshire.
Youell, B. (2006). *The learning relationship: Psychoanalytic thinking in education.* London: Karnac.

Chapter 4
Widening Educational Participation: Masculinities, Aspirations and Decision-Making Processes

Penny Jane Burke

Introduction

This chapter focuses on the decision-making processes involved in accessing higher education. I draw on my ESRC funded research (RES-000-22-0832) on masculinities and men returning to study, which aims to understand the ways that gendered identities shape and impact on men's experiences of access courses and their educational aspirations. Thirty-nine men took part in two in-depth interviews, and all were participating in London access or foundation programmes. Although the primary focus of the study was on gender and masculinity, my theoretical perspective understands gendered identities as complex formations that intersect with multiple identifications and social positions, including age, class, dis/ability, ethnicity, nationality, race, religion and sexuality. My analysis in this chapter attempts to make sense of complex identity formations across multiple sets of differences and the ways that these might shed light on the processes of decision making that the men were engaged in as learners. The analysis is contextualised in relation to policies of lifelong learning and widening participation which to some extent frame the men's decisions, aspirations and choices about where and what to study and their dispositions and sensibilities as (potential) higher education students.

Social inclusion and widening educational participation are central concerns in lifelong learning policy, both in UK and EU policies (DfEE 1998, 1999; European Union 2004). Participation in learning has been identified as a mechanism by which to tackle social exclusion and to improve national economic competitiveness, often overshadowing concerns with social equity and justice in education (Morley 2000, p. 230). Lifelong learning policy constructs a 'knowledge society' of individual and

---

Reprinted by permission of Taylor & Francis Group (http://www.informaworld.com) from British Educational Research Journal, 32/5 (2006), Penny Jane Burke: Men accessing education: gendered aspirations.

P. J. Burke (✉)
School of Education, Roehampton University, London, UK
e-mail: p.burke@roehampton.ac.uk

flexible learners, and a key problem is seen as lying with those who lack the aspirations to capitalise on the range of learning opportunities freely available to all.

> The discourse of lifelong learning in the UK is one that favours individualism and instrumentalism, embedded within structures and organisations that are themselves gendered, raced and classed. (Jackson 2003, p. 366)

I draw on research on men, masculinities and educational participation to shed light on the processes of decision making that the men engage in and the relationship between this, their decisions about participating in higher education and their gendered aspirations. I conceptualise processes of decision making as tied in with complex sets of shifting identities which shape the men's aspirations. The men's aspirations and decisions are discursively re/fashioned through complex negotiations made within social contexts, structures and relations.

Lifelong learning policy that aims to tackle social exclusion necessitates a theorised understanding of classed, gendered and racialised identity formations (Webb 1997; Anderson and Williams 2001; Reay 2001; Archer et al. 2002) in order to expose the complex operations of inequality within sites of lifelong learning. Many strategies to widen educational participation have ignored the insights of theoretical work that attempts to understand the relationship between complex power relations, social inequalities and gendered identities. As a consequence, much lifelong learning policy tends to be informed by taken-for-granted assumptions that have not been critically examined, problematised or addressed (Archer et al. 2003), often exacerbating educational inequalities (Burke 2002). Hegemonic discourses of 'social exclusion' are themselves embedded in problematic assumptions about cultural deficit and working-class and minority ethnic failure (Archer and Leathwood 2003).

In this chapter, in order to understand the men's decisions and aspirations, I draw on the body of literature that points to identity as productive of complex forms of exclusion in lifelong learning (see, e.g. Mahony and Zmroczek 1997; Thompson 2000; Reay 2001; Reay et al. 2002; Youdell 2006; Burke and Jackson 2007). This literature conceptualises identity as discursively produced, as well as structural and tied to concrete material conditions. It explores the complex intersections of identity, including age, class, dis/ability, ethnicity, gender, race and sexuality, and the ways that these intersect in unpredictable and fluid ways to re/produce structural inequalities and discursive misrecognitions.

Educational aspirations and decisions are discursively fashioned through complex formations of identity and identifications. Regulatory and competing discourses make available a range of classed, masculine and racialised identities within and outside of educational fields. The men are engaged, as are all subjects of and in the social world, in an ongoing process of becoming (students of higher education) and of complex sets of identification (Hall 1992, pp. 287–288): the subtle, shifting and active recognition of self and other. Masculinity as a concept highlights 'differences in power and experience between groups of men' (Archer 2003, p. 14) and supports a sociological analysis of the ways that decisions and aspirations are socially contextualised and embedded in complex gendered relations. As 'configurations of practice', masculinities are produced through social relations which include 'differences and hierarchies among men' (Connell 2000, p. 23). Within different social contexts, such as schools and colleges, men are 'incited to adopt certain practices of "masculinity" and, hence, to display themselves as incumbents of certain categories of masculinity on particular occasions' (Martino 1999, p. 240). The men's accounts reveal 'how centrally class as well as gender is implicated in psychic processes' (Reay 2001, p. 223), and a detailed analysis uncovers the interconnections between the auto/biographical, cultural, discursive, emotional and material in the re/fashioning of gendered aspirations across individual histories.

In this chapter I draw on a qualitative study of 39 men taking access and foundation programmes in three further education colleges and one university in London. The in-depth interviews focused on the men's educational memories, histories and experiences. The interview transcripts are not analysed as reflecting an objective reality, but as discursive and partial accounts of the men's memories and experiences which are produced in the specific situation of an interview. It was explained in the interview that pseudonyms would be used, for the sake of anonymity, and each participant was invited to select their own. Interestingly, in the majority of the cases the men selected their pseudonym with minimal consideration and little hesitation which suggests that the names are connected in some way to their sense of self. The men were selected under two sets of criteria: (1) that they were categorised by the college/university as home students and (2) that they were participating in an Access to Higher Education course, a Foundation degree or, in the case of the university, a Science and Engineering Foundation Programme (SEFP). The colleges and university were selected for their London location, their demographic differences and because they offered access and/or foundation programmes. It is noteworthy that although they are all home students, the men's countries of origin include Pakistan, Iraq, Bangladesh, Columbia, Kenya, Sudan, Belize, Spain, Nigeria, Bulgaria, Angola, Jamaica, Ghana, Portugal, Poland, Italy, Cyprus and England. Their ages ranged from 18 to 54. The men's generational and national diversity offers an analytic richness to a critical examination of decisions and aspirations across shifting and contradictory masculine identifications.

Widening Participation: Policy Contexts and Frameworks

Although widening participation (WP) has become a key policy discourse in England with particular orientations since the New Labour government's period in office, the project to widen access and participation in higher education has a long history, with competing perspectives and approaches Within these competing perspectives, there has been a strong commitment to redress the structural inequalities in higher education by targeting historically under-represented groups and developing support mechanisms to increase their participation in higher education. Access to Higher Education courses in England were initially developed with such aims in mind, and there was a clear strand of social justice running through this project (Kirton 1999; Burke 2002). Similarly, in the United States, a radical tradition exists whereby affirmative action policies were put into place to redress unequal participation patterns across different social groups and to encourage in particular the participation of Black students in higher education (Allen et al. 2005).

Jones and Thomas (2005) helpfully outline three contrasting approaches to WP, although the lived reality of widening participation is perhaps far messier than this represents. The first approach Jones and Thomas categorise as the 'academic approach'. This strand emphasises attitudinal factors such as 'low aspirations'. In this approach, activities to raise aspirations are prioritised and these are located at the peripheries of universities with 'little or no impact on institutional structure and culture' (p. 617). The second approach that they outline is the 'utilitarian approach' which similarly focuses on attitudinal factors, including again the notion of 'low aspirations'. The second approach is also concerned with lack of traditional academic qualifications and is embedded in a deficit understanding of WP. Jones and Thomas thus characterise the 'utilitarian approach' as the 'double deficit model' (p. 618) and one that particularly emphasises the relationship between higher education and the economy. The third approach they identify as 'transformative', which focuses on the needs of under-represented groups in higher education. They argue that higher status institutions are more likely to take the 'academic approach', less prestigious institutions are more likely to take the 'utilitarian approach', leaving little space for transformative approaches to higher education (p. 627).

In England, as most 'non-traditional' entrants to higher education are concentrated in the post 1992 new universities, the hegemonic discourse of widening participation is strongly framed by the utilitarian approach, and this is significantly influenced by the 'logic of neoliberal globalisation' (Jones et al. 1999, p. 238). Within this context, there is a firm acceptance that the economy and marketplace are at the centre of the project to widen participation as a key policy imperative. With notions of the market at the centre of WP policy, the key role of HE is constructed as enhancing employability, entrepreneurialism, economic competitiveness and flexibility (Morley 1999; Thompson 2000; Burke 2002; Archer et al. 2003; Bowl 2003). Neoliberal market oriented approaches significantly shape meanings of widening participation, including what and whom higher education is for (Burke and Jackson 2007).

Davies and Saltmarsh explain that neoliberalism

> espouses 'survival of the fittest' and unleashes competition among individuals, among institutions and among nations, freeing them from what are construed as the burdensome chains of social justice and social responsibility. Populations are administered and managed through the production of a belief in each individual in his or her own freedom and autonomy. (Davies and Saltmarsh 2007, p. 4)

The focus of neoliberalism is on the disciplining/ed individual who engages continuously in the project of self-improvement where it is up to the individual to make sure that he or she can 'get ahead'. Lifelong learning in this context becomes a central tool of neoliberal self-disciplinary mechanisms, so that every individual has the responsibility to participate in lifelong learning in order to gain credentials to enhance their employability, continually responding to and responsible for meeting the requirements of a changing, dynamic and unstable global market. Neoliberalism erases collective sensibilities and social responsibility, rendering social inequality as secondary to individual mobility, firmly positioning individuals as 'consumers' of, and equal players in, the free market of lifelong learning and higher education.

Neoliberalism thus takes attention away from the ways that identities are implicated in complex social inequalities and reduces education to a technology of self-improvement for individual workers and consumers competing in a global market. Although the WP policy discourse makes rhetorical gestures towards eradicating exclusion from the different sites of lifelong learning, including higher education, the neoliberal reconstruction of 'exclusion' is one that firmly asserts responsibility to the individual named and identified as 'excluded'. Furthermore, the hegemonic neoliberal discourse of WP tends to operate around contradictory claims: on the one hand, the claim of the 'classless society' or the 'death of class' and, on the other, the powerful ways that 'class is invoked in moves to draw young people from deprived areas into HE' (Lawler 2005, p. 798). In similar ways, issues of gender equality are seen as irrelevant in WP policy debates, but reappear as a national concern in relation to the perceived crisis of masculinity and the claim that women are taking over the university (Quinn 2003). WP policy is a part of the broader neoliberal technologies of self-regulation in which subjects come to understand themselves as responsible for the production of a self with the skills and qualities required to succeed in the new economy (Walkerdine 2003, p. 239). Issues of structural inequality and cultural misrecognition become hidden in WP policy discourse, and rather individuals are called upon to take up the challenge of WP. Such a challenge is located in a wider neoliberal project of self-development and improvement through participation in lifelong learning opportunities which are presented as meritocratic and available to all who have the potential to benefit.

However, this is not to say that discourses of transformation and social justice are not still at play to some extent in WP policy, as this quote from the Higher Education Funding Council for England demonstrates:

> Widening participation addresses the large discrepancies in the take-up of higher education opportunities between different social groups. Under-representation is closely connected with broader issues of equity and social inclusion, so we are concerned with ensuring equality of opportunity for disabled students, mature students, women and men, and all ethnic groups. (HEFCE 2006)

The problematic of this excerpt becomes apparent, though, with close analytical attention to the framing policy text which places emphasis on individuals from under-represented groups taking responsibility to change their aspirations, dispositions and values (Gewirtz 2001). This emphasis has significantly altered relations between the individual and the state and has led to a shift from government to governance, 'signalling a move away from a citizen-based notion of rights associated with a sense of the public, to an individualistic client-based notion of right based on contractual obligations' (Blackmore 2006, p. 13). Just as individual students are responsible for their self-improvement, individual teachers and WP practitioners are responsible to raise the aspirations of young, disadvantaged individuals identified as having potential. I have argued elsewhere that aspirations are not individually formed, but are relational and interconnected with complex auto/biographies, multiple identifications and social positionings and are discursively produced within schools, colleges and universities (Burke 2006). What is not considered in the hegemonic discourses of WP is the necessity of transforming education institutions in order to address seriously the deeply embedded structural inequalities and discursive misrecognitions that exist across intersections of age, class, dis/ability, ethnicity, gender, inter/nationality, race, religion and sexuality. These complex inequalities are intricately intertwined with longstanding cultural and discursive mis/representations which produce discourses of derision (Ball 1990) and pathologised subjectivities (Skeggs 2004). In critiquing what she names as the narrow skills-driven approach to WP policies, Carole Leathwood warns that such policies are likely to fail if they refuse to engage with the complex reasons why different social groups might be resistant to education in relation to their negative experiences of learning in formal institutions:

> The current lifelong learning strategy is likely to fail if the narrow skills-driven approach which alienates potential learners continues to be pursued. There is already a healthy resistance to participation from many who regard the education on offer as middle-class and alien, and without any attempts to address the reasons for such resistance, and to ensure that educational opportunities offer positive and relevant experiences and benefits, many of those who are intended recipients of lifelong learning are likely to continue to resist it. (Leathwood 2006, p. 52)

Indeed, those entering higher education from 'different' backgrounds are often seen as potentially contaminating of university standards, and as a result a key policy strategy is to protect the quality of higher education by creating new and different spaces for those new and different students (Morley 2003). For example the Government White Paper, *The Future of Higher Education*, reads:

> Our overriding priority is to ensure that as we expand HE places, we ensure that the expansion is of an appropriate quality and type to meet the demands of employers and the needs of the economy and students. We believe that the economy needs more work focused degrees—those, like our new foundation degrees, that offer specific, job-related skills. We want to see expansion in two-year, work-focused foundation degrees; and in mature students in the workforce developing their skills. As we do this, we will maintain the quality standards required for access to university, both *safeguarding the standards of traditional honours degrees and promoting a step-change in the quality and reputation of workfocused courses.* (DfES 2003, p. 64, emphasis added)

In this excerpt, WP is being explicitly linked with concerns about 'safeguarding the standards of traditional honours degrees'. The text implies that opening access to new student constituencies has the potential to have a negative effect on traditional university spaces which need to be protected against the entry of 'non-traditional' students. It also assumes that the appropriate level of participation for those new student constituencies is work-based degrees rather than traditional honours degrees. This leads policy in the direction of creating new and different kinds of courses for new and different kinds of students without addressing that these differences are shown to be classed, gendered and racialised by research in the field (HEFCE 2005; Reay et al. 2005). In analysing their interviews with working-class students, Reay et al. (2005, p. 85) explain:

> Choice for the majority [of working-class students] involved either a process of finding out what you cannot have, what is not open for negotiation and then looking at the few options left, or a process of self-exclusion.

In this way, the WP policy agenda is not able to challenge the status quo, or redress the legacy of the under/mis-representation of certain social groups in traditional forms of higher education which carry with them status and esteem. As a result enduring hierarchies, privileges and inequalities remain untouched whilst new forms of unequal social relations are being created (Burke 2002). This logic constructs 'WP students' in very particular ways and leaves notions of deficit in place. Traditional student identity is subtly held in place so that the traditional university undergraduate is re-constituted as white-racialised and middle-classed. The 'WP student' is constituted as 'Other', deserving of higher education access, but only to 'other' kinds of courses and institutions.

Aiming Higher[1] and Raising Aspirations

In this section, I interrogate the hegemonic policy discourse of 'raising aspirations' which forms a significant focus of widening participation policy. I will deconstruct this discourse to unearth the assumptions and values underpinning it and to identify its implications for widening educational participation and for the men's aspirations and decisions.

Aimhigher has been the key policy initiative in England to work towards the government's goal of increasing participation levels in higher education towards 50% of 18–30-year-olds by the year 2010. This initiative aims to 'raise the aspirations' of talented individuals from disadvantaged social-economic backgrounds. Aimhigher has undoubtedly made a valuable contribution to WP, for example, by providing useful and accessible information to parents and pupils and supporting them in making important decisions about their future participation in education. However, the hegemonic discourse of 'raising aspirations', which underpins the Aimhigher framework, is problematic in the ways that it produces deficit constructions of 'disadvantaged' communities and conceptualises aspirations as individual and linear (Burke 2006).

The main work of Aimhigher staff has been seen as 'raising the aspirations' of young people who stand out as having special talent and potential despite their social positioning. The discourse locates problems of deficit in individuals who are pathologised through the discourse of 'social exclusion' (Gewirtz 2001; Skeggs 2004). The problem lies in the processes of identifying who has potential—and who does not—and the assumption is that such processes are objective and fair and unconnected from wider social inequalities. Gillborn and Youdell (2000) demonstrate in their study that the construction of ability within schools continues to be a highly classed, gendered and racialised process. The notion of 'potential' is highly subjective and rests on assumptions about ability and on privileged ontological dispositions (i.e. those coded as young, able-bodied, middle-class, white and heterosexual). Raising aspirations is constructed as an individual self-improvement project, facilitated by the new WP labour force, which occurs outside of social relations and the micropolitics of educational organisations (Morley 1999). Within this

---

[1] Since writing this chapter, it has been announced that funding for Aim Higher has ceased.

framework, the complex social and personal histories in which particular forms of knowledge and capital have been privileged and particular bodies have been coded as knowledgeable are ignored. Rather, knowledge and knowing is constructed as objective, apolitical, decontextualised, disembodied and detached from the legacy of the misrecognition of the cultural capital, literacy practices and knowledge of historically marginalised groups (Apple 2006).

Raising aspirations is connected to the neoliberal policy discourse of social exclusion which has been critiqued by sociologists (e.g. Gewirtz 2001; Archer et al. 2003) to expose the ways that it leaves the operations of power unexamined. Shifting the attention to 'exclusion' and away from structural inequalities and discursive misrecognitions operates as a mechanism to reprivilege particular cultural practices and values. The heterogeneity of British society is framed in terms of 'diversity', and yet the complex differences and inequalities behind diversity are silenced. Importantly, sociological work emphasises that identities are produced within the discursive sites and practices of schools, colleges and universities (Mac an Ghaill 1994). Excluded identities themselves are constructed, performed, named and produced within schools, colleges and universities (Youdell 2006). The emphasis on individual aspirations misses out the significant interconnections between a subject's aspirations and their classed, racialised, (hetero)sexualised and gendered identities, ignoring the social and cultural contexts in which subjects are constructed, and construct themselves, as having or not having potential, or indeed not choosing to participate in higher education for a range of valid reasons (Archer and Leathwood 2003). Aspirations themselves are formed through social relations and identity positions; they are negotiated and renegotiated within the social contexts that the individual is situated: they are not linear in formation, but cyclical, iterative and reflexive (Burke 2006). Aspirations are tied to gendered identities in complex ways that require close and qualitative analytical attention.

Decision-Making Processes and Formations of Aspirations

Aspirations are discursive and closely tied in with structural differences and inequalities. The men taking part in this research expressed high levels of aspiration, which is not altogether surprising, considering these are men who successfully accessed education through different alternative-entry programmes. However, the ways in which they articulated their aspirations requires close analysis to reveal the connections between their individual aspirations, complex decision-making processes negotiated with others, policy and wider discourses (such as neoliberalism) and classed, gendered and racialised identities. The processes by which the men re/constructed their aspirations in the interviews involved taking up, rejecting, challenging and remaking identifications across space and time at local, cultural and global levels. The processes were also closely tied to structural and material im/possibilities as well as the different sets of capital (e.g. cultural, linguistic and social) un/available to the men. A myriad of influences shaped the men's shifting and contradictory aspirations and decisions including family, community, friends and teachers, as well as national and religious identifications. This section will begin to explore the men's accounts to shed light on some of the critiques made of WP policy above and to consider the ways that decision making and formations of aspirations are shaped by masculinities and neoliberalism.

There are many examples of contradictory aspirations in the men's accounts, influenced by family, friends and uncertain and shifting identifications. Dragon, born in Pakistan, is an 18-year-old student participating on a Science and Engineering Foundation Programme (SEFP) at an East London University. Dragon is significantly influenced by his parents' perspectives and also by his national and religious sense of self. His early aspirations are attached to his strong sense of loyalty to his family and the hegemonic discourses around being a man in his local community. His response below constructs an imagined heterosexual, responsible family man who conforms to the expectations of his extended family. He talks about his own plans in relation to the wider community with which he identifies, explaining that 'we' usually marry at the age of 24.

> Interviewer: If you can recall two years back, when you were sixteen, what would you have imagined yourself doing at twenty six?
> Dragon: I would imagine doing my job and hopefully married as well. Because we usually get married about twenty four. And just a normal house, a car as well, and I've actually tried to do my practical car test and failed twice. But I am going to try again. Third time.

In expressing his aspirations in the interview, he constructs different versions of himself that are able to fit in with both his Pakistani and English identifications. He tries on different versions of manhood: being a businessman, a dentist, a doctor, and these are tied in with the varied contexts of his everyday life, moving in and out of different cultures and expectations. Some of these are attractive to him, due to the embodied identifications that such masculinities carry, such as being a businessman and wearing a suit. Other aspirations are shaped around what he believes is available to him or not, the level of competition involved and the kinds of careers his family would desire for him.

> Interviewer: What was your dream job, before starting your A levels, what did you imagine…?
> Dragon: Before it was just a business manager, because I went into the City and saw these businessmen with their suitcases and suits, and coming out of big buildings, and I thought—yeah, this is something I want. But before coming over here, because doing science engineering its biology engineering as well, so maybe I can do this and try for medicine, or dentistry, which I was really interested in, but dentistry is hard competition. I would have to actually do this and then a degree in biology or something, a science subject, and then apply. And still there might not be a guarantee of me getting in, which is why I left that.

In the context of his national identifications as a Pakistani man, his hopes for the future are modest and safe, careful not to rock the boundaries of his community and family. He imagines himself primarily as a husband and father, able to support his family through a secure job.

> Interviewer: What about now, if you think yourself ten years ahead, what do you see?
> Dragon: Just a normal person with a job, hopefully, and a wife and kids and nothing too much.

Yet, in the discursive context of the interview, and the specific prompts used by the interviewer, he also expresses contradictory dreams that are challenging to these normalised versions of being a man within his community.

> Interviewer: What would be a dream come true, in jobs?
> Dragon: Oh I'll be very rich, going around to countries with my job and be a very important person. Not like a politician or anything, but close to that. And have a massive house, probably in America. I visited America and the houses over there are really nice. Very big. And one more thing, which I want to try to make possible, is to become a cricketer. I'm a really huge fan of cricket. I'm not actually in any clubs at the moment, and people say I should join. And I'm OK, I can play good as well. Not really good. But just good. So that's one of those dreams I think is achievable with a bit of practice.

Dragon plays around with discourses of success and heterosexual masculinity, having a huge house and being 'a very important person', such as a cricket celebrity. He is drawn back-and-forth between 'dream' and 'realistic' aspirations in the interview, and he fashions his 'realistic aspirations' around being modest, responsible and unselfish, characteristics he associates with what it means to be a Muslim man.

> Interviewer: OK, now you've described to me the big dream. What would you realistically expect of yourself?
> Dragon: I think a job that just pays well, just to manage my family and house. Expenses and…maybe just occasionally holidays and things. That's fine. Because really my religion does say that you don't really need much, and if you do have much you just give, so you are equal to everyone. So I just don't want too much. Just enough will be fine.

Unsurprisingly perhaps, families are a recurring theme in the men's accounts about their educational decision making, and mothers seem to play a particularly central role in the men's decisions. However, sociological analysis helps illuminate the social and relational dimensions of decision making and aspiration, rather than simply focusing on individual mothers and families. Such an analysis takes account of the complex power relations within families and the gendered relationship between mothers and sons. It also highlights the fragile line that mothers walk when they are supporting their children in making the 'right' educational choices and decisions: a thin line between regulating and policing decision-making processes and being caring and supportive.

Ali, a 19-year-old SEFP student originally from Iraq, speaks specifically about his mother's important influence in processes of decision making about his choice of what and where to study. In his account, his mother is unable to strike the almost impossible balance of simultaneously being a friend and a responsible parent. Ali describes the double-edged sword of parental expectations, and relates his difficulties with A levels as an effect of the pressure his mother exerted over his schoolwork. Ali defines his family's background as middle-class, and his account fits closely in with wider expectations of (middle-class) parents and sociological literature on the relationship of middle-class parents to their child's education (Power et al. 2003).

> Ali: I would say my mum, she had a big influence, because I always had to do…she asked me if I had done my work or had not done my work, how am I doing in the school, am I doing fine? […]…even though when somebody insists that you have to do the work you

start to hate it. That's one of the reasons now I find it a bit hard with A levels, to keep up with my work, because always I've been told—we came all the way from back home, here, for you to study and to be better. And that put more pressure on me. And when you pressure someone he wouldn't do as good as he wants.

Later in the interview, though, Ali talks about his admiration for his mother, who was able to overcome what he describes as a set of catastrophic events, and through her own determination made the decision to come to the UK to escape the 'constant pain' of living in invaded Iraq. He explains that his mother comes from a wealthy background and became a single mother after the death of his father. Concerned for Ali's safety due to the war, she made the 'tough decision' to move with the children to England. Ali explains that his mother had specific aspirations for him to pursue a career in medicine, while Ali wanted to go into physics. Although he was not motivated to study, he put effort into his GCSEs because it would have been 'cruel' in his eyes to do any differently considering the sacrifices his mother made to seek refuge in the UK for his safety.

Ali: Yes, even though I was trying to do something in physics I didn't tell my mum. She always wanted me to be a doctor, or something prestigious. So I had to just say—OK. That's when I really tried…actually from GCSE I started to drift away from my studies, trying to avoid the subject, because my mum, she tells me to go and study. I tried to avoid it. So when it came to doing the other subjects, it would be a bit cruel if I said for my mum, because it was for myself. But I would say for mum, because I know she got through so much hassle to get us here. But I thought it would be rewarding, even though I didn't make it. Still I passed.

Ali explains how he came to decide to pursue engineering, which involved sensitive and careful negotiations with his mother. Engineering, he explains, fits in better with his 'personality' than medicine, and he seems to take up neoliberal discourses around entrepreneurialism, ambition and self-determination. This again exposes the complex processes involved in decision and aspiration making which, in Ali's case, is linked to his mother's perspectives, her auto/biography and its relationship to his experiences, his self-identifications and hegemonic discourses around acceptable careers for young men in the UK.

Ali appears to position himself in relation to neoliberal discourses of success and determination. He constructs himself as immune to any social constraints because he has a goal and so he is able to overcome anything through his individual determination and self-belief. In this way, he might be seen as the ideal 'widening participation student' who constructs himself in relation to discourses of meritocracy and sees success as available to all men who work hard, adapt to 'British culture' and are willing to give 'whatever it takes' to succeed. Ali explains:

First of all, when I came from Iraq, for me it doesn't make a difference wherever I go. Wherever I go I feel home, for some reason I don't know. People say they are homesick and stuff, but for me I just adapt to it because I have to. Because I've got a goal, which is to be successful. So whatever it takes, I will.

Many of the men in this research had complex experiences of migration, and their aspirations are formed between and across competing discourses about forms of masculinity and aspiration in different familial, national and cultural contexts. In some of the men's accounts, 'British culture' is idealised and contrasted to their 'home cultures'. Furthermore, the theme of families and parenting is different across the data set, as the older men also form their decisions in relation to their own identifications as parents. For example, when Skiddo is asked what he has learned in his access course, he answers in terms of gaining broader values as a father, specifically values of love and respect. Skiddo is a 30-year-old Access to Health studies, Nursing and Midwifery student at an East London further education college from an African background. He is self-defined working-class. His account resonates with Gewirtz' critique of New labour policies that were focused on working on the marginalised to become more like white, middle-class parents (Gewirtz 2001).

> At home? You can never compare them because what I have learned here is respect and love, and you don't have that from the teachers there. If I was back home the love that I have for my daughter, I don't believe I should have now, because there you just believe everybody is looking after themselves. Some parents, they don't even see their kids for days, weeks, but they live in the same house, get out in the morning, come back in the night, and don't even check to see if they are asleep well. Too many things I have learned I can never compare them, because it depends on the society. It is not a bad thing for them, but it is just a way of life in that part of the world.

Although there are generational differences in the men's accounts, there are also similarities. Like Ali, Skiddo takes up neoliberal discourses of flexibility, individualism and adaptability in explaining his decisions and aspirations, but also ideal-type student-dispositions. Both Skiddo and Ali explain their decisions through familiar narratives of positive thinking, working towards a goal, staying focused and moving forward. They both take up neoliberal discourses in making sense of their migration experiences and in coping with the challenges that face them, both as students and as living in new cultural environments. For example, Skiddo says:

> I would say I am the type of person, I adapt to any situation and any environment very quickly. When I left my country I left everything behind me, but I never thought about who I was and what I left, and stuff. I just think there is a challenge ahead of me. So I would say when I left there I forgot what I used to do. I would think that part of being a businessman inside me, probably might do something part time like that. But now I am focused on doing what I want to do now.

Although the kinds of discourses Skiddo draws on have resonance with the success narratives of neoliberalism, he also locates himself firmly in relation to the tribal values of his home community:

> Bamlake, Bamlake is a very proud tribe. So I am proud to be a Bamlake. They are business inclined and hard working. Most people from this tribe are always doing well.

In this way, Skiddo constructs his student-dispositions as related directly to the tribal community to which he continues to have a strong sense of belonging. This is an interesting insight that challenges the UK policy focus on individual parents and helps to shed light on the strengths that minority ethnic students bring to access courses from their experiences of broader forms of support offered beyond immediate family relations.

Complex and Contradictory Masculine Aspirations

Drawing on interviews with men participating in access and foundation pro-grammes, I have argued that lifelong learning policy, with its related discourses of social inclusion and widening participation, is too narrowly focused on simplistic notions of 'raising aspirations' which are embedded in discourses of individualism, meritocracy and neoliberalism. This focus not only leaves hidden intricate opera-tions of power, privilege and inequality but also constructs certain groups as lacking and inferior as compared to a core community of 'included' citizens who are seen as having the right kinds of values, skills and aspirations.

The interviews explored aspiration making across time, by examining the men's auto/biographies and memories, and across space, by considering the impact of changing cultural and geographical contexts and competing masculine identifica-tions. In highlighting classed, generational, national and racialised differences, I have argued that individual aspirations are discursively constituted formations, al-ways contextualised and produced within complex social relations. The men's deci-sions and aspirations are produced through their masculine identifications and in-tricate re/negotiations with others, in relation to changing trans/national discursive fields. They are also shaped by wider neoliberal discourses that implicate them in the project of self-improvement and in disciplinary technologies of self-regulation.

This chapter argues for a theorised and nuanced approach to understanding de-cision making and formations of aspiration that accounts for identity, context and social relations. Policy developments that aim to tackle social exclusion and injus-tices must take into account the discursive nature of aspiration making. Utilitarian approaches to WP are stuck at the attitudinal level, unable to capture the complex-ity of decision making about educational participation. It is crucial to understand that aspirations are not constructed exclusively at the individual level, but are tied in with complex structural, cultural and discursive relations and practices. Policy initiatives such as Aimhigher undoubtedly made an important contribution to life-long learning and widening participation, but were also in danger of exacerbating social inequalities and misrecognitions further through deficit constructions. The men's accounts illuminate the complexity of decision making and aspiration form-ing, which are relational, negotiated and contextualised.

References

Allen, W. R., Jayakumar, U. M., Griffen, K. A., Korn, W. S., & Hurtado, S. (2005). *Black under-graduates from Bakke to Grutter: Freshmen status, trends and prospects, 1971–2004.* Los Angeles: Higher Education Research Institute, University of California.

Anderson, P., & Williams, J. (2001). *Identity and difference in higher education: 'Outsiders With-in'.* Aldershot: Ashgate.

Apple, M. W. (2006). *Educating the "right" way: markets, standards, God, and inequality.* Lon-don: Routledge.

Archer, L. (2003). *Race, masculinity and schooling: Muslim boys and education.* Berkshire: Open University Press.

Archer, L., & Leathwood, C. (2003). Identities, inequalities and higher education. In L. Archer, M. Hutchings, & A. Ross (Eds.), *Higher education and social class: Issues of exclusion and inclusion.* London: Routledge Falmer.

Archer, L., Leathwood, C., & Hutchings, M. (2002). Higher education: A risky business. In A. Hayton, & A. Paczuska (Eds.), *Access, participation and higher education.* London: Kogan Page and Stylus.

Archer, L., Hutchings, M., & Ross, A. (2003). *Higher education and social class: Issues of exclusion and inclusion.* London: Routledge Falmer.

Ball, S. (1990). *Politics and policy making in education.* London: Routledge.

Blackmore, J. (2006). Unprotected participation in lifelong learning and the politics of hope: A feminist reality check of discourses around flexibility, seamlessness and learner earners. In C. Leathwood, & B. Francis (Eds.), *Gender and lifelong learning: Critical feminist engagements.* Oxon: Routledge.

Bowl, M. (2003). *Non-traditional entrants to higher education: They talk about people like me.* Stoke-on-Trent: Trentham.

Burke, P. J. (2002). *Accessing education effectively widening participation.* Stoke-on-Trent: Trentham.

Burke, P. J. (2006). Men accessing education: Gendered aspiration. *British Educational Research Journal, 32*(5), 719–734.

Burke, P. J., & Jackson, S. (2007). *Reconceptualising lifelong learning: Feminist interventions.* London: Routledge.

Connell, R. W. (2000). *The men and the boys.* Cambridge: Polity.

Davies, B., & Saltmarsh, S. (2007). Gender economies: Literacy and the gendered production of neo-liberal subjectivities. *Gender and Education, 19*(1), 1–20.

DfEE. (1998). *The learning age: A renaissance for a new Britain.* London: The Stationery Office.

DfEE. (1999). *Learning to succeed—A new framework for post-16 learning.* London: The Stationery Office.

DfES. (2003). The *future of higher education.* London: The Stationery Office.

European Union. (2004). *The new generation of community education and training programmes after 2006.* Brussels: European Commission.

Gewirtz, S. (2001). Cloning the Blairs: New labour's programme for the re-socialization of working-class parents. *Journal of Educational Policy, 16*(4), 365–378.

Gillborn, D., & Youdell, D. (2000). *Rationing education: Policy, practice, reform and equity.* Buckingham: Open University Press.

Hall, S. (1992). Introduction: Identity in question. In S. Hall, D. Held, & T. McGrew (Eds.), *Modernity and its futures.* Cambridge: Polity.

HEFCE. (2005). *Young participation in higher education.* Bristol: Higher Education Funding Council for England.

HEFCE. (2006). *Widening participation: A review.* Bristol: Higher Education Funding Council for England.

Jackson, S. (2003). Lifelong earning: Working-class women and lifelong learning. *Gender and Education, 15*(4), 365–376.

Jones, R., & Thomas, L. (2005). The 2003 UK Government Higher Education White Paper: A critical assessment of its implications for the access and widening participation Agenda. *Journal of Education Policy, 20*(5), 615–630.

Jones, C., Turner, J., & Street, B. (1999). Introduction. In C. Jones, J. Turner, & B. Street (Eds.), *Students writing in the university: Cultural and epistemological issues.* Amsterdam: John Benjamins.

Kirton, A. (1999). Lessons from access education. In A. Hayton (Ed.), *Tackling disaffection and social exclusion: Education perspectives and policies.* London: Kogan Page.

Lawler, S. (2005). Introduction: Class, culture and identity. *Sociology, 39*(5), 797–806.

Leathwood, C. (2006). Gendered constructions of lifelong learning and the learner in the UK policy context. In C. Leathwood, & B. Francis (Eds.), *Gender and lifelong learning: Critical feminist engagements.* Oxon: Routledge.

Mac an Ghaill, M. (1994). *The making of men: Masculinities, sexualities and schooling.* Buckingham and Philadelphia: Open University Press.

Mahony, P., & Zmroczek, C. (Eds.) (1997) *Class matters: 'working-class' women's perspectives on social class.* London and Bristol: Taylor & Francis.

Martino, W. (1999). 'Cool boys,' 'party animals,' 'squids' and 'poofters': Interrogating the dynamics and politics of adolescent masculinities in school. *British Journal of Sociology of Education, 20*(2), 239–263.

Morley, L. (1999). *Organising feminisms: The micropolitics of the academy.* Hampshire: Macmillan.

Morley, L. (2000). The micropolitics of gender in the learning society. *Higher Education in Europe, 25*(2), 229–235.

Morley, L. (2003). *Quality and Power in Higher Education.* Milton Keynes: Open University Press.

Power, S., Whitty, G., & Wigfall, V. (2003). *Education and the middle class.* Buckingham: Open University Press.

Quinn, J. (2003). *Powerful subjects are women really taking over the university?* Stoke-on-Trent: Trentham.

Reay, D. (2001). Finding or losing yourself?: Working-class relationships to education. *Journal of Education Policy, 16*(4), 333–346.

Reay, D., Ball, S., & David, M. (2002). 'It's taking me a long time but I'll get there in the end': Mature students on access courses and higher education choice. *British Educational Research Journal, 28*(1), 5–19.

Reay, D., David, M., & Ball, S. (2005). *Degrees of choice: Class, race, gender and higher education.* Stoke-on-Trent: Trentham.

Skeggs, B. (2004). *Class, self, culture.* London: Routledge.

Thompson, J. (2000). Introduction. In J. Thompson (Ed.), *Stretching the academy: The politics and practice of widening participation in higher education.* Leicester: NIACE.

Walkerdine, V. (2003). Reclassifying upward mobility: Femininity and the neo-liberal Subject. *Gender and Education, 15*(3), 237–249.

Webb, S. (1997). Alternative students? Conceptualizations of difference. In J. Williams (Ed.), *Negotiating access to higher education: the discourse of selectivity and equity.* Buckingham: SHRHE and Open University Press.

Youdell, D. (2006). *Impossible bodies, impossible selves: Exclusions and student subjectivities.* Dordrecht: Springer.

Chapter 5
Innovatory Educational Models for Women Returners in Science, Engineering and Technology Professions

Clem Herman, Barbara Hodgson, Gill Kirkup and Elizabeth Whitelegg

Introduction

Women returning to work after a break have been the target of programmes and initiatives within the adult and higher education sectors for many years: they have also been the focus of government concern at times of skills shortages. Often drawing on feminist principles and pedagogies, such initiatives have generally aimed to empower women and raise their awareness of gender issues at the same time as offering skills and training in preparation for employment (Coats 1996; Ellen and Herman 2005; Phipps 2008). The initiative discussed in this chapter has its roots in these traditions but, by using an online environment, the government has been able to offer a new programme to a wider and more diversely distributed target group, as well as focussing on the needs of a specific group: women already qualified in Science, Engineering or Technology (SET) subject areas.

The chapter begins by outlining the continuing problem of under-representation of women and girls in SET including the specific needs of women in these sectors. We then discuss the background to, and rationale for, a recent programme of support measures developed by the UK government, one of which is an innovative online course which was developed by an established network of educators with a commitment to gender issues. The course, aimed at women SET graduates who want to return to work in this employment sector after a career break, is described and its impact discussed. We, the authors of this paper, are all members of the team responsible for creation and delivery of this course. We have also been involved (along with an external independent team) in evaluating how well the course has achieved its objectives. In this context, we are action researchers; the research data continue to be collected on the course, and changes to the course are made iteratively in response to this research and to other aspects of the environment. We end this chapter by generalising from our experience to make some recommendations for taking forward this kind of innovatory educational model for women returners in other

C. Herman (✉)
Department of Communication and Systems, The Open University, Milton Keynes, UK
e-mail: c.herman@open.ac.uk

S. Jackson et al. (eds.), *Gendered Choices,* Lifelong Learning Book Series 15,
DOI 10.1007/978-94-007-0647-7_5, © Springer Science+Business Media B.V. 2011

areas. The recommendations are relevant within a global context, but this chapter is mainly concerned with UK employment priorities, and the models discussed were developed to meet these.

Background to the Problem of Women's Careers in SET

Despite changes in science curricula in the UK and elsewhere over the past two decades, participation in SET at higher education level and in careers remains highly gender segregated. Predictions that compulsory study of science for all up to age 16 would result in more girls flowing through the educational pipeline into SET careers have resulted in disappointingly small increases in numbers. Educational choices, particularly for girls and particularly in science, are influenced by a complex web of interacting factors so that changes in curricula alone are unlikely to alter the situation radically to result in significantly increased numbers of girls choosing to study SET subjects (Murphy and Whitelegg 2006). This situation is replicated at an international level with many other studies showing similar patterns in other countries, and leading to global concerns about the consequences of such continued inequality.

The analogy of a leaky pipeline has commonly been used to illustrate the decline in the participation of girls and women in SET through the education system and into careers. For a minority of young women who do choose to continue with their study of SET beyond compulsory schooling into higher education and beyond, the pipeline narrows and leaks more rapidly as they encounter more and more barriers and constraints to their progress at each stage (Rees 2001). This is illustrated by a study of young women members of the Institute of Physics who were embarking on research careers in physics. The study (Whitelegg et al. 2002) revealed direct and indirect gender barriers to progression via perceived institutional employment practices and the prevalent male culture or atmosphere in physics research which created what has been called a 'chilly climate' for women. This perception of a 'chilly climate' is not unique to working in physics research, or specific to a lab environment (Erwin and Maurutto 1998).

As revealed in this and other comparable studies, the male culture in SET is seen as being more confrontational and self-confident, and encourages sharing of new ideas and contacts within a small, usually all-male circle. Female students are often reluctant to challenge this, feeling themselves to be in a fairly powerless position, and are more likely to try to work within the culture. Those women who have gained established positions in SET careers can be an important source of support and act as positive role models for the younger females. However, because there are few of them, their achievement becomes very visible, and failure can have a disproportionately negative effect.

Women's perceptions of a career path in SET research reveal concerns which relate to: the long hours' culture; the difficulty of returning to work after a career break (especially when a gap in candidates' publication records counts against them); the need to get back up to date and the difficulty of doing this; the challenge of combining research work with childcare, and the difficulty of working part-time when employed on research grants.

These issues emerge further down the career pipeline and are not evident to young graduates. The situation in physics is mirrored to a greater or lesser extent throughout the other SET areas. In engineering, the 'chilly climate' manifests itself by the use of gendered language and forms of address to refer to engineers, men-only social circles and the necessity of a female engineer becoming 'one of the lads' to belong; sexual visibility and harassment are also a problem, as is the limited range of topics available for conversations, and invisibi ity as a professional (Faulkner 2006). Even in the Biological Sciences, where the participation of girls is initially greater than in other areas of SET, the numbers of females working at the higher levels in research or management careers are not representative of the numbers who embark on this subject. This situation has not changed over several decades.

UK Government Responses

The UK has seen a renewed awareness of this problem over the past decade at a national policy level, prompted initially by the perceived shortage of a skilled labour force in SET employment sectors. As a response, the Government commissioned a review of the supply of scientists and engineers as part of its strategy to improve the UK's productivity and innovation performance. The review identified several factors, specifically some contributing to the supply difficulties faced by the female SET workforce(Roberts 2002). However, the Roberts Review, as it is known, acknowledged that it was not within its scope specifically to consider the issue of the shortage of women in SET, so Baroness Susan Greenfield was asked to prepare a separate report (Greenfield 2002) specifically to look into this. In addition to identifying the need for training in SET, at around the same time the Department for Trade and Industry published the Maximising Returns report (People Science and Policy Ltd 2002) which, amongst other things, identified that a large pool of female SET graduates had returned to employment, but were working in non SET sectors. This raised awareness not only of the need to make SET careers attractive places for women to participate in, but also of the need to tackle the problems that women encountered when returning to work in SET after a career break.

As mentioned at the start of this chapter, initiatives to support women in SET and women returners have been in existence in the UK for many years (see Phipps 2008), but many of these were short lived and local. One of the key recommendations of Baroness Greenfield's report was to 'reduce fragmentation of efforts and to enable stakeholders to play an active and effective part in change' (Greenfield 2002, p. 9). This recommendation led to the setting up of the UK Resource Centre for Women in SET (UKRC)[1] whose brief was to act as an umbrella organisation for all bodies who were concerned with women in SET in the UK and to hold funds

---

[1] http://www.ukrc4setwomen.org/.

for implementing many initiatives such as mentoring, networking and returners' schemes for women. In addition, it was tasked with: improving statistical monitoring; advising and working with SET employers and professional bodies; raising the profile of women in SET; running an expert women's database; producing good practice guides and developing a means of recognising good SET employers. The importance of these tasks was further underlined by another Government-commissioned report in 2006 from the Women and Work Commission (Women and Work Commission 2006) who were asked to examine the causes of the gender pay and opportunities gap and to recommend ways to close it within a generation. The report recommended that a £20 million package should be provided to pilot a range of measures designed to enable women to change direction and progress in their jobs and careers.

Many of the initiatives identified as necessary to improve the presence of women in SET were already in place at this time in various parts of the UK. They were organised by a plethora of organisations drawing on funding from a variety of sources. Many ran very successfully for a few years, and then collapsed due to a cessation of funding (see, for example, the discussion of the Open University's Women In Technology scheme in later sections). 'Return to work' schemes are an example of this sort of initiative which the UK Resource Centre for Women in SET (UKRC) was asked to take forward and develop on a national rather than local scale. Working in partnership with a national education provider, The Open University, which already had a track record of successfully providing educational opportunities for women, provided the synergy to launch a major new initiative to tackle this problem.

Distance Education for Women

In the UK, distance education has been extremely successful at encouraging adult women's participation in SET and other subjects of study, both as novices in the field and as 'returners'. Distance education, as its forerunner correspondence education, has provided many women, in many countries, with their only chance to learn when other educational institutions were inaccessible to them. As a system for women specifically, it can be traced back to 1873 and the Society to Encourage Studies at Home, which offered distance education to adult women in the East Coast of the United States (Watkins 1991).

The evidence suggests that this is a form of education that many women still find more accessible and flexible than other forms of education at specific times in their lives (Lunneborg 1994; Swarbrick 1980; Kirkup and von Prümmer 1997). (In 2006, for example, women were 61% of Open University undergraduates.) But there are aspects of the system of distance education that have been criticised. A specific gender-related criticism is that distance education has reinforced the isolation and domestication of women in the home, rather than emancipating them through participation in a public educational space (Farnes 1988). Distance education has also been criticised for being a 'Fordist' model of industrial production applied to education (Peters 1983): something that large-scale distance institutions, now calling themselves 'Mega-Universities' (Danie. 1996), are no longer ashamed of. They would argue that digital technologies applied to large-scale educational systems allow them to become flexible, accessible, post-modern institutions. In this chapter we sympathise with that position, arguing that digital technologies have allowed us to produce something innovatory for our women students. However, we take seriously those well-argued critiques of digital technologies that consider them to be gendered (Adam 1998; Wyatt et al. 2000). Research evidence of the impact on women of digital technologies when applied to learning (e-learning) is contradictory. A number of studies find women disadvantaged when using e-learning, while others, for example Selwyn (2007), have argued that in Western universities, although many aspects of computer-based activity (e.g. playing games and downloading music) are still gendered as male, e-learning is seen by many students as being a female activity. A number of reports by the Pew Internet and American life project have shown that women and girls are more active than men and boys in many aspects of online social networking (Pew 2008). We believe that when e-learning is carefully designed to match the resources and learning preferences of women students, it can be very successful.

Many Open University women students are investing in their own professional updating and education so as to prepare themselves better to re-enter the workforce; they are already 'flexible workers' (Robins and Webster 1999) engaged in lifelong learning, taking personal responsibility for developing their own employment-related skills and knowledge. These women have always made up a significant part of the OU student population. As they moved in and out of the labour market, often combining family responsibilities with part-time employment, they looked to escape female work ghettos with poor career prospects and low pay by retraining in new areas, and obtaining academic credentials. Others, already professionally qualified, used the OU to keep themselves intellectually active or updated in their field while they took career breaks for family reasons. One of the first special initiatives for women's education in the OU was for women already qualified in SET fields.

The Women into Technology (WIT) Scheme for Women Returners

In the 1970s and 1980s the Open University had recruited women to its science and technology courses in higher numbers than traditional universities. In the mid-1980s women were 16% of all students on OU technology courses and 37% of students on entry level Science courses. In 1980 Swarbrick established the first Open University scheme, funded by the UK Manpower Services Commission, and in partnership with Loughborough University, to prepare women qualified in engineering and technology, who had left paid employment for family reasons, to return to technological work. The programme was designed to promote confidence, knowledge and skills in career planning, and broaden and update existing technical knowledge. The programme included special counselling, a residential preparatory weekend and a choice of studying from a wide range of distance learning courses in technology subjects which could contribute towards a degree level qualification. In the 1980s OU distance learning technologies included paper-based materials, television and radio broadcasting, audio materials (on tape) and some computer-based activities using networked teletype machines located in local study centres, supported by local tutors. Once they were all studying their mainstream SET courses, students had little contact with each other. This isolation of pre-internet distance education was a well-recognised problem, and a great deal of effort was spent encouraging students to find ways to keep in contact with each other after the residential experience.

Swarbrick and Chivers described the rationale for using distance education as follows:

> The retraining needs of experienced women engineers who wish to retrain and return to work after several years at home are not necessarily the same as those of the young male trainees who are normally found in college classes. There are problems of distance and travel to college, lack of childcare facilities, inconvenient timetabling, apart from the inappropriateness of courses. (Swarbrick and Chivers 1985, unnumbered page)

Between 1982 and 1985, 118 women received bursaries and completed the programme. Many returned to SET employment soon after the end of their studies (Kirkup and Swarbrick 1986). The scheme was so successful that in 1985 it was expanded to offer similar bursaries to women who wanted to enter science and technology professions for the first time. Eventually changes in government funding meant that the scheme could no longer be funded because it did not fulfil new criteria (Swarbrick 1986, 1987), and, like many an excellent gender equality projects, it ceased when its funding stopped. The success of the WITS scheme also raised awareness of gender issues more widely within the Technology Faculty, and the subsequent introduction of curriculum and pedagogical changes contributed to an increase in the numbers of women students (Bissell et al. 2003).

However, despite the success of programmes like WIT, there was a continued problem of women's representation in SET at a UK and international level during this time as evidenced, for example, by the SIGIS report (Faulkner 2004). The need for direct intervention to support women returners re-emerged on the political agenda in the UK with the publication of the Maximising Returns report (People Science Policy 2002) which highlighted the national importance of bringing women back into SET employment. The subsequent setting up of the UK Resource Centre for Women in SET in 2004, with the Open University as a core partner, provided the resources to develop a new online course for women returners. Although the experience of the WIT scheme was an inspiration in formulating the new programme, it was clear that there would be enormous advantage in delivering the course online, making use of the most up-to-date learning technologies in order to attract a wider audience.

A Feminist Institutional Network for SET Activities

With public resources limited and subject to competition in their allocation, the ability to act quickly to take advantage of external initiatives for women's education depends usually on the prior existence of an individual or a small group of gender activists within an organisation. As part of the national Women into Science and Engineering (WISE) campaign,[2] a new activist group was created within the OU which was subsequently able to support and promote WIT, and helped extend its life. The group developed its own momentum, aiming to expand work on the participation of women students and staff in SET subjects in the University.

The WISE group at the OU provided an interfaculty space for the development of interdisciplinary perspectives and mutual networking and support. It worked on the development of interdisciplinary Women's and Gender Studies courses, creating strong critical analysis of gender, and inserting SET content into these courses (Kirkup and Keller 1992). It supported research activity by group members on women in SET fields, within and outside the OU (e.g. Carter and Kirkup 1991; Whitelegg et al. 2002; Donovan et al. 2005; Ellen and Herman 2005), promoted gender awareness of the needs of women students in the SET disciplines in the University, and advised on the design of course materials. Members of the network were also involved in external national initiatives and campaigning groups, such as the Women's Engineering Society, Women in Physics Group of the Institute of Physics and the UK Association for Women in Science and Engineering (AWISE).

One aspect of the group's power lay in the influence its members wielded in various arenas including national campaigns that led to the creation of the UK Resource Centre for Women in SET (UKRC).

An Online Course for Women Returners to SET—An Integrated Model

Over time, membership of the OU group of activists changed. Some members retired, or were pulled into working for other projects and new members joined who had different experiences of working outside the University in women's education in SET. This changing body provided an underlying continuity, while being re-energised with new people with new ideas. Several members of the OU network were key in setting up the UKRC and the associated campaign which was launched in 2004 to support women's re-entry into SET employment and research careers known as the RETURN Campaign. A key component of the national strategy was to be a special initiative for women returners to SET, developed by the OU for online

---

[2] WISE began in 1984 and was run by the Engineering Council and the UK Equal Opportunities Commission to promote the participation of girls and women in SET education and careers. The campaign still exists and continues to work particularly with schools on these issues.

delivery: T160[3]. This was the first time such a scheme for returners had been offered in such a format and on such a large scale, and it was intended to attract women who were geographically isolated or unable to study at conventional institutions. At the same time, with the unique tutorial structure of the Open University and additional activities provided by the UKRC network of regional hubs based in Scotland, Wales and three English regions, participants were able to benefit from localised support in their own area. The possibilities of adding other kinds of networking in addition to face-to-face meetings were much greater in this project than in the WIT scheme.

In order to meet the needs of women from a range of academic backgrounds, the course was designed to offer a generic programme of personal and professional development rather than trying to update specific technical knowledge or skills. However, the online nature of the course was also intended to be a vehicle for students to renew and expand existing IT skills that would be of value in their subsequent employment. The course was designed to run over a period of 10 weeks and to be accessed via a dedicated website and online discussion areas. The learning outcomes of the course illustrate the broad nature of the material covered. Participants would: analyse their personal career and educational history, including the development and updating of their CV; identify their professional skills and highlight their training needs; explore the impact of gender in the workplace and develop skills to increase employability, such as job searching, interview and negotiation skills, networking and communication, as well as producing a career action plan.

Course materials were designed to help to address the barriers facing women returners, with emphasis on the SET-specific issues. An important tool introduced within the first week of the course is an electronic portfolio that enables women to collect evidence of their achievements and collate paid and unpaid work experience, including an evaluation of skills and abilities gained. This was found to be a valuable tool that could be taken away by students for use after the end of the course (Herman and Kirkup 2008). Reflective activities that enable women to examine critically their careers to date were built into early sessions of the course. For example, a 'lifeline activity' requires students to reflect on their achievements as well as the challenges in their lives by asking them to portray these as 'highs and lows' on a chart.

The course was designed to provide practical outcomes that would help move women towards their stated goals. Two main outputs were included in the assessment requirements that could be essential tools for future career development: namely a CV and an action plan. The CV (or 'résumé') is checked and commented on as part of the first course assessment, and feedback on it is incorporated into a revised version submitted for final assessment. The action plan with clear time limited goals provides a template for continued progress for 6 months beyond the end of the course, and included a commitment to contact another student at the end of this period.

---

[3] All Open University courses are known by Faculty initials as part of a unique course code—in this case T stands for Technology where the course is located.

With the support of national government and European funding, the course has been free of charge to participants, including reimbursement of travel and childcare expenses for attending two face-to-face tutorial sessions. While not all women have attended these sessions, for many this opportunity to meet other women in similar situations and to resume social networking in a professional capacity proved to be important in regaining their confidence: this has been an important theme throughout the course and in the subsequent support provided by the UKRC network of regional hubs. This is underpinned in the course by material on networking that explores how to make and maintain useful contacts, encouraging women to join online networks to enhance their own sphere of influence. Additional face-to-face networking events, held in conjunction with UKRC regional partners, have proved very popular, offering women practical experience of networking in a formal professional environment (including activities such as 'speed networking'). The course also features the stories of nine 'role model' women who have successfully returned to work after their own career breaks, highlighting important personal issues such as work–life balance. Indeed, the exploration of work–life balance is an important theme throughout the course, and reflections by students on this topic highlighted the difficulties they encountered in reconciling multiple roles (Herman 2006). While the course aims to encourage and support these women in their return to employment, it is also important to allow them to explore the difficulties they could face both practically and emotionally in reconciling family and work commitments, and to develop an understanding of how these conflicts can be shaped by gendered assumptions about domestic and workplace roles.

Students use a range of online discussion forums to structure and carry out course activities, creating a sense of intimacy and shared experience. The OU has had experience of using online group activities for learning since the late 1980s, and the course team understood how to design online activities for maximum participation (Salmon 2002). In addition, there is an online activity where guests from industry and the research community are invited as 'visiting experts' to answer students' questions over a two week period. Questions have ranged from specific issues about working in particular academic and industrial sectors to more generic questions about how to reconcile work and family life.

Collaboration between the OU and other UKRC partners has enabled the course to be accompanied by a range of other support activities which added value: mentoring; work placements; individual advice and guidance, and networking events co-ordinated with the aid of a central database of returners held at the UKRC national headquarters. The significance of this integrated model was highlighted by the external project evaluation report: 'This coherence is innovative and significant to the service user, who can expect support at several points during her preparation and search for a return to SET employment' (Webster 2007).

Mentoring has been one of the key support activities provided. Course participants register to have a one-to-one mentor or join a peer mentoring circle in which they mutually support other women returners in the same situation as themselves, meeting regularly as a group after their initial training from one of the mentoring co-ordinators. Student feedback, which we discuss later, suggests that these local support networks are crucial for developing and building self-esteem as well as contacts which are invaluable in seeking employment. Indeed, networking has been a central component of the integrated model. While on the course, women are encouraged to identify and join relevant networking organisations including professional institutes and learned societies, and national/international organisations and groups supporting women in SET. The final component of the integrated model has included the provision of work placements for some participants in order to give them relevant up-to-date work experience.

The Outcomes of an Online 'Returners' Course

Between 2005 and 2007 the T160 course had over 700 women participate in five cohorts and has contributed significantly to the overall national objective of supporting the return to work of women qualified in SET. Since 2008, after the initial funding period elapsed, the course has been integrated into the OU's mainstream provision and continues to support about 100 returners per year.

An evaluation of the course and its impact on participants was conducted in 2007 involving three groups of students (458 participants). Data were collected from registration forms, an online survey (63% return rate) and a selected, representative sample of 19 interviews (Dale et al. 2007). The illustrative participant comments used below are all taken from this evaluation.

Results indicate that difficulties and barriers are still likely to be encountered in returning to work, and these are very similar to the barriers highlighted in the SET Fair report (Greenfield 2002). Most of the participants had taken a career break, usually, but not always, because of children. Their average age was 40 with most in the age range 30–50 years. Most had been unemployed for over three years. Some were 'underemployed' (i.e. working at a skill level below that of their qualifications and experience) or working in some other field in order to be able to have local, flexible or part-time employment. They were all SET graduates with a range of subject backgrounds—31% Physical Sciences and Mathematics, 23% Biology, 15% Computing and IT, 11% Engineering, with the rest having backgrounds in specialised or inter-disciplinary fields. Difficulties and barriers to returning to work were identified as:

- Lack of work experience (71%)
- Out-of-date skills (70%)
- Lack of confidence (57%)
- Lack of available work at an appropriate level (57%)
- Location of employers (51%)
- Lack of interview practice (49%)
- Lack of contacts (49%)
- Unavailability of part-time work (46%)
- Finding child care (26%)

The majority of course participants said they were planning to return to work on completion of the course, or in the near future. About a third wanted full-time employment, and about a quarter wanted part-time employment. A significant number were exploring opportunities for self-employment and portfolio careers. More than 20% believed that they would require further training before they were likely to be successful in their aspirations. Some women were hoping to use their scientific and technical skills differently, perhaps as technical writers or scientific journalists. Others, who were disenchanted with the culture of SET, both in academia and industry, were seeking to take their SET qualifications and skills elsewhere. About half expected to seek employment at a lower level than they had enjoyed before they took a career break. A variety of reasons contributed to this expectation: many felt the need for re-training and re-skilling before they could establish themselves at the same level; many were looking for part-time work to start with; for some, employment opportunities were location-limited; it was not clear how one might change career, but immediately work at an equivalent level. Some women reported experiences of having felt the need to 'drop down a level' and then having to deal with resentment from bosses who felt intimidated because they were less qualified than the returners.

Participants had three main objectives for studying the course:

- To help them return to paid work (66%)
- Personal development (54%)
- To help change career (37%)

More specifically they wanted to know about options open to them after their career break, and needed to develop knowledge of, and confidence in, current recruitment and selection procedures.

These objectives align with the purpose, design and learning outcomes of the course, and most participants felt that their objectives for taking the course had been met. When asked about the impact of the course on their lives, most comments were extremely positive and emphasised the importance of the personal development:

> The course has enabled me to look at my needs and wants. It has made me aware of my personal barriers to returning to a work environment and has started me looking at ways I can overcome them. (IT graduate, 48 years old)

Most participants were very positive about the impact of the course on their skills, confidence and future prospects. The emphasis and support in developing a CV was universally appreciated, and doing company research was felt to be really useful. An improved CV, in particular, had boosted their confidence in their future careers. 'I feel more confident...that I have better career prospects' (Technician, 27 years old). 'It really helped to see longer-term and has given me more confidence.' (IT graduate, 49 years old)

For some the experience bore immediate fruit:

> I got a job and am so happy! I would not have applied for the job without T160 guiding my thoughts and motivating me. It also gave me the confidence to apply high and now I realise

that it was not beyond my capabilities, also, and I would have had a much less impressive CV and cover letter without the course. (Psychologist, 36 years old).

The online networking aspects of the course were perceived as valuable by many:

I am very happy I took this course. I am very aware now that I am not the only SET trained woman who is not employed. It has also given me the opportunity to form a network. (Chemist, 28 years old)

Some would have liked more opportunity for face-to-face networking on a more local basis, or continued contact within the framework set up by the course. A few participants, however, did not fully grasp the nature of an online course, and they missed out on electronic networking possibilities. Because T160 is a relatively short course, some participants only understood the nature of the online communication possibilities too late in the course to benefit greatly.

One part of the course focussed on structural gender-based barriers to employment in SET. Many found this helpful as they realised that their lack of success in finding career paths to return to was often due to structural and institutional rather than personal factors. The converse of this was that some participants felt disheartened and discouraged by the analysis of institutional discrimination. The course tried to mitigate this anticipated feeling of disempowerment. A theoretical gender perspective encouraged the sharing of experiences of dealing with gender issues in a work environment.

Those participants who had started with the objective of returning to work or changing career had not necessarily been able to do so within the short time-frame of the course, but they did feel well prepared to go forward. They had developed five-year goals and action plans and written inspiring, but realistic visions. They had re-examined their goals, their achievements and their skills. They described having clearer objectives, greater focus and were often much more optimistic: indeed many had now changed their plans.

…the course has made me examine my motives, and I've altered my objectives. I am much clearer in my own mind. (Geologist, 51 years old)

…spending time focussing properly on the thought of returning to work instead of just thinking about it in passing…. I have reconsidered my original career which I had previously dismissed the idea of returning to. (Chemist, 49 years old)

…to be honest my life is now changing completely – sometimes I can't believe it! (Technician engineer, 40 years old)

Inevitably, the balance the course took in addressing issues did not suit everyone. Some participants felt that there was too much emphasis on the needs of women returners with children and insufficient attention given to issues of location, age and updating of skills. Career breaks happen for many reasons, some from choice, others not. There was also concern that the course was not challenging enough for highly qualified women. A short course like this cannot address, in equal measure, all the barriers facing these women. However, our data suggest that it has been successful in supporting women to develop confidence, improve their career focus and initiate action. It has enabled participants to up-date some general skills and help them assess the need for further training. It has facilitated the formation of personal networks and, through the wider RETURN campaign of the UKRC, introduced participants to existing support networks. It has enabled some to experience individual mentoring and national peer mentoring circles, and to access work placement and 'returner' fellowship schemes.

Conclusion and Recommendations

There are five interesting lessons for other projects in women's education that come out of this one. These are to do with: distributed learning course design; inter-organisational partnerships for educational provision; the importance of buy-in and leadership from the top in organisations in order to achieve culture change; the importance of internal, informal networks of gender activists; the impact on women's identities of provision and support for women 'returners'.

The feedback from participants and the high level of positive outcomes (over 300 out of the original 700 are known to have gone on to employment or further study at the time of writing) show that an online course, plus integrated local support, can offer a successful model for the re-integration of women returners following a career break. This course confirms the experience that distance education can be accessible, flexible and the preferred mode of formal education for retraining to return to work, or for developing the careers of many adult women. While similar resources may not be easily available to small education and training providers, it is clear that more extensive use can be made of online tools for developing supportive networks by those who design courses for adult women. Extensive use of the internet among women in the developed world makes it easier to use online social networking tools to build communities for women who are geographically isolated, or working in the domestic environment, and this does not necessarily incur expensive infrastructure development. The particular online and distributed pedagogical model that this course has adopted has enabled students to draw on national resources and networks while being very involved with local support activity, developing local knowledge and networking.

The individual responses of the women who were supported through the RETURN campaign, including the T160 course, indicate that these women were able to (re)-identify themselves as scientists and engineers, while envisaging and relocating themselves in the current SET employment landscape. Engagement with a group of women in very similar positions allowed them time to reflect on and plan for their future careers. Having direct access to role models and mentoring, to many different networks and to a variety of support services, at national and local level, all contributed to a sense of progress and change of direction with which these women felt confident and comfortable. Their experiences should contribute to and enhance the services and support available for future returners, and perhaps also influence the SET employment climate.

This integrated model of support provided by the OU and the network of UKRC partners, within the context of a strong commitment to collaboration and partnership, has been vital to the success of the course at a national level. Being both national and local, it draws on the strengths of both, and is likely therefore to be more robust than the local courses that we have been more familiar with in the past. While small organisations and community education providers may not have access to national level partners, the networking capacities of the internet would also enable a consortium of small providers to create, at a more local level, something similar to the course and partnership we have described here.

Working in partnership with a national organisation, such as the UKRC in this instance, enabled access to influential policymakers, professional bodies and senior managers in SET industries. Changes to culture and working practices will only take place if those in high level positions proactively support change, so opportunities provided by access to such people of influence are an important factor in achieving progress for women's career development in SET employment.

Our experience is an example of the importance of the development of informal networks of gender activists in educational institutions. New methods of online networking might make it possible to strengthen these networks and keep them live during quiet/inactive periods. We suggest that universities and further education colleges, for example, should actively support informal internal networks of staff with a particular interest in women's education, and allow space for their activities. Such networks usually ask for very little in the way of institutional resources: they rely mainly on the small amounts of time members give to them. However, these networks provide the institution with the capacity to bid for funding when special initiatives for women are announced. They provide a location for external parties to make contact with for future projects. They provide the support base that individual innovators need if their projects are to be sustainable. They also provide continuity between different funded projects because in the gender field we are used to sporadic funding and periods of scarce resources.

The particular issues faced by women in SET continue to be significant despite many years of policies, interventions and initiatives. Wider social and cultural issues continue to play an important role, and despite good intentions there is no 'once and for all' educational solution to the 'leaky pipeline' in SET. For the foreseeable future, women's careers will involve time away from employment as women still take primary responsibility for childcare and family work. Consequently, there will continue to be a need for special educational initiatives to help women return to SET employment after a career break, to allow both them and the State to take advantage of the previous investment in their education and skills. However, employers and policymakers must ensure that educational activity is combined with changes to workplace practices and culture which will enable retention and progression for women in their careers. A closer partnership between educational providers, employers and professional organisations could ensure the availability of re-training and part-time working opportunities at all levels of a career.

Acknowledgements The T160 Course and associated services for women returners described here have been funded by the European Social Fund (ESF) Equal Programme and the UK Government's Department for Trade and Industry (DTI) through the UK Resource Centre for Women in SET. We are grateful to the women who participated in the T160 course with such enthusiasm, and who shared their stories with us; to the course team; tutors; evaluators and colleagues from the UK Resource Centre for Women in SET, as well as other networks for women in SET who contributed to the success of the course.

References

Adam, A. (1998). *Artificial knowing: Gender and the thinking machine*. London: Routledge.

Bissell, C., Chapman, D., Herman, C., & Robinson, L. (2003). Still a gendered technology? Issues in teaching ICT at the UK Open University. *European Journal of Engineering Education, 28*(1), 27–35.

Carter, R., & Kirkup, G. (1991). Redressing the balance: Women into science and engineering at the Open University. *Open Learning, 6*(1), 56–58.

Coats, M. (1996). *Recognising good practice in women's education and training*. Leicester: NIACE.

Dale, A., Ellis, F., & Jackson, N. (2007). Evaluation *of T160 'Science, Engineering and Technology (SET): A course for women returners'*. *Internal report*. Milton Keynes: Open University.

Daniel, J. (1996). *Mega-universities and knowledge media*. London: Routledge Falmer.

Donovan, C., Hodgson, B., Scanlon, E., & Whitelegg, E. (2005). Women in higher education: Issues and challenges for part-time scientists. *Women's Studies International Forum, 28*, 247–258.

Ellen, D., & Herman, C. (2005). Women's training revisited: Developing new learning pathways for women IT technicians using a holistic approach. In J. Archibald, J. Emms, F. Grundy, J. Payne, & E. Turner (Eds.), *The gender politics of ICT* (pp. 251–264). Middlesex: University Press.

Erwin, L., & Maurutto, P. (1998). Beyond access: Considering gender deficits in science education. *Gender and Education, 10*(1), 51–69.

Farnes, N. (1988). Open university community education: Emancipation or domestication? *Open Learning, 1*, 35–40.

Faulkner, W. (Ed.). (2004). *Strategies of inclusion: Gender in the information society. Final report* (Public version of SIGIS Deliverable D08). Aug 2004, ISSTI/University of Edinburgh, ISBN 1 872287 74 3.

Faulkner, W. (2006). *Gadget girls and boys with their toys*. Research briefing. Bradford: UK Resources Centre for Women in SET. http://www.ukrc4setwomen.org/html/resources/ukrc-publications/GadgetgirlsandboyswiththeirtoysHowtoattractandkeepmorewomeninengineering.html?pub_id=26. Accessed 30 July 2010.

Greenfield, S. (2002). *SET fair: A report on women in science engineering and technology*. London: Department of Trade and Industry.

Herman, C. (2006). *Achieving a harmonious work–life balance: Myth or reality? Experiences of women returning to work in science, engineering and technology*. Science Policy Meets Reality Conference, University of Prague, 1–2 Dec 2006.

Herman, C., & Kirkup, G. (2008). Learning in transition: The use of eportfolios for women returners to science engineering and technology. *Innovations in Education and Teaching International (IETI), 45*(1), 67–76.

Kirkup, G., & Keller, L. (1992). *Inventing women—science, technology and gender*. Oxford: Polity.

Kirkup, G., & Swarbrick, A. (1986). *Women in technology. A report to the training division of the manpower services commission on the first year of option 1 for women with no technologi-*

cal qualifications who wish to enter technology (unpublished report). Milton Keynes: Open University.

Kirkup, G., & von Prümmer, C. (1997). Distance education for European women: The threats and opportunities of new educational forms and media. *European Journal of Women's Studies, 4*(1), 39–62.

Lunneborg, P. (1994). *OU Women: Undoing educational obstacles*. London: Cassell.

Murphy, P., & Whitelegg, E. (2006). *Girls in the physics classroom: A review of research on the participation of girls in physics* (pp. 1–61). London: Institute of Physics.

People Science and Policy Ltd. (2002). *Maximising returns to science, engineering and technology careers* (p. 76). Warwick and London: Institute for Employment Research, University of Warwick and Department of Trade and Industry.

Peters, O. (1983). Distance teaching and industrial production: A comparative interpretation in outline. In D. Seward, D. Keegan, & B. Holmberg (Eds.), *Distance education: International perspectives* (pp. 95–113). New York: Routledge.

Pew Internet and Social Life Project. (2008). Various reports at http://www.pewinternet.org/PPF/r/230/report_display.asp. Accessed 30 July 2010.

Phipps, A. (2008). *Women in science, engineering and technology: Three decades of UK Initiatives*. Stoke-on-Trent: Trentham.

Rees, T. (2001). Mainstreaming gender equality in science in the European Union: The ETAN Report. *Gender and Education, 13*(3), 243–260.

Roberts, G. (2002). *SET for success: The supply of people with science, technology, engineering and mathematics skills*. London: Department for Trade and Industry and Department for Education and Skills.

Robins, K., & Webster, F. (1999). *Times of the technoculture. From the information society to the virtual world*. London: Routledge.

Salmon, G. (2002). *E-tivities. The key to active online learning*. London: Routledge Falmer.

Selwyn, N. (2007). E-Learning or she-learning? Exploring students' gendered perceptions of education technology. *British Journal of Educational Technology, 38*(4), 744–746.

Swarbrick, A. (1980). To encourage the others: Women studying technology. *Teaching at a Distance, 17*, 2–14.

Swarbrick, A. (1986). Women in technology: A scheme for women engineer returners. *European Journal of Engineering Education, 11*(3), 339–349.

Swarbrick, A. (1987). Women in technology. In M. Thorpe & D. Grugeon (Eds.), *Open learning for adults* (pp. 103–116). London: Longman.

Swarbrick, A., & Chivers, G. (1985). *Evaluation of the women in technology scheme*. Paper presented at the Third GASAT Conference, London, 13–18 Apr 1985.

Watkins, B. L. (1991). A quite radical idea: The invention and elaboration of collegiate correspondence study. In B. L. Watkins & S. J. Wright (Eds.), *The foundations of American distance education*. Dubuque: Hunt.

Webster, J. (2007). *Empowering and enabling women returners: Evaluation report on JIVE return services*. UKRC internal report. http://www.theukrc.org/. Accessed 31 July 2010.

Whitelegg, E., Hodgson, B. K., Scanlon, E., & Donovan, C. (2002). *Young women's perceptions and experiences of becoming a research physicist*. Proceedings of 12th International Conference of Women Engineers and Scientists, 27–31 July, Ottawa, Canada. Paper reference no. 167, p. 5.

Women and Work Commission. (2006). *Shaping a fairer future*. London: Department of Trade and Industry.

Wyatt, S., Henwood, F., Miller, N., & Senker, P. (Eds.). (2000). *Technology and in/equality. Questioning the information society*. London: Routledge.

Chapter 6
Women's Choices Shattered: Impact of Gender Violence on Universities

Esther Oliver

Introduction

Different expressions of violence in our societies affect women. This chapter analyses the way in which violence occurs in universities. Forms of misogyny and discrimination encountered by female academics and students are translated into barriers which hamper their educational and professional plans, affecting their lifelong learning processes and having an impact on their lives. The evidence presented in this chapter is obtained from academic literature in the field and from the voices of research participants. Those who took part in the research are mainly involved in dealing with this issue in UK universities. The data point to two different types of findings. First, that the university is still a male-dominated domain in which different forms of misogyny and discrimination occur, affecting female academics and students. Second, in this context, different forms of violence become barriers which have a negative impact on the educational and professional plans of some women and, by extension, on their lives in society as a whole. This chapter contributes towards breaking down the stereotype view that only some specific groups of women are affected by this problem. On the contrary, this problem can affect both female students and staff, since violence against women crosses as many boundaries in the academic field as it does in society as a whole.

In order to understand the wider concept of violence against women, a good place to start is with the definition contained in the *Declaration on the Elimination of Violence against Women* (United Nations 1993), which was established in the UN General Assembly resolution 48/104 of the 20th of December 1993:

> For the purposes of this Declaration, the term 'violence against women' means any act of gender-based violence that results in, or is likely to result in, physical, sexual or psychological harm or suffering to women, including threats of such acts, coercion or arbitrary deprivation of liberty, whether occurring in public or in private life. (Article 1)

E. Oliver (✉)
Department of Sociological Theory, University of Barcelona, Barcelona, Spain
e-mail: estoliver@googlemail.com

S. Jackson et al. (eds.), *Gendered Choices*, Lifelong Learning Book Series 15,
DOI 10.1007/978-94-007-0647-7_6, © Springer Science+Business Media B.V. 2011

The definition of violence in this declaration includes the physical, sexual and psychological violence which occurs within the family, in the general community and which is perpetrated or condoned by the State.

I will first discuss more detailed definitions provided by several authors of the diverse forms of this phenomenon within the university context. Fitzgerald et al. (1988), for example, created a research tool entitled *The Sexual Experience Questionnaire* (SEQ), which aimed to facilitate comparative results and to reach a common definition of what sexual harassment is. Their definition of sexual harassment, based on Till's categories (Till 1980), is considered to be one of the most commonly used definitions for research in this field (Toffey Shepela and Levesque 1998; Kalof et al. 2001). Fitzgerald et al. (1988, p. 157) identified five general areas of sexual harassment: *gender harassment* (generalised sexist remarks and behaviour); *seductive behaviour* (inappropriate and offensive, but essentially sanction-free, sexual advances); *sexual bribery* (solicitation of sexual activity or other sexually related behaviour based on a promise of rewards); *sexual coercion* (coercion of sexual activity based on a threat of punishment); *sexual assault* (gross sexual imposition or assault). The later work of Kalof et al. (2001) indicates how this typology was revised to incorporate a new concept. These authors argued that sexual harassment is a behavioural construct consisting of three separate dimensions: *gender harassment* (including verbal and nonverbal behaviour which does not aim for sexual cooperation, but conveys degrading, hostile or insulting attitudes); *unwanted sexual attention* (this consists of verbal and nonverbal behaviour such as repeated request for dates, intrusive letters and phone calls, touching, grabbing and gross sexual imposition or assault) and *sexual coercion* (which consists of unwanted sexual attention linked to job- or course-related losses or benefits which are either explicit or implied and consist of bribes or threats to achieve sexual cooperation) (Kalof et al. 2001, p. 285).

Drawing on this broad concept of violence against women suggests there is a need to analyse the structures of power relationships which still prevail in university contexts. Indeed, understanding these structures can contribute towards clarifying why some circumstances favour contexts which are prone to the emergence of gender violence. According to Osborne (1995), it is related to maintaining male privileges, social control, silencing women, and gender domination in academia. Furthermore, other research specifically highlights the negative effects that unequal conceptualizations of gender relationships can have in actually generating violent conduct (Bondurant 2001).

The research presented in this chapter is linked to the research framework developed by Safo CREA's[1] Women's Group,[2] which stresses the need to go deeper into the study of the different forms of violence which affect all kinds of women in today's societies. This group also stresses the importance of the analysis of new forms of masculinity which can contribute towards overcoming this violence.

---

[1] CREA is the Centre of Research in Theories and Practices that Overcome Inequalities, at the University of Barcelona.

[2] http://www.pcb.ub.es/crea/en/gdona_en.htm.

Work in the present chapter draws on contributions from international academic literature in the field and the findings obtained from the qualitative empirical data collected. These empirical data have been collected in the frame of a postdoctoral research project entitled *Gender-based violence at universities* (2006–2008), developed in the United Kingdom and supported by the Department of Innovation, Universities and Business, Generalitat de Catalunya. In the development of this research, it is important to mention the collaboration with the research team of the I+D+I (a research and development project at national level) *Violencia de género en las universidades españolas* (Gender violence in Spanish universities), coordinated by the University of Barcelona (CREA 2005–2008).

An exhaustive literature review was carried out using major standard comprehensive international bibliographical sources (the ten first international journals with the highest impact factor as ranked by the ISI Journal Citation Report on Women's Studies, and two internationally relevant academic databases (Sociological Abstracts and ERIC)). Moreover, other significant references from the field (mainly quoted in these initial sources or identified as being relevant during the research process) were included in the framework of the academic literature which was analysed.

In addition, between September 2007 and April 2008, I developed the field work stage of my study. I followed a qualitative methodology with a communicative orientation (Flecha and Gómez 2004), which is the methodological approach followed by several research projects[3] of the Framework Programme of the European Commission (1999). This approach highlights the role of the subjects in the whole research process (i.e. promoting their participation in the definition of the interview guides or asking for their feedback on the main results obtained). Following this methodology, I conducted ten interviews with professionals involved in the definition or the implementation of mechanisms to combat sexual harassment in universities. Amongst the research participants there were eight women and two men who all had positions of responsibility in university bodies in charge of the implementation of equality or anti-harassment policies in nine different UK universities. I also carried out eight daily-life stories with women and two with men, involved in feminist organisations, women's associations in universities or student's unions. These research participants carry out work in organisations which are concerned with this phenomenon or are actively involved in providing responses to female students and academics who have suffered sexual harassment within the university context. The difference between the interviews and the daily-life stories is that the former are more oriented towards obtaining information on the institutional perspective of the topic while, in the second case, the focus is on collecting knowledge and perceptions from people not part of university management.

The qualitative field work explored the interviewees' understandings of two main issues: (1) the barriers which affected women's lifelong learning processes and professional plans related to the persistence of sexual harassment in academia

---

[3] http://www.ub.es/includ-ed/.

and (2) the elements which can contribute to overcoming all forms of violence against women within this context.

In this chapter I will specifically explore the data related to the way in which the barriers identified are an expression of the fact that universities are still male-dominated domains which allow different forms of misogyny or discrimination against women to occur. Each section of this chapter combines references to the academic literature with quotations from my fieldwork. The first section describes another side of the university context, which contains complex hierarchical barriers and power relationships, favouring the development of attitudes of hostility to women, such as different forms of sexual harassment. The argument in the second section of this chapter is focused on exploring how these barriers have an impact on the way in which female students experience their educational paths, or on the way in which female academics develop their professional plans. Finally, I will highlight new insights about this phenomenon.

Violence Against Women Also at Universities

Statistical data show that the level of violence against women in society as a whole is reflected in violence at universities. The campaign launched by the Council of Europe in 2006, entitled *Stop domestic violence against women*, maintained that one-fifth to one-quarter of all women have experienced physical violence at least once during their adult lives, and more than one-tenth have suffered sexual violence involving the use of force. Secondary data provided by this campaign also indicate that about 12–15% of all women have been in a relationship involving domestic abuse after the age of 16.[4]

The figures available from different research projects, mainly carried out in non-European countries, and which specifically focus on the university context, also demonstrate high rates of the different forms of violence suffered by college women (both students and faculty staff) and perpetrated by dating partners, boyfriends or professors in universities. Gross et al. (2006), for example, based their study on a sample of 935 undergraduate female college students and demonstrated that 27.2% of women report that they faced unwanted sexual experiences after enrolling in college. Kalof et al. (2001) also indicated that women are victims of sexual harassment perpetrated by college professors and instructors. Out of a sample of 525 undergraduates, they found that 40% of the women and 28.7% of the men had been sexually harassed by male faculty members. Both studies were conducted in the United States.

However, very little detailed research evidence is available about the way in which this violence affects female academics and students in European universities. One such research project is an I+D+I (Research and Development) project

---

[4] http://www.coe.int/t/dg2/equality/domesticviolencecampaign/source/PDF_FS_Violence_Campaign_E.pdf.

entitled Violencia de género en las universidades españolas[5] (Gender violence in Spanish universities) (CREA 2005–2008). This study has opened up a new field of knowledge within the study of gender violence in Spain. In the UK context, some universities have records of the sexual harassment cases which occur every year. However, academic literature based on researching these data is still limited. One such study (Lee 2006) undertook an analysis of the fact that academics (mainly women, but also some men) face bullying or harassment perpetrated by students in university settings in the United Kingdom, focusing in particular on academics being bullied or harassed by students, and showing that this violence can occur in both directions.

These studies indicate that so far it has only been possible to see the tip of the iceberg with regard to a reality which is still relatively unknown or studied in our universities. As Dziech and Weiner (1990) stated when they undertook one of the first studies in the United States on sexual harassment in universities, the lack of news about violence against women in European universities does not necessarily mean good news.

Universities as Male-Dominated Domains

Female staff and female students come across different types of barriers when they are confronted by sexual harassment within the university context. The analysis of these barriers points to the fact that few of these cases are reported and to the need for a better definition of effective responses to combat sexual harassment within academic contexts. In this section, I will provide some evidence of these constraints.

First, universities are still male-dominated institutions which contain complex hierarchical and power relationships. Grauerholz (1996), for example, explains how some universities are embedded in institutional and social structures that make it difficult for women to report encounters of abusive situations. This author points out the hierarchical nature of universities which still place men in authoritarian and powerful positions and increases the vulnerability of women. This can be increased, for example, when most of the governing bodies and managerial structures are still male-dominated, as several research participants highlighted:

> Particularly in this university [...] which is, as you know, further behind other universities, it is still very traditional and generally very male-dominated, so it is important that [...] several campaigns, such as a kind of raising of awareness or a specific thing [...]. (Participant in a daily-life story no. 3)

Dziech and Weiner (1990) mention other reasons why women in universities are more vulnerable such as the hazy institutional authority in universities, the temporariness of the academic positions many women hold and the academic conserva-

---

[5] This research was directed by Dr. Rosa Valls, professor at the University of Barcelona. Her research team is composed of members of seven Spanish universities: http://www.pcb.ub.es/crea/proyectos/violencia/index.htm.

tism which still prevails in these institutions. They also mention the huge resistance to change, the distribution of power and the fact that the institutional changes which are promoted are so slow.

Jocey Quinn also analysed the unequal distribution of power between men and women in universities through an international research project consisting of in-depth interviews with women working in universities in different countries. She states: 'It was rare for women to reach the highest positions in their universities and those who had more power were scarcely feminist. Women struggled to gain representation on decision-making committees, and once there, they were made to feel invisible and even ridiculous' (Quinn 2003, p. 26).

According to the indicators for 'Women and Science'[6] created by the European Commission (1999), 'the feminisation ratio amongst senior academic staff' (grade A), between 1998 and 2002 in the EU-25 level[7] moved from 14.0% in 1998 to 16.4% in 2002. However, the percentage of women in the most senior positions is still very low: the distribution of women amongst academic staff by grade was 14% for grade A (more senior positions) and 41% for grade D (less senior positions) in the EU-25. At a UK[8] level, this distribution between women in universities is simi-lar (14% for grade A and 46% for grade D).

Second, some circumstances create an adverse environment for women in some academic contexts which makes it difficult for them to break the silence which sur-rounds sexual harassment when it happens (Benson and Thomson 1982; Fitzgerald et al. 1988; Dziech and Weiner 1990; Osborne 1995). Osborne (1995), for example, mentions the existence of a *chilly climate* in her study which she carried out in a Ca-nadian university. She demonstrates the devaluation and marginalisation of women in some university contexts reflected by the curricula, or through the use of sexual and racist stereotypes in class.

Gross et al. (2006) also mention the impact of sexist stereotypes on the attitudes and beliefs of college men and women, for example, those which associate rape with physical force, violence and with completed intercourse. According to these authors, these situations mean that some of the sexual harassment suffered by wom-en in universities is not labelled or reported, because it is regarded as acceptable.

This adverse environment for women is also evident in the hostility or the lack of response from some institutions when women decide to complain or to report the harassment they have experienced. Some research participants, for example, stress the lack of effective responses to some cases:

> [...] two years ago a female student in a college was attacked late at night by another male student, and she has marks on her body [...] she went to talk to somebody in her college

---

[6] http://ec.europa.eu/research/science-society/women/wssi/downindi_en.html#As.

[7] The following countries are included in the label EU-25: Austria, Belgium Flemish speaking community, Belgium French speaking community, Cyprus, Czech Republic, Germany, Denmark, Estonia, Greece, Spain, Finland, France, Hungary, Ireland, Italy, Lithuania, Luxembourg, Latvia, Malta, The Netherlands, Poland, Portugal, Sweden, Slovenia, Slovakia, United Kingdom.

[8] http://ec.europa.eu/research/science-society/women/wssi/pdf/10_academicstaff_grade.pdf.

about the situation [...], but [the attitude was] there is nothing we can do at all. (Participant in a daily-life story no. 4)

We hear about staff who say, who feel very hopeless and say, even if I had made a complaint, [...] I don't believe that things will get better as a result of complaining. (Interviewed person no. 6)

Wagner and Magnusson (2005), identify strategies within some higher education institutions aimed at silencing women academics who have been victims of sexual harassment: these include stigmatization or indifferent attitudes in response to their experiences. The same attempts to silence women were also highlighted by participants in my research:

You try to go on with things and move forward and you go to sit in the bar, and that person is there and she told her tutor that and her tutor said: oh you should probably not go to the bar then, and that was the attitude, which is absolutely ridiculous [...]. (Participant in a daily-life story no. 3)

A similar feeling is found when women have to face mistrust from others, or are considered trouble-makers or to be partly responsible for what happened. The problem identified above is compounded for the complainant by the punitive reaction transmitted by the institution to some women who decide to complain:

[...] so I mean in this particular case a woman made a complaint about harassment [in her university], [...] and she put in this complaint and described what was happening [...] if she complains of being harassed, she is punished for complaining [...]. (Participant in a daily-life story no. 3)

There are many indications of the pressure on some women to remain invisible within academia. In one of the few studies found on this topic carried out in the UK, for example, Thomas (2004) argues that effective responses to sexual harassment in universities should not be taken for granted even when sexual harassment policies or equal opportunity policies are implemented. In addition, Eyre (2000) argues that some university environments create conditions under which some forms of sexual harassment are naturalised by the dominant discourse, even amongst feminist academics.

Specifically, the lack of support and solidarity between female academics and students is another barrier to overcoming abusive situations for women in academia (Benson and Thomson 1982; Dziech and Weiner 1990; Cowan 2000; Eyre 2000). Cowan (2000), for example, analyses the way in which the lack of solidarity between female students contributes to increasing and reproducing a climate of hostility amongst women in universities. She studies the way in which women can contribute towards the perpetuation of sexual violence when they support the idea of blaming the victims. Cowan concludes that these women's hostility towards other women may impede women's participation in the movement against gender violence. On the other hand, Benson and Thomson (1982) indicate that this lack of solidarity can also be found within the female academic community, amongst themselves or directed at female students, when they ignore or do not support other women who are in a more vulnerable situation.

This lack of solidarity amongst women in some academic contexts was high-lighted in my own research data:

> I think there should be more women in the policies and in the procedures for female solidar-ity [...] quite a lot of women don't support each other because then they will be attached to being involved with sexual harassment because it damages their career. So there is a divi-sion [...] because it affects your own life and your own career. (Participant in a daily-life story no. 6)

Based on these contributions, it can be clearly observed that different forms of vio-lence against women affect academic women and female students, and that the uni-versity is not immune from such violence which is prevalent in our wider society.

To summarize:

- Universities are still mainly male domains and contain complex and hierarchi-cal power relationships which make it difficult for violence against women to receive appropriate acknowledgement. Such circumstances can increase the vul-nerability of some women, mainly those who face abusive situations.
- Some of the barriers that women come across in these environments hinder women's opportunity to break the silence and to become more visible when they have experienced abuse.

Emotional and Professional Barriers to Women's Educational Plans

When analysing the forms of discrimination and barriers which affect the social, educational and economic development of women, it is very important to take ac-count of misogyny in the wider society. Behind the difficulties that some women experience, many academic studies reveal behaviour, attitudes and values involving scorn, discrimination or the sexual abuse of women, also within university contexts (Burt 1980; Dziech and Weiner 1990; Reilly et al. 1992; Stombler 1994; Ayres Bo-swell and Spade 1996; Boeringer 1999).

This hostility towards women is discovered in some social contexts which pro-mote it in many different forms (Forbes et al. 2006). Some authors establish a clear connection between certain beliefs and the development of behaviour linked to sexual harassment and assault (Reilly et al. 1992). Based on a study containing a sample of 920 students (534 college women and 386 college men), Reilly et al. found significant positive correlations between men's self-reported tolerance for sexual harassment, adversarial sexual beliefs, rape-myth acceptance and the likeli-hood to rape or be a sexual victimiser. This is referred to as *continuum of misogyny*.

This underpins the treatment of academic women by male peers or male faculty members in some universities. The emphasis on women's submission in certain so-cialisation processes (Yancey and Hummer 1989; Kalof 1993; Stombler 1994) and on female subordination in patriarchal societies (Dziech and Weiner 1990) and its institutions (such as universities) can also contribute towards explaining it. Stalker

(2001) establishes a link between the misogyny which still exists in societies today and the barriers that women face during their participation in education. The expectations of women, and of what their role in families should be, increase social pressure on them when they decide to continue their education. This pressure is an added barrier to their learning process and sometimes translates into disillusionment and failure. The main barriers to women's educational and professional plans identified in this study can be divided between those which have an impact on their personal and emotional lives and those which have a direct impact on their educational and professional plans.

Regarding the barriers which have an impact on the personal and emotional lives of women, one difficulty which has been highlighted in academic literature and in testimonies collected in my own empirical research is the low rates of reporting abuse. In many cases women affected suffer from isolation and do not report their aggressors (Dziech and Weiner 1990; Stombler 1994). Research participants also stress the difficulties that some female students have when coming to terms with the situation they have experienced:

> Some students deal with it by pretending it doesn't happen. I know a couple of cases, I am going to put it in a box and I am going to continue my studies while I am here, and although I always told them to go to a counsellor, it is very much their choice how to deal with the event or the incident. (E02: Interviewed person no. 2)

This lack of reporting and silence is accompanied in some cases by different feelings, identified as a deep sense of shame, a decrease in emotional stability, an increasing tendency to blame themselves, an extended belief that harassment is inevitable, a lowering of self-esteem and a negative impact on the personal growth process (Benson and Thomson 1982; Marks and Nelson 1993; Eyre 2000; Wagner and Magnusson 2005). One of the research participants also explained her perception of the impact harassment can have on women:

> Someone who is psychologically undermining you, telling you are rubbish, putting you down, being horrible to you and at the same time, there is any tendency you might have […] I have done something wrong, this is my fault […]. (Interviewed person no. 4)

Some women also develop a fear of reprisals by male peers or male supervisors if they finally decide to report the aggressor. These fears become even greater when women perceive that the structures of power in universities favour an environment in which sexual harassment is tolerated and not condemned:

> She decided she didn't want to go to the police because it can be a long case, and they live in the same college together […] so they possibly meet on a daily basis because each college has one-hundred students (approximately), and she was very concerned about the social stigma and she decided not to do anything. (Participant in a daily-life story no. 4)

Certain authors also highlight the fear of being considered a trouble-maker or the potential effect reporting someone could have on women's careers and a concern for their reputation within organisations (Toffey Shepela and Levesque 1998). These authors point to such issues as factors which influence women's decisions not to report instances of sexual harassment. In addition, Dziech and Weiner (1990) write that the key to understanding women's responses to harassment is to be found in the

education and socialisation of some women into certain kinds of gender identities
which can increase their vulnerability. At the same time, and according to the argument presented at the beginning of this section, the socialisation processes experienced by some men, which are rooted in misogynistic values, can also have a deep
effect on increasing women's vulnerability.

As a result of the lack of an effective response by universities to cases of sexual
harassment, and also as a consequence of the harmful effects that these situations of
abuse have on them, some women are disappointed by the approach taken. This has
an impact on their educational and professional plans. Some develop negative opinions and perceptions of the university as an institution and of male academics as
professionals (Marks and Nelson 1993), or they lose confidence in the effectiveness
of the sexual harassment policies which are implemented in universities (Thomas
2004). Some women might also develop (or increase) a feeling of mistrust in their
relationships with the opposite sex, and sometimes adopt strategies to reduce their
chances of encountering the perpetrators (Benson and Thomson 1982; Reilly et al.
1986).

However, the strategies to avoid potential situations of harassment become extremely difficult when male faculty members or professors are the aggressors and
college women are the victims. This is because female students are in a subor-
dinate position, or because female academics are less powerful than senior male
colleagues. Participants in the field work explained specific circumstances which
complicate this situation:

> [...] when you are doing a dissertation on a particular piece of romantic poetry, a very spe-
> cialised dissertation, and you got a supervisor who is the unique specialist in this area, and
> then you have one-on-one supervision with this person you know, every couple of months,
> or every month, and then there is a problem now [...] a harassment problem or even other
> kinds of problems, but then it is pretty much impossible to get another supervisor and so,
> this is kind of the problem with the supervisor relationship [...]. (Participant in a daily-life
> story no. 3)

Another type of negative impact which particularly affects women who have been
sexually abused or harassed is a decrease in the quality of their work. Some of them
lose confidence in their own work and in some cases they reduce the effort they de-
vote to it (Reilly et al. 1986; Fitzgerald et al. 1988). Consequently, these situations
make it more difficult for women to develop the ability to learn to their full potential
(Wagner and Magnusson 2005). It affects their self-esteem and increases the possibility that they will decide to give up their commitment to their careers in male-
dominated academic areas (Benson and Thomson 1982). Indeed, these analyses
make it explicit that sexual harassment is a form of sexism which interferes with the
ability of women to get an education or undertake a job (Dziech and Weiner 1990).

Some women's choices are influenced to the extent that some of them decide to
stop attending classes at university, or to drop out of a course in order not to come
across the perpetrator again. This happens when universities have not developed
effective measures to penalise male academics who are the perpetrators of sexual
harassment. For the same reason, some women decide to change their advisor or professor or give up their academic careers in male-dominated areas. In the most severe

cases, a few women decide to withdraw from university (Reilly et al. 1986; Fitzgerald et al. 1988; Dziech and Weiner 1990; Marks and Nelson 1993; Toffey Shepela and Levesque 1998). This issue emerged in the data collected for the present study:

> I think there are plenty of people for whom the stress [...] is the result of some form of harassment. Occasionally, we hear that people have decided to leave university as a result of this. We have got some evidence that people respond by being ill and not coming to work, or just by low levels of work, [...] if people feel that they cannot complain, they get trapped in a situation [...]. Evidence from individual cases that have come to the harassment network. (Interviewed people no. 6)

Sexual harassment not only affects female students, but also female professors and staff. Farley (1978) carried out a study of sexual harassment in jobs which affected women in the 1970s. Amongst the cases she explored, she included some illustrative quotes which reflected the effect that harassment by superiors had on academic women:

> I hadn't been teaching that long when the dean of my college was all over me for sex. He was terribly insistent and I repeatedly refused. The next thing I know he suspended me from teaching; of course, he gave me all sorts of other reasons. I couldn't believe what was happening. Can you imagine when the dean is saying all these terrible things? [...] Even if you win it presents a terrible image. (Farley 1978, p. 109)

Although there are some 30 years between Farley's investigation and my own study, interview data suggested that this problem persists. One research participant warned of the fears some people had of jeopardising their own careers if they go ahead with reporting someone after being harassed or bullied:

> People are very scared to come forward because they think by coming forward they will jeopardise their careers. [...] It can happen in a very subtle way [...] I am going to give you a bad reference. (E04: Interviewed person no. 4)

Finally, it is also relevant to take into account that the impact of sexual harassment in universities affects not only the lives and educational and professional plans of the women who are victims of it, but also the professional and personal lives of the people who support them. Dziech and Weiner (1990), for example, describe the way in which sexism on campus creates a second order of sexual harassment victims: those who advise, support, and rule in favour of the primary victims. Indeed, the people who become involved in the situation of women who have experienced sexual violence, who express solidarity towards them, and help to change this situation in universities can also be affected by large social and institutional pressure, or by reprisals.

Recommendations

The initial findings, supported by an analysis of the literature and of my own data, suggest the need for further research. There is a need to analyse violence against women, not as something which affects individual women, but as a collective problem which needs to be addressed by the actual university structures (Stombler 1994; Grauerholz et al. 1999; Wagner and Magnusson 2005). On some occasions, measures oriented towards solving these situations have been focused on individual victims of sexual harassment in order to analyse their particular circumstances and to explain why it has happened to them. However, international research stresses the shortcomings of such an individualistic perspective and the need to analyse the phenomenon in a way that takes into account its origins in social institutionalisation. The tacit acceptance of violence is rooted in beliefs and in value systems which are embedded in models of hegemonic masculinity which undervalue women. Therefore, new insights should emphasise the problem at an institutional level (Reilly et al. 1986; Nicholson et al. 1998).

There is also a need to analyse ways and define methods to overcome hostility towards women in universities (Toffey Shepela and Levesque 1998; Grauerholz et al. 1999). In that sense, research efforts are required to analyse ways to promote non-acceptance of sexual harassment and to transform university environments which are hostile to women into supportive, egalitarian and dialogic spaces (Ayres Boswell and Spade 1996; Potter et al. 2000). The main aim of these new insights should be to promote a change in the ideas which undervalue the perception of women in sexual and affective relationships, and to promote reflection on the consequences of unhealthy sexual and affective relationships (Charkow and Nelson 2000). More effort should be made to intervene in the social dynamic of universities and in the way social structures impact on gender relations (Ayres Boswell and Spade 1996; Grauerholz et al. 1999; Eyre 2000; Wagner and Magnusson 2005). One of the ways to do that is by developing more supportive environments for women.

Educational interventions can be an effective way to encourage a change in attitudes and values related to forms of violence against women (Fonow et al. 1992; Reilly et al. 1992; Ayres Boswell and Spade 1996; Toffey Shepela and Levesque 1998; Potter et al. 2000; Gross et al. 2006). Moreover, educational efforts can increase women's awareness of the potential for victimisation in some intimate situations with acquaintances or dating partners (Reilly et al. 1992). These educational efforts can contribute towards promoting reflection on the role of communication in changing sexual relationships and on the role of power and myths in sexual assaults (Potter et al. 2000). Research findings also suggest the need to further explore and start working on the preventive socialisation of gender violence at early educational stages, in order to prevent sexual harassment of children and teenagers before it begins (Gómez 2004; Valls et al. 2008).

Further recommendations, stemming from the main points in this section, relate to the need to analyse ways to improve the recruitment of female faculty members in different positions, at every level of the hierarchical structures in universities (Grauerholz 1996). It is important to guarantee the presence of female faculty members at every level in order to make universities more hospitable environments for women (Osborne 1995). In addition, increasing the presence of female students in every department, including those such as engineering that are currently male dominated, may be a way to promote their transformation into study environments which are free of gender discrimination.

Finally, Thomas (2004) suggests the need to carry out a systematic evaluation of the impact of sexual harassment policies implemented in universities in order to progress towards creating effective responses. Feedback from these evaluation procedures can provide important clues to help guarantee that the measures undertaken have a significant impact on overcoming this problem.

In developing mechanisms for support and solidarity among women, I would like to stress the significance of informal networks of women when facing difficulties and obstacles to reporting someone (Grauerholz et al. 1999; Banyard et al. 2005). Equally significant is the promotion of informal networks of solidarity amongst women to support those who have experienced sexual harassment, in order to complement the formal structures defined by universities for complaints (Grauerholz et al. 1999). These types of networks, based on the positive impact of feminist interaction, can draw on more collaborative relationships. They can also be founded on friendship and relationships involving trust, and can overcome some of the constraints to reporting or making a formal complaint.

Conclusions

Evidence obtained from academic literature and qualitative data shows that some universities are still male-dominated domains in which there are many barriers affecting mainly women. One of these barriers is the existence of different forms of gender violence. The basis of these findings is a broad definition of violence against women which includes not only physical violence, but also sexist attitudes and comments, different forms of scorn, sexual coercion, harassment or sexual assault. This is a wide concept which suggests the need to examine male power structures in universities and their impact on contexts which can favour situations involving gender discrimination or gender violence.

Despite the limitations of research published at a European level on this topic, international research (mainly from the United States) provides significant data on the rates of violence against academic women (both students and faculty members). These studies indicate that more knowledge is needed in order to understand better how this phenomenon emerges in universities.

To conclude, I would like to stress the impact that the prevalence of forms of gender discrimination in the university context has in society as a whole. Sexual harassment or violence against women is related to social institutionalisation and the acceptance of practices rooted in a system of beliefs and values which are embedded in the models of hegemonic masculinity which persist in our societies and which undermine women. The prevalence of these situations in universities can have a deep impact on the lifelong learning processes of women, on the opportunities for women to have a successful academic career and to obtain a good quality job. Consequently, this problem is a clear indication of the work that still needs to be done in order to achieve full equality between men and women in our societies.

References

Ayres Boswell, A., & Spade, J. Z. (1996). Fraternities and collegiate rape culture: Why are some fraternities more dangerous places for women? *Gender and Society, 10*(2), 133–147.

Banyard, V. L., Plante, E. G., Cohn, E. S., Moorhead, C., Ward, S., & Walsh, W. (2005). Revisiting unwanted sexual experiences on campus. A 12-year follow-up. *Violence Against Women, 11*(4), 426–446.

Benson, D. J., & Thomson, G. E. (1982). Sexual harassment on a university campus: The confluence of authority relations, sexual interest and gender stratification. *Social Problems, 29*(3), 236–251.

Boeringer, S. C. (1999). Research note: Associations of rape-supportive attitudes with fraternal and athletic participation. *Violence Against Women, 5*(1), 81–89.

Bondurant, B. (2001). University women' acknowledgment of rape. Individual, situational and social factors. *Violence Against Women, 7*(3), 294–314.

Burt, M. R. (1980). Cultural myths and support for rape. *Journal of Personality and Social Psychology, 38*(2), 217–230.

Charkow, W. B., & Nelson, E. S. (2000). Relationship dependency, dating violence and scripts of female college students. *Journal of College Counselling, 3,* 17–28.

Cowan, G. (2000). Women's hostility toward women and rape and sexual harassment myths. *Violence Against Women, 6*(3), 238–246.

CREA Centre of Research in Theories and Practices that Overcome Inequalities (2005–2008). Violencia de género en las universidades españolas. Funded by the Women's Institute and the Spanish Social Affairs and Labor Ministry

Dziech, B., & Weiner, L. (1990). *The lecherous professor. Sexual harassment on campus.* Urbana Champaign: University of Illinois Press.

Eyre, L. (2000). The discursive framing of sexual harassment in a university community. *Gender and Education, 12*(3), 293–307.

Farley, L. (1978). *Sexual shakedown. The sexual harassment of women on the job.* New York: Warner.

Fitzgerald, L. F., Shullman, S. L., Bailey, N., Richards, M., Swecker, J., Gold, Y., Ormerod, M., & Weitzman, L. (1988). The incidence and dimensions of sexual harassment in academia and the workplace. *Journal of Vocational Behavior, 32,* 152–175.

Flecha, R., & Gómez, J. (2004). Participatory paradigms: Researching 'with' rather than 'on'. In B. Crossan, J. Gallacher, & M. Osborne (Eds.), *Researching widening access: Issues and approaches in an international context* (pp. 129–140). London: Routledge.

Fonow, M. M., Richardson, L., & Wemmerus, V. A. (1992). Feminist rape education: Does it work? *Gender and Society, 6*(1), 108–121.

Forbes, G. B. Adams-Curtis, L. E., Pakalka, A. H., & White, K. B. (2006). Dating aggression, sexual coercion, and aggression-supporting attitudes among college menas a function of participation in aggressive high school sports. *Violence Against Women, 12*(5), 441–455.

Framework Programme of the European Commission, D. G. X. (1999). Eurobarometer 51.0. Europeans and their Views on Domestic Violence Against Women.

Gómez, J. (2004). *El amor en la sociedad del riesgo.* Barcelona: El Roure.

Grauerholz, L. (1996). Sexual harassment in the academy: The case of women professors. In M. S. Stockdale (Ed.), *Sexual harassment in the workplace. Perspectives, frontiers and response strategies* (pp. 29–50). Thousand Oaks: Sage

Grauerholz, L., Gottfried, H., Stohl, C., & Gabin, N. (1999). There's safety in numbers: Creating a campus advisers' network to help complainants of sexual harassment and complain receivers. *Violence Against Women, 5*(8), 950–977.

Gross, A. M., Winslett, A., Roberts, M., & Gohm, C. L. (2006). An examination of sexual violence against college women. *Violence Against Women, 12*(3), 288–300.

Kalof, L. (1993). Rape-supportive attitudes and sexual victimization experiences of sorority and nonsorority women. *Sex Roles, 29*(11/12), 767–780.

Kalof, L., Kimberly, K. E., Matheson, J. L., & Kroska, R. B. (2001). The influence of race and gender on students self-reports of sexual harassment by college professors. *Gender and Society, 15*(2), 282–302.

Lee, D. (2006). *University students behaving badly.* Staffordshire: Trentham.

Marks, M. A., & Nelson, E. S. (1993). Sexual harassment on campus: Effects of professor gender on perception of sexually harassing behaviour. *Sex Roles 28*(3/4), 207–217.

Nicholson, M. E., Maney, D. W., Blair, K., Wamboldt, P. M., Saxton Mahoney, B., & Yuan, J. (1998). Trends in alcohol-related campus violence: Implications for prevention. *Journal of Alcohol and Drug Education, 43*(3), 34–52.

Osborne, R. L. (1995). The continuum of violence against women in Canadian universities. Toward a new understanding of the chilly campus climate. *Women's Studies International Forum, 18* (5/6), 637–646.

Potter, R. H., Krider, J. E., & McMahon, P. M. (2000). Examining elements of campus sexual violence policies. Is deterrence or health promotion favored? *Violence Against Women, 6*(12), 1345–1362.

Quinn, J. (2003). *Powerful subjects. Are women really taking over the university?* Stoke on Trent: Trentham.

Reilly, M. E., Lott, B., & Gallogly, S. M. (1986). Sexual harassment of university students. *Sex Roles, 15*(7/8), 333–358.

Reilly, M. E., Lott, B., Gallogly, S. M., Caldwell, D., & DeLuca, L. (1992). Tolerance for sexual harassment related to self-reported sexual victimization. *Gender and Society, 6*(1), 122–138.

Stalker, J. (2001). Misogyny, women, and obstacles to tertiary education: A vile situation. *Adult Education Quarterly, 51*(4), 288–305.

Stombler, M. (1994). 'Buddies' or 'slutties': The collective sexual reputation of fraternity little sisters. *Gender and Society, 8*(3), 297–323.

Thomas, A. M. (2004). Politics, policies and practices: Assessing the impact of sexual harassment in policies in UK universities. *British Journal of Sociology of Education, 25*(2), 143–160.

Till, F. J. (1980). *Sexual harassment.* A report on the sexual harassment of students. District of Columbia, National Advisory Council on Women's Educational Programs.

Toffey Shepela, S., & Levesque, L. L. (1998). Poisoned waters: Sexual harassment and the college climate. *Sex Roles, 38*(7/8), 589–611.

United Nations. (1993). *Declaration on the Elimination of Violence Against Women.* UN. General Assembly, A/RES/48/104.

Valls, R., Puigvert, L., & Duque, E. (2008). Gender violence amongst teenagers: Socialization and prevention. *Violence Against Women, 14*(7), 759–785.

Wagner, A., & Magnusson, J. L. (2005). Neglected realities: exploring the impact of women's experiences of violence on learning in sites of higher education. *Gender and Education, 17*(4), 449–461.

Yancey Martin, P., & Hummer, R. A. (1989). Fraternities and rape on campus. *Gender and Society, 3*(4), 457–473.

Chapter 7
Part I: Conclusion

Irene Malcolm, Sue Jackson and Kate Thomas

The work in the present section of the book can be located in a tradition of women's learning that draws on feminist principles and pedagogies to empower women in seeking non-gendered choices. Women's learning through shared experience and networking, which is an important focus in the chapters above, emerges as a theme that resonates in discussions of work and identity in subsequent sections of the book. In Chap. 6 Olivier reveals the crucial role played by solidarity among women to support those affected by gender violence. Networking and sharing experience emerge in women's concerted action to support more equitable learning relationships. This leads in one example to the inception of a new learning programme (Chap. 5) and in another to new approaches to learning relations (Chap. 3). In the chapters above, mutual support helped women to develop learning to address unequal power relations (Chap. 6) or to enter workplaces where power relations contribute to women's under-representation (Chap. 5).

The problem of gendered learning is related to deficits in the workforce capacity. At the same time, women's exclusion in areas such as SET has a wider detrimental effect on society. Networks (face-to-face and mediated through technology) sustain progress in women's learning, supporting and enabling them to address the cultural changes needed to make workplaces conducive to their careers, opening up new identity possibilities. As the chapters in this section demonstrate, gendered choices in learning are significant in women's (and men's) marginalisation.

The authors in this section offer an alternative vision that promotes women's contributions and the importance of their shared experience. They suggest new possibilities that can contribute to effective and equitable learning. These forms of learning are important in promoting inclusive cultures that can inform future workplaces. The analysis of learning experiences in this section of the book forms the

I. Malcolm (✉)
School of Education, Social Work and Community Education, University of Dundee, Nethergate, Dundee, DD1 4HN, UK
e-mail: i.z.malcolm@dundee.ac.uk

S. Jackson et al. (eds.), *Gendered Choices,* Lifelong Learning Book Series 15, DOI 10.1007/978-94-007-0647-7_7, © Springer Science+Business Media B.V. 2011

background to considerations of organisational cultures as constraining or facilitating: a theme that is developed in the discussions that follow. The gendered nature of learning pathways has far-reaching implications for women's work which is the theme of the next section of the book.

Part II
The Agenda for Gender in Workplace Learning

Chapter 8
Part II: Introduction

Kate Thomas, Sue Jackson and Irene Malcolm

Part I addressed the impact of policies and current methodological approaches on gendered learning pathways and choices. While acknowledging gender challenges for men as well as women within lifelong learning, the chapters in Part I particularly highlighted women's experiences as central to the development of their learning choices. The chapters in Part II move our focus to the world of work to consider gendered choices at different stages of the employment lifecycle and in different employment and learning contexts.

Three of the chapters address issues of work-based learning and gender from an UK perspective (Chaps. 9, 10 and 11) and these are complemented by Chap. 12 which presents an Iranian perspective on education and economic participation. While there are obvious cultural and economic differences between the sites of study, it is nevertheless instructive to note the synergies between them in terms of barriers to female participation and progression. Similarly, the themes addressed are applicable beyond the immediate contexts of the chapters; all four highlight the interaction of lifelong learning, in this case work-based learning, and gender and explore the ways in which this interaction is mediated by structural constraints, occupational status and age. All place gender firmly on the work-based learning agenda in addressing gendered choices and gendered experiences of learning, the workplace and organisational cultures.

Globalisation and the rapid development of communications and information technologies have acted as significant drivers for a refocusing of work-based and work-related learning within the UK in order to meet the demands of the 'knowledge-driven economy' (Webb et al. 2006, p. 564). For example, the Leitch report (2006) urged the UK to set itself higher skills ambitions in order to become 'world class' in a globalised world. Its recommendations included improving levels of intermediate skills, increasing numbers of apprenticeships and boosting the percentage of adults

K. Thomas (✉)
Schools and Colleges Partnership Service, University of the West of England,
Frenchay Campus, Coldharbour Lane, BS16 1QD Bristol, UK
e-mail: kate2.thomas@uwe.ac.uk

S. Jackson et al. (eds.), *Gendered Choices,* Lifelong Learning Book Series 15,
DOI 10.1007/978-94-007-0647-7_8, © Springer Science+Business Media B.V. 2011

qualified to Level 4[1] and above to over 40%. In Chap. 11, Anita Walsh reminds us that there is an acceptance that 'workplaces need to be conceptualised more clearly as learning environments' (Billett 2006, p. 38) and certainly, UK curriculum and qualification developments increasingly emphasise work-related knowledge and skills. For example, a key feature of the new diploma qualification for 14–19 year olds is 'an insight into what work is really like' (14–19 Diplomas 2009). The Foundation degree, an intermediate higher education qualification was introduced in England specifically to 'provide graduates...needed in the labour market to address shortages in particular skills' (QAA 2004, p. 1) and aims to 'equip people with the relevant knowledge, understanding and skills to improve performance and productivity' (www.fdf.ac.uk).

In the global knowledge economy and in the educational response to it, 'core workers are expected to be active lifelong learners' (Stevenson 2002, p. 2), able to adapt and respond to rapidly changing demands. Yet 'there is little explicit recognition that the ways in which the learner–worker is placed in the knowledge economy are gendered, "raced" and classed' (Webb et al. 2006, p. 564). All chapters in Part II consider the barriers faced by women in taking 'responsibility for their own employability' (Webb et al. 2006, p. 565) whether these are funding regimes which constrain opportunities for retraining (Chap. 9); unequal access to workplace learning opportunities (Chap. 11) or entrenched expectations that Iranian women will prioritise familial obligations over economic participation (Chap. 12).

In Chap. 9, linking back in particular to Chap. 5's consideration of women returning to careers in SET, Linda Miller considers the relationship between gendered employment choices and career decision-making at early and later stages in the lifecourse. A gender segregated workforce has exacerbated the challenge of the UK's skills deficit and, Miller claims, specifically disadvantaged women in the development of a high skills economy and in pay comparison with men. Drawing on empirical evidence from a range of data sources, she considers what factors help or hinder younger and older women to contemplate a broader range of employment. In particular, she asks whether older women are more likely to be conditioned by traditional beliefs and lifestyle choices and therefore more reluctant to change or develop careers in atypical sectors such as construction and engineering? Miller reflects on different models of career choice and Mercer's work on the renegotiation of self in mature students in HE/FE to argue that greater confidence and self-knowledge mean older women are more open to atypical career choices. However, she concludes that because retraining is essential to career and employment choice in later life and because funding regimes discriminate in favour of younger learners, older women's career choices are likely to be limited by opportunity and available funding. Conversely, younger women's 'employment choices are more gendered, confined by self-concept and school and college discourses including information, advice and guidance' (Chap. 9).

---

[1] Level 4 of the National Qualifications Framework (NQF) for England, Wales and Northern Ireland is equivalent to the Certificate in Higher Education in the Framework for Higher Education (FHEQ).

Suzanne Hyde continues to explore the tensions between government policy and women's experiences in Chap. 10. Like Miller, she focuses on the experiences of older women in an English context, but as with Chap. 9, her findings and conclusions are far more widely relevant. Hyde employs a life history analysis approach to the learning journeys of low-paid, female, union members attending a range of union-funded courses in the workplace. The involvement of unions in the workplace learning agenda has created its own tensions, not least because shifts in emphasis towards funding for younger learners, and skills for older learners, together with a contraction in liberal adult education have significant implications for equality, class, gender and race. Hyde considers the 'implications for a "feminised" model of learning and its relationship to the current skills agenda' (Chap. 10).

The learners' stories reveal a complex relationship between non-instrumental and instrumental motivations for workplace learning. Whereas individuals' non-instrumental reasons for learning contradict the skills focus of the workplace learning agenda, their learning is nevertheless shown to have considerable instrumental benefits to the individual and to the organisation. Learners reported increased confidence and self-esteem as well as positive changes to workplace relationship and career development. Instrumental reasons for workplace learning were also more complex than they first appeared, particularly where the courses involved were reflective rather than competence-based. Hyde concludes that a distinction between soft and hard outcomes of skills-related learning is, like the agenda itself, too simplistic. How much more complex is the picture when gender and other equality issues are considered?

Anita Walsh demonstrates this complexity in Chap. 11, with a detailed examination of the evolution of work-based learning into an accredited 'equivalent' of academic knowledge and a consideration of the effect of gender on access to workplace learning. Walsh argues that the lifelong learning debate now recognises the 'sociality' of knowledge, knowledge and learning produced through social practices (Chap. 11); her chapter traces the positioning of workplace learning as a widening participation tool within higher education and as a key mechanism for upskilling the workforce within the knowledge economy. However, rather than expanding career and educational horizons, Walsh argues that without a greater degree of critical reflection and changes to organisational and structural constraints, this wider recognition of workplace learning reinforces existing gendered divisions in the workplace, rather than providing opportunities for wider participation in higher education.

Walsh shows how the gendered, classed and 'raced' nature of paid employment results not only in unequal access to workplace learning, but to an inequality of impact. In the lower occupational levels of the labour market where roles are markedly gendered and women predominate, the impact of work-based qualifications such as the National Vocational Qualification (NVQ) has been, Walsh argues, to confine women to those occupational areas. This continues the impact of the hidden curriculum in schools which directs girls towards 'feminine subjects'. She also concludes that the fact that women represent the majority of part-time learners on Foundation degree courses linked to low-status, low-paid roles suggests that this means of widening participation in higher education is reinforcing occupational segregation.

Walsh points out that 'learning intensive' and 'learning deprived' work environments can and do occur within the same organisation with women less likely to be able to access 'learning intensive' environments at graduate and higher levels of seniority than men. Where women with formal qualifications gain access to 'learning intensive' environments, they are vulnerable to a lack of critical reflexivity which perpetuates gendered organisational practices and to structural constraints of childcare and part-time working on their labour market choices. Overall, Walsh argues that there is a failure to recognise that women in all sectors of the labour market require access to educational opportunity including workplace learning at different points throughout their lives.

Women's changing relationship with the workplace at different points in their lives is a theme also taken up in Chap. 12. While authors Narjes Mehdizadeh and Gill Scott focus on issues and barriers specific to Iran, their perspective nevertheless consolidates this section's wider theme of inequality in educational provision and labour force participation. The contradictions in the relationship between Iranian women's high rates of educational achievement and low rates of economic activity are highlighted in the specific barriers to labour force participation experienced by graduate mothers. Mehdizadeh and Scott place these issues in the wider frame of development and citizenship, noting that the latter too often reflects male entitlement to education and employment and that women's agency plays an essential but too often unrecognised role in development.

In common with other chapters in Part II, the authors argue that women's economic participation and therefore access to work-based learning, is limited by societal beliefs, attitudes and care responsibilities. Since 1989, both education and employment in Iran have remained dominated by societal beliefs and norms which dictate a domestic role for women. Women remain restricted to employment in particular, largely public sectors, notably health, education and social care. Structural problems with Iranian workplace learning mean that this does not offer a remedial or alternative course of action once women are in employment. Social barriers exist to female entrepreneurship. The authors therefore argue that despite significant increases in Iranian women's rates of educational achievement, in confining women to particular subjects and sectors and in failing to connect curricula to the requirements of the Iranian economy or the possibilities of a knowledge economy, women's educational achievement has not proved economically liberating.

Mehdizadeh and Scott conclude their chapter by highlighting the experience of Iranian graduate mothers, reinforcing the theme of the tensions between policy and experience which has run throughout this section. Access to childcare provision, they argue, is as important to developing women's labour force participation as the development of a knowledge-based economy. Yet a national requirement on Iranian employers to provide childcare for female employees has resulted in restricted female recruitment. Similarly, a positive emphasis on the development of women's economic participation in national policy is at the very least, hampered by a restatement of the 'strength of the family institution' within which women's caring role is automatically assumed.

References

14–19 Diplomas. (2009). http://www.dcsf.gov.uk/14-19/. Accessed 30 April 2009 (Web only).

Billett, S. (2006). Constituting the workplace curriculum. *Journal of Curriculum Studies, 38*(1), 31–48.

Foundation Degrees. (2008). http://www.fdf.ac.uk. Accessed 30 April 2009 (Web only).

Leitch, S. (2006). *Prosperity for all in the global economy—World class skills.* Chicago: HM Stationery Office.

QAA. (2004). Foundation Degree qualification benchmark. http://www.qaa.ac.uk/reviews/foundationDegree/benchmark/FDQB.pdf. Accessed 11 May 2009.

Stevenson, J. (2002). Concepts of workplace knowledge. *International Journal of Educational Research, 37*(1), 1–15.

Webb, S., Brine, J., & Jackson, S. (2006). Foundation degrees and the knowledge economy. *Journal of Vocational Education and Training: Special Issue on Gender matters. Perspectives on women, work and training, 58*(4), 563–576.

Chapter 9
Women Work-Based Learners: Factors Affecting Lifelong Learning and Career Opportunities

Linda Miller

Introduction

This chapter sets out the policy background behind attempts to encourage women to enter gender-segregated areas of work in England. It then considers factors within individuals themselves and within the work environment that facilitate or, conversely, inhibit attempts to encourage women to move into gender-segregated occupations. The chapter also examines current funding policies in England and considers whether these support or inhibit attempts to encourage women to re-train and gain high-level qualifications in atypical, gender segregated, areas.

Before moving on to consider these issues, however, some explanation needs to be given regarding the way in which UK policy is developed now, following the establishment of the devolved governments of Wales and Scotland. Much of the current skills policy is being driven by the conclusions of the Leitch review (Leitch 2006), which concluded that, for the UK to become a world leader in skills by 2020, attainment at most levels of skill would need to be doubled. Subsequent to the Leitch review, a UK-wide Commission for Employment and Skills was established.

Although the Commission for Employment and Skills now directs skills policy for the UK, the UK government decides training and funding policy only for England, rather than for the UK as a whole. Policies relating to training and funding in England are implemented through the Department for Business, Innovation and Skills (BIS)[1]. Different policies—for example, on what level qualifications to offer or prioritise, and how to fund them—are set and followed in Scotland and Wales.

While policies emanating from BIS apply only to England, policies developed by the Department for Work and Pensions (DWP) and relating to employment issues

---

[1] BIS has had responsibility since its inception in June 2009. Between June 2007 and June 2009 responsibility for this policy area lay with the Department of Innovation, Universities and Skills (DIUS) and before that the Department for Education and Skills (DfES).

L. Miller (✉)
Institute for Employment Studies, Brighton, UK
e-mail: linda.miller@employment-studies.co.uk

S. Jackson et al. (eds.), *Gendered Choices*, Lifelong Learning Book Series 15,
DOI 10.1007/978-94-007-0647-7_9, © Springer Science+Business Media B.V. 2011

apply within Scotland and Wales as well as within England. Therefore, while any broader issues regarding occupational gender segregation and gender-differentiated patterns of qualification apply across the UK, discussion of specific policies in this chapter (such as funding through Train to Gain) relate only to England.

The broad issues pertaining to gender segregation in work, education, and training are considered next.

Gender Segregation in Work and Education

Despite the long-standing existence of legislation outlawing sex discrimination, many (in fact most) sectors nonetheless remain strongly gender-segregated after 30 years of sex discrimination legislation. This is the case irrespective of what level of employment is considered. Entries to education and training programmes typically mirror the patterns of segregation observed in employment. At school level there remain strongly gender-segregated patterns of qualification, with concerns being particularly focused on the low numbers of females in schools taking science qualifications.[2] Gender imbalance in entry to such subjects at ages 16 and 18 then has a subsequent impact on registration patterns for university courses, with relatively small numbers of women choosing to take 'STEM' subjects (science, technology, engineering and mathematics) at university.

Within the work-based learning and further education arenas there are similar segregated patterns of entry to apprenticeships. The Cassels review of apprenticeships in 2001 revealed that registrations for the (then) modern apprenticeships showed identical patterns of gender segregation to those seen in adult employment; further analyses undertaken by Miller et al. (2004) as part of research commissioned by the Equal Opportunities Commission (EOC) to inform the General Formal Investigation (GFI)[3] into occupational gender segregation revealed that little had changed since Cassels recommended action to address these segregated entry patterns (Cassels 2001). Recent analyses reported by the Trades Union Congress have confirmed that there has been little progress in the four years since then (TUC 2008).

Such segregated patterns of education and training serve only to reinforce patterns of occupational gender segregation within the workforce. Gender segregation has increasingly become a focus for government attention in recent years, and there are several reasons for this. First, there is a set of issues that might best be summarised under the heading of the 'skills deficit'. One such issue is the shortage of

---

[2] Although this finally seems to be changing: Trends in 'A' (Advanced) level results reveal that females are gradually increasing their share of science 'A' levels; data are available from the UK Resource Centre for Women (www.setwomenresource.org.uk).

[3] The Equal Opportunities Commission has statutory powers under the Sex Discrimination Act to instigate a General Formal Investigation where there is prevalent gender segregation in employment and training; the work looked at employment, education and training in five strongly segregated areas, but looked in particular at the situation regarding apprenticeships.

people entering some of the more strongly segregated areas of the economy, such as construction and engineering, which means that employers are effectively being forced to look outside their traditional recruitment pool for potential recruits.

Secondly, the government has stated its intention to move towards a 'high skills economy', and indeed, this is also part of the strategic goals of the European Union (EU) for all its member states. The EU Lisbon Summit meeting in 2000 set out its intention to make the EU 'the most competitive and dynamic knowledge-based economy in the world' and indicated that there would be a need for investment in education and training to address the subsequent skill requirements. In the UK, the gender gap in qualifications is seen as contributing to the national skills deficit that impedes progression towards a 'high skills economy'. The 2003 White Paper *21st Century Skills, Realising Our Potential* (DfES 2003) identified intermediate level skills deficits in female workers as a cause for concern—in particular 'skills gaps in…intermediate skills at apprenticeship, technician, higher craft and associate professional level' (DfES 2003, p.12). The White Paper also indicated that women's labour market disadvantage was linked to this lack of skills and stated that it was the government's intention to increase the skill levels of all under-represented groups in society, but particularly women workers who are typically locked in a 'narrow range of low level manual occupations' and in part-time work where training opportunities are limited. It was also noted that older women tend to have lower levels of qualification than younger ones.

Lastly, membership of the EU imposes a requirement upon the government to address perceived weaknesses in the labour market. The Employment Action Plan (EAP) for the UK for 2003 identified the gender pay gap and occupational segregation as two issues that needed to be addressed by government policy. The main actions identified by the Government in the 2003 EAP to address gender segregation comprised largely of actions focussed on the science sector along with reference to increasing promotion of work–life balance, increased childcare provision and financial incentives. The EAP also identified the EOC's General Formal Investigation into gender segregation as being part of the UK's actions to address occupational segregation, although the EOC is independent of the government and therefore not what one might normally consider to be part of a National Action Plan. It should be noted, though, that the focus on occupational gender segregation had disappeared by the time that the 2004 EAP was produced.

The above sets out three of the reasons why the UK government has become more interested in recent years in encouraging women to gain qualifications and move into sectors in which they have traditionally been under-represented. However, there is another, arguably much stronger, reason why the government wants to encourage more women to consider areas of work more traditionally associated with men, and one that might also be expected to be persuasive for the majority of women, too. On average, today, women still remain far more poorly paid than men—current EOC estimates are that there is an 18% 'gender pay gap' between the average female and male employee in the UK. John Forth and his colleagues at the University of Essex have estimated that occupational segregation accounts for a significant proportion of this pay gap between women and men—some 20% for full-time workers and 14% across all workers (Forth et al. 2003). The argument, then, is that if women could be persuaded to enter jobs in atypical sectors such as engineering and construction, this would go some way towards reducing the inequalities in pay between women and men.

In principle, then, there are jobs, and well-paid jobs at that, into which we might expect to see women flocking in their thousands—but they do not. So the first question has to be, why is this? The 2003 White Paper implied that 'the problem' lies with older women, and, furthermore, the implication was that older women are somehow making perverse decisions both in not actively seeking to attain the intermediate level qualifications that would bring increased financial rewards, and in failing to consider sectors that are far better paid than those in which the majority of women work.

So, first, let us consider the position of older women in the jobs market. One possible explanation for older women's reluctance to consider atypical areas of work might be that older women grew up at a time when cultural beliefs about gender stereotypes were stronger and, as a result, are more attached to traditional ideas about the feminine sex-role stereotype and 'female identity' and, because of this, prefer to avoid atypical areas of work. Is there any evidence that older women have more stereotypical beliefs or are more 'set in their ways' and reluctant to change?

Research into changes in sex-role stereotypes over time indicates that, as might be expected, older people do hold more traditional beliefs regarding appropriate sex roles for women and men. Furthermore, researchers such as John Archer (Archer 1999) have demonstrated that occupational identity is a central part of our self-concept, and therefore it might be reasonable to conclude that, if older women have more traditional sex stereotypes, then they would be more likely to reject masculine occupations as being incongruent with their self-concept, or at least with that part of the self-concept that relates to sex-role stereotypes and appropriate roles for men and women.

However, it would appear that this is not the main reason why older working women do not choose to retrain and enter more highly paid male areas of work. The main reasons seem to lie in more pedestrian factors—mostly to do with training and funding opportunities. If anything, the research evidence that will be described in the following sections indicates that, nowadays, the trend is for women to become more open minded with age regarding possible job options and training—at least in principle. But there are barriers to overcome, and largely these lie outside the self, not within. These issues will be explored in the following sections, starting first with evidence relating to younger women and then moving on to consider the position of older women.

The Decisions of Younger and Older Women

Encouraging younger women to consider atypical areas of study and work might initially be considered an easier task than persuading older women. However, as already indicated, the entry statistics for qualifications such as GCSEs (the General

Table 9.1 Proportion of females in advanced apprenticeships in selected sectors. (Source: Miller et al. 2004)

Female share, advanced apprenticeships	
Occupational area	*Percent*
Construction	1.2
Engineering	2.7
Information technology and electronic services	15
Plumbing	0.6
Childcare	99.0

Certificate of Secondary Education), 'A' (Advanced) levels, degree programmes and the various vocational equivalents (Young Apprenticeships (YAs), National Vocational Qualifications (NVQs) and apprenticeships) suggest little progress over the past decade, with the great majority of subjects remaining strongly gender-segregated. The apprenticeship statistics that we obtained as part of the EOC's GFI (shown in Table 9.1) revealed that apprenticeships showed the same extremes of gender imbalance as were seen in employment statistics (Miller et al. 2004).

In other words, very little change in the patterns of career/training choices was seen amongst this younger group of women. This is despite the fact that the Learning and Skills Council—the body that currently funds most non-HE, post-compulsory education—is one of the public sector bodies that has a statutory duty to encourage equal opportunities—in this case, in education and training.

It is fair to comment that, even given the existence of this statutory duty, there are various reasons that could explain why such patterns of segregation might nonetheless still be seen. One explanation could be that young women are already so strongly 'feminine stereotyped' by the time they reach age 16 that they simply do not wish to consider strongly male-stereotyped areas. In fact, recent work by Millward et al. (2006) does seem to confirm this: Millward and her colleagues found that individuals' own sex-role stereotyping impacts on job preferences, with more strongly feminine-stereotyped girls (that is, girls who rate themselves as being more 'feminine' on a measure of sex-role stereotyping) being the least likely to be attracted to masculine occupations.

However, research by Miller and Hayward (2006) has revealed two key findings relating to this point: The first is that the extent to which perceptions of stereotyping influence girls' 'liking' for various careers reduces with age,[4] suggesting that it might in fact be easier to persuade older females than younger ones. The second was that perceptions of stereotyping are slightly less influential than the extent to which an occupation is seen as segregated. Table 9.2 is reproduced from Miller and Hayward (2006) and shows the correlations of pupils' ratings of the extent to which they believed they would like various jobs with the extent to which they viewed those jobs as predominantly male- or female-stereotyped (defined as the extent to which they 'should be' performed mainly by one or the other sex) and male- or

---

[4] Although this appears not to be the case in males, for whom if anything, rigidity with regard to career choice seems to be a problem that is more 'set in stone' than amongst females.

Table 9.2 Correlations of occupational preference ratings with occupational gender segregation (OSRSI) and occupational sex-role stereotyping (OGSI) indices for 23 occupations for boys and girls in four age groups. (Source: Miller and Hayward 2006)

		Boys	Girls
OSRSI correlated with occupational preference	Age range 14–15	0.648**	−0.648**
	Age range 15–16	0.772**	−0.759**
	Age range 16–17	0.729**	−0.470*
	Age range 17–18	0.782**	−0.189
OGSI correlated with occupational preference	Age range 14–15	0.645**	−0.638**
	Age range 15–16	0.779**	−0.749**
	Age range 16–17	0.724**	−0.517*
	Age range 17–18	0.779**	−0.288

$*p<0.05; **p<0.01$

female-segregated (defined as the extent to which they are actually performed by one sex or the other).

The data show that young women become more positively disposed towards atypical jobs as they grow older, suggesting that it might be easier to persuade older women to consider jobs in atypical areas than younger women. In the next section therefore I move on to consider some of the factors other than the extent to which a job is stereotyped that may contribute towards career decisions made later on in life.

Changing Careers

It is easy to envisage the career trajectory for many females, for whom the career path starts with the decision at 16 to enter a job in a stereotypically female area of work. Following some time in that job—and possibly after having a family—she may start to think that this is perhaps not what she wants to do for the rest of her life and begin to think about what her options are. By this time she is older and, often, more confident, and may start to look around at other jobs in the organisation (or elsewhere). At this point she may recognise firstly, that other jobs bring better rewards, both personal and financial; and secondly, that she herself is just as capable as some of the individuals she sees in those other roles.

There is research that backs up this model of the way in which women start to change the way in which they think about themselves and about their potential job options with increasing age and experience: For example, in another piece of research commissioned by the EOC as part of the GFI into occupational segregation Dale et al. (2005) report how many of the women they interviewed said that they had only come to the atypical work area later on in life, often after having overcome obstacles to get there.

By this time they were more mature and had more confidence and therefore were more able to consider and deal with other—perhaps masculine—work environments. Although research does suggest that sex-role stereotypes become less important with increasing age, this may not however necessarily be of central importance in understanding how this change process occurs. An alternative explanation arises from the fact that, with increasing age we are presented with many more opportunities to see evidence of our own abilities and therefore with opportunities to re-assess ourselves, and this may well lead us to consider areas of work that we had previously dismissed. This explanation derives from the work of Daryl Bem (Bem 1967), who suggested that we make judgements about ourselves using the same sorts of information that we use to make judgements of other people. So eventually, over time, we build up an idea of ourselves as someone who (perhaps despite our earlier trepidations) is rather good at some particular skill. Much of the literature on older learners reinforces this view. For example the Dale et al. study cited above reported that women said that being able to work in atypical areas such as carpentry, ICT, and mechanical engineering had 'given them a new understanding of what they could achieve' (Dale et al. 2005, p.12).

It is perhaps appropriate at this point also to consider some of the models of career choice. A very great number of theories have been proposed to explain the bases for individuals' career choice. The two I would like to focus on are, firstly, one that considers the various factors that become salient at different stages of development (proposed by Linda Gottfredson) and, secondly, one that examines the way in which individuals' changing circumstances and self-perceptions impact on choice (proposed by Donald Super). Both of these theories would seem to be of use in understanding the way in which women's career decisions may alter with age.

The Gottfredson model of career choice (Gottfredson 1981) suggests that an individual's interests and abilities assume importance rather later in the lifecourse than do factors such as the extent to which the job is sex-role stereotyped (and congruent with the individual's gender) and the status of the occupation (see Table 9.3). This is in line with the suggestions made above, that individuals become more aware of their abilities and interests with age. Gottfredson's model suggests that sex typing is so central to the individual's self concept that they will not willingly abandon this in making a career choice. However, it should be noted that subsequent research has indicated that, in fact, individuals will abandon sex type of job more willingly than the Gottfredson model suggests—mostly through necessity, as the majority of high prestige jobs tend to be those done mostly by males (e.g. see Hesketh et al. 1990).

The final stage of the Gottfredson model sees 'field of work' being decided upon at age 14 plus. However, this need not necessarily imply that the individual remains fixed in their view from this point on and at this point it is useful to consider the

Table 9.3 Components of Gottfredson's model of career circumscription and compromise. (Source: Gottfredson 1981)

Age	3–5	6–8	9–13	14 plus
Elements	Little vs. big	Gender	Social class and intelligence	Personal interests, values and competencies
Characteristics	Adult roles	Sex type	Prestige	Field of work

ideas of Donald Super (1957; 1990). Super proposed the idea that people can cycle repeatedly through the stages of career choice when major changes or transitions occur, with these choices being based on their self-perceptions and their self-concept. In other words, Super's conceptualisation of career choice explicitly acknowledges the fact that people change, and their ideas about themselves in turn change with age. If we combine this idea with Gottfredson's model then we can start to see how additional information about our abilities can become incorporated into later decisions about careers and training. The stages described by Gottfredson's model are shown in Table 9.3. If we combine the ideas of Super with this model then we can see that the '14 plus' column could be extended to become a series of columns that reflect major transition and choice points. In fact, a similar idea has recently been proposed by Mercer (2007) to explain the process of renegotiation of the self and the self-change, development and growth that she hypothesises takes place in mature students in further and higher education.

For girls, the Miller and Hayward (2006) data shown in Table 9.2 suggest that the significant shifts in their opinions about jobs start to take place around about the age of 17 or 18. The main point to make here of course is that this change in perceptions occurs beyond the age at which young people have made the qualification choices that effectively set their career path for several years.

This means that, if a woman decides to move into an atypical area of work after this age, she will most likely need to re-train. The next step then would be to contemplate gaining the qualifications necessary for entry to that new career path. But, despite government rhetoric on the need to increase the skills base of adults in the UK, this is where the real hurdles start. These issues are considered next.

'I've Decided to Re-train'

What happens if women[5] want to change career later in life? Is re-training possible? The first point to note is that there are several different factors that go into making re-training 'possible'. The first is willingness, and institutions such as Birkbeck, which provide access to degree programmes through part-time study, are testimony to the fact that older people are more than willing to return to learning, when it is made accessible. And that last caveat regarding accessibility is central to ensuring that people who *want* to learn *can* learn. Access issues—access in terms of geography, timing of provision and funding of learning options—are foremost amongst decisions to return to learning, and these factors are arguably even more potent barriers to learning in the vocational arena than in academia.

What is the situation confronting a woman seeking to re-train in a vocational subject? First, patchy provision is more likely to be an issue in the vocational sector. In research into the factors influencing choice of course upon leaving school,

---

[5] Or, indeed, men: the same hurdles outlined in this section apply equally to men seeking to change career direction.

lack of choice was cited by more adults as a reason for their decision by those who had taken a vocational award than by those who had followed an academic course (Miller et al. 2000a). Second, recent research into the reasons for individuals dropping out from further education revealed that 8% of early leavers said that the times of the course did not suit their working hours and 6% said it was too difficult to balance the course with other commitments (Simm et al. 2007).

However, the main problem confronting a woman who decides to re-train is likely to be funding. Despite Government rhetoric apparently promoting lifelong learning, an apprenticeship is likely to be almost completely out of the question: even if a woman wishing to re-train managed to persuade an employer to take her on as an apprentice in the new area of interest, then she (and more to the point, the putative employer) will probably find that she is not eligible for funding for an apprenticeship, for in England statutory funding for apprenticeships ends at age 25, and in reality now it mostly ends at 19.[6]

In addition, despite the UK Government having flagged up the need for more people in the workforce to attain higher-level skills, the majority of the funding policy developments in England for work-based learning for the past three or four years have focussed on level 2 awards (rather than level 3). The Train to Gain (TtG) initiative (and its forerunner the Employer Training Pilots which ran for three years before Train to Gain was introduced), is now the main funding route for work-based training outside of standard apprenticeship funding. There are three issues to note regarding this funding programme. One is that until very recently—until late 2006—only training up to level 2 was funded via this strand. The second is that full funding is provided to attain a first level 2 only, so if the individual already has a qualification at level 2 then TtG will not provide the opportunity to re-train.[7] And note that a 'first level 2' is defined as equivalent to five GCSEs at grades A–C. Therefore many people who might not consider themselves to have any relevant vocational qualifications but who did a handful of GCSEs at school—indeed, who really do not have any vocational qualifications, for a handful of elderly GCSEs[8] is unlikely to be of much use in changing career path—will nonetheless find themselves ineligible for funding under this programme.

In its original incarnation this funding stream also did nothing to help any older individuals—men as well as women—to gain the coveted level 3 (intermediate level) qualifications that the Government considers to be key to economic prosperity.

---

[6] Conflicting policies often lead to funding being inadequate to achieve all Government targets. Although the Government is keen to raise the number of individuals with level 3 qualifications, a seemingly greater priority in recent years has been to reduce the number of young people (those aged under 19) not in education, employment or training (NEET). This has led to a prioritisation of funding for under 19 s, along with a consequent curtailment of funding for those aged over 19. Although the Government announced changes to funding for older people in 2007, this has had very little impact; this is discussed at the end of the chapter.

[7] Although there are signs very recently (2009) that the rules regarding this point are starting to be applied less stringently now.

[8] Or the older GCE 'O' levels and Certificate of Secondary Education (CSEs); all of these are considered 'equivalent' to a level 2 award.

To be fair, and as indicated above, this changed in 2006 to allow funding towards a level 3 qualification, and 'level 3 pilots' are currently being trialled and evaluated at various locations around England. These include two level 3 pilots in the London area aimed specifically at women and, elsewhere in England, pilots for 'level 3 jumpers': individuals who do not have a level 2 qualification (i.e. who do not even have five GCSEs) but who are deemed to be employed in jobs that would support their direct entry to a level 3 qualification without first completing a relevant level 2 qualification. This is only part funding though: the entitlement is for the cost for attaining a level 2 award and the individual or employer is required to make up the difference. It is also questionable quite how many such individuals exist (that is, working in level 3 jobs with no qualifications). There is also part-funding for individuals who have a level 2 award to progress to a level 3, but again this requires either the individual or, more likely, the employer, to pay the additional amount, (and this is less than the entitlement for individuals who do not have a first level 2) and again, it should be pointed out that this is to support progression in the individual's *current* employment.

The intention is that the level 3 strand of the funding programme will be rolled out nationally in due course. So, it is appropriate to ask, will roll-out of funding under TtG help women gain access to the training courses required to start a career in a new sector? Well, probably not. While *in principle* the funding does provide an entry route into training, the money is made available *only* for employee training and *only* via the employer—the employer has to agree the training for existing employees. The first and most obvious point to be made therefore is that this funding is available primarily for people who are already employed,[9] and the training is focused on their current job. Therefore while this may help existing employees to engage in further development, it does nothing to help women who want to move out of traditional female areas of employment (nor, indeed, males who wish to change employment area).

In the event of an employer deciding to recruit an unqualified woman into an atypical area of work, then in principle they would be eligible to receive funding for training for a level 2 or for part-funding towards a level 3, once the level 3 funding is extended nationally. We should perhaps ask how probable it is that employers will take on unqualified women in traditionally male areas of work? On grounds of current evidence this does not seem very likely. Although there has been much rhetoric about the need for employers to recruit women in order to avert 'the skills crisis', it remains questionable quite how willing the average employer is to take on women—even qualified women—in traditionally male areas of work. While there may have been some movement on this point, our research undertaken as part of the EOC GFI into occupational gender segregation indicates that there may still be quite some way to go yet:

---

[9] Some limited funding is available for unemployed people through Job Centre Plus, albeit with restrictions.

The potential employer said, 'This is a job for big strong men. We don't want women coming in here with their hormones. You can't keep your nails clean if you work here, you know. We want to keep this factory all male.'
We had a roofer ring up to advertise for an apprentice, and he said, 'Well I don't think my wife would like it if I had a nice young dolly bird up on my roofs.' Miller et al. (2005)

It should be noted that the first of the employers quoted above had said this while interviewing a young woman who had already completed most of a level 2 apprenticeship programme at a well-known, reputable training company in the area and who was now seeking a position as an advanced (level 3) apprentice. The quotes serve to demonstrate just how unwilling some employers remain to take on females as trainees or apprentices (irrespective of whatever the law may say) despite in other respects being seen as falling into the more 'positive' end of the training attitudes spectrum, since they were in general favourably disposed towards employing and training apprentices. A persistent problem in the UK, and one with which many Sector Skills Councils are currently grappling, is the fact that many employers are unwilling to employ and train apprentices at all—or indeed to train any staff—and prefer to recruit only trained staff. Therefore, women wishing to retrain stand no chance of being considered by such employers and, as the evidence reveals, irrespective of whatever the law might say in this regard, only a sub-set of those who do take on and train apprentices are willing to take on females—even those who are already part-qualified.

It would not be true to say that the Government is entirely unaware of the implications of its funding policies for adult learners who wish to engage with the lifelong learning agenda. In 2008 the White Paper *'World Class Apprenticeships: unlocking talent, building skills for all'* (DIUS 2008) announced Government plans to make apprenticeships available for up to 30,000 older workers and to increase in general the number of places on level 3 programmes. In reality, though, few of these adult apprenticeships have actually materialised. In addition, while increased numbers of funded apprenticeships for older workers in principle potentially might resolve some of the barriers to vocational re-training for older people, in reality the intention to fund many of these apprenticeships through the Train to Gain funding strand means the proposed changes will provide little help for older women wishing to train in any areas other than those in which they are already employed. Therefore, while these new proposals are broadly welcomed, the intention to route funding via employers means that many—and probably most—of the barriers for women outlined in this chapter are likely to remain in place.

In other words, women are prevented by age, by any existing, possibly irrelevant, qualifications they may hold and by dint of being in existing employment from gaining access to funding for re-training. The only remaining option is training that is made available through Job Centre Plus; however, seeking funding through this route would require any employed woman who was considering a career change to first resign, bringing consequent restrictions on benefits, which any woman with children is particularly likely to try to avoid incurring.

Therefore, the funding regime currently in place essentially militates against women wishing to re-train, rather than assisting them. In fact, the current funding regime does virtually nothing (aside from facilitating access to career development loans) to assist anyone—men as well as women—who wishes to change career direction, even if they wish to move into areas of work for which the country has an urgent need for more skilled individuals. In particular, the funding regime actively works against the government rhetoric regarding the need for more women to move into higher-skilled and more lucrative areas of work. This leaves funding by the individual themselves (either through their disposable income or via a career development loan) as the sole route available, and countless reports in the past have pointed to the fact that women typically have far less disposable income than do men, making it much less feasible that they will be able to afford to fund any re-training themselves either directly or via a loan (and this is without considering related issues such as whether vocational programmes are available at times convenient to people who are employed or indeed at a convenient location).

Start Them Off Young?

Given the fairly limited success to date in encouraging older females into atypical areas, the Government has started to think about targeting younger groups of learners. Young Apprenticeships (YAs) are vocational awards taken by pupils aged 14–16 while at school. Typically, young apprentices go to a college or private training provider for the training (usually a day a week), and also they undertake work placements across the two years of the programme.

The education and training partnerships that submitted bids to offer these qualifications were required to state in their applications how they would address equal opportunities issues. The then DfES (now DCSF[10]) commissioned the Institute for Employment Studies (IES) to examine the extent to which the provider partnerships had achieved a more diverse group of pupils over the first two years of the programme. At present it is rather a patchy picture with only occasional pockets of good practice (Newton et al. 2006; Newton et al. 2007). The IES team discovered that one of the ways in which some providers have been trying to encourage a more diverse group of learners is to offer 'taster' sessions—short sessions either in the college or training environment in which they can gain some practical experience of the subject. This would appear to be a sensible approach, since one of the factors that has been identified as making females less likely to move into atypical areas of work is a lack of any relevant experience in that area—i.e. having no experience to use as a basis upon which to make a decision about whether or not they have the ability to cope with the various activities involved in a subject.

The Government is currently very keen on taster sessions and is trying to encourage more providers to offer these.[11] But will the sessions really help? At present,

---

[10] Part of DfES became DCSF while part became DIUS, now BIS.

[11] And indeed, the outcomes of the IES work includes a toolkit that can be used by education providers to help them design taster sessions in a way that ensures they will attract a more diverse

with just a few exceptions, it rather looks as though tasters are reaching only those young people who have already more or less decided on an area, rather than really providing opportunities to those who are not already attracted to the subject. But if tasters were offered more widely—perhaps on a semi-compulsory basis, to ensure that young people are exposed to areas of work which they might otherwise have no experience of, which is one suggestion that has been put forward—would they help?

My own work on how people make judgements about their own performance on novel and complex tasks suggests that tasters need to be designed carefully; handled wrongly, this approach could end up doing more harm than good. In this final section I am going to consider what happens to men's and women's confidence when exposed to short practice sessions, after which I will return to the question of sex-role stereotyping and decisions about atypical areas of work.

The first of the studies (Miller 1991) used a design in which participants were asked to make a rating of their confidence after receiving instructions for a complex problem-solving task but before starting a short practice session; they were then asked to make a second rating at the end of the practice session but ahead of a test session. Half received feedback during the practice session and half did not. In terms of performance, there was no difference in the numbers of errors made by females in comparison to males; nonetheless, for females undertaking the task with feedback (which told them how many of the items they had answered correctly or incorrectly), their confidence fell after the short practice session; males' confidence rose.

In a second study the same basic design was used. in that participants were given instructions, followed by a practice session followed by a test session. However, in this version of the task, participants could elect to work through as many practice items as they liked (up to a maximum of 20) before starting the test phase. In this study participants were asked to fill out the Personal Attributes Questionnaire (PAQ; Spence et al. 1974) to give an assessment of the extent to which they were sex-role stereotyped.[12] One point is worth noting. While there was no actual difference in the number of practice items chosen by males or females (irrespective of any difference in expressed confidence), participants who had scored highly on the 'feminine' scale of the PAQ chose significantly more practice items (in fact, double the number) than did the more masculine participants.

---

group of young people. The toolkit is available as a free download at: http://www.employment-studies.co.uk/pubs/summary.php?id=444&page=2.

[12] Since the PAQ was introduced Spence and her colleagues have revised their views so that now, the PAQ is conceptualised as measuring 'gender differentiating personality traits' rather than sex-role stereotyping per se, with the gender differentiating dimensions being labelled 'instrumentality' and 'expressivity'. Recent assessments (e.g., see Miller et al. 2000b) indicate the scale still has validity in differentiating between males and females, with males on average continuing to assess themselves as more 'instrumental' (originally the 'masculine' dimension) than do females, while females continue to assess themselves on average as more 'expressive' (originally the 'feminine' dimension) than do males.

Taken together, these two studies suggest that, first, a limited amount of practice with feedback can serve to undermine women's confidence; and secondly, 'feminine' stereotyped women (who still remain the largest of the four population 'subgroups' obtained when women are grouped using instruments such as the PAQ or Sandra Bem's 1974 Bem Sex Role Inventory) may be particularly discouraged by limited experience on difficult tasks in which there is a likelihood of witnessing failure in the early attempts.[13] Given that taster events feature practical sessions of necessarily limited duration, this suggests that this new approach to engaging with atypical groups needs close examination to ensure that short sessions do not serve to reduce the confidence of some young people.

Lifelong Learning Outside the Vocational Arena

The focus of this article has primarily been on women who wish to make career changes that would require vocational training. In particular it has considered the implications of Government funding policies for women seeking to re-train and gain level 3 vocational qualifications. However, it is not just in the vocational arena that Government policies are likely to have particularly severe implications for women. The White Paper that announced the introduction of adult apprenticeships was shortly followed, in September 2008, by a consultation letter sent out by the Secretary of State for Innovation, Universities and Skills, which stated the Government's intention to withdraw support for students within HE who choose to study for 'Equivalent Level Qualifications' (ELQs), that is, for a qualification at the same (or lower) level as that already held by the individual. The Secretary of State argued that this was because it was better to focus what funding there was on individuals entering higher education for the first time, or pursuing a qualification at a higher level than they already held; it was not fair to expect the public purse to support individuals in gaining a second qualification at the same or lower level and, therefore, funding would be withdrawn from these individuals. Thus the same restrictions are now being applied to those seeking to change career by gaining a second academic award as have been applied to those who sought to change career by studying for vocational awards; funding is now effectively denied to all individuals who hold an existing qualification.

There would be few problems with this policy were it the case that all initial education decisions were based on sound advice and a full understanding of the occupational options available to individuals consequent upon their qualification choices. But we know that guidance and advice on qualifications and careers is one of the weakest points of current provision. We know that many women—even highly educated women—opt into certain areas of work not through any informed choice but because they are unaware of what other options may be available to them

---

[13] And, in fact, the same is true of 'feminine' stereotyped men, although generally speaking these constitute a very small sub-group.

(Hurstfield et al. 2006). Consequently, many often end up in low-paid jobs that then render them unable to pay for training that would in turn allow them to move into better-paid areas of work and out of the poverty trap.

Rubery and Rake (2000) have commented on the failure of the UK government to assess the gender impact of new policies and integrate such assessments into its policy analyses. The decisions to scrap support for equivalent-level qualifications and to fund apprenticeships for older workers through Train to Gain both appear to be further examples of the Government's failure to assess the potential gender impact of its policies; both these decisions are likely to have far more severe implications for women than they will for men.

Conclusions

There appears to have been an assumption in much of the equalities work that older women are not so favourably disposed towards jobs in atypical areas as are younger women, and that most effort should be focussed on removing the barriers to younger women who wish to enter education, training and work in atypical and strongly segregated sectors. An overview of the research suggests instead that older women have more confidence and that this, combined with their previous employment experience, makes them more likely to consider atypical areas of work. However, older women are more likely to be caught in a funding trap if they want to re-train. Above the age of 25 they are ineligible as individuals for any statutory funding, while any funding channelled through the Train to Gain funding programme would be focussed on their current job, rather than on preparing them for a significant job change. Set against this, younger girls are more concerned about the views of their peers, less confident about being the odd one out in a group, less able to stand up to bullying and more likely to have inaccurate views of the jobs (Miller et al. 2005; Millward et al. 2006); although they can get funding to go into these areas, very few choose to do so.

As indicated earlier in this chapter, some of the recent work, such as that by Millward and her colleagues, suggests that job choice is influenced by the nature of the individual's own sex-role stereotyping (at least in younger people). John Archer's work too suggests that jobs form a central part of self-identity. Although there is some evidence of cultural shifts in sex-role stereotyping (Miller et al. 2000b), these shifts are slight and the majority of people—even young people—remain consistently gender sex-typed (that is, males remain largely masculine-sex-typed and females remain largely feminine-sex-typed).

Taken together, this might suggest that any expectation of achieving a completely even gender balance across occupations is unrealistic, at least in the foreseeable future. This is not to say that we should not continue to offer a full range of opportunities to all individuals. However, irrespective of whether psychological factors such as extent of sex-role stereotyping do actually constitute a barrier to expanding the career opportunities of women, what we can be certain of is that the current funding policies most definitely do not help. What is also evident is that they do not help men either. The focus of funding policies for older workers on the development of workers in their existing jobs has effectively cut off support for any worker wishing to change career and, in so doing, cut off the potential supply of new and enthusiastic recruits into areas of skills shortage.

The White Papers set out the Government's position in trying to encourage women to gain higher-level skills and move into more lucrative areas of work. However, there will need to be far more thought given to the supporting and enabling policies that are needed to make this a reality; rather than joined-up policies, there currently seem to be joined-up barriers in place. At present, these policy barriers appear to constitute far more of a hurdle than do any deficiencies in confidence deriving from self-identity.

Acknowledgements I would like to thank my colleagues Jim Hillage, Becci Newton and Marie Strebler for helpful discussions on this chapter.

References

Archer, J. (1999). *The nature of grief: The evolution and psychology of reactions to loss.* New York: Routledge.

Bem, D. J. (1967). Self-perception: An alternative interpretation of cognitive dissonance phenomena. *Psychological Review, 74*(3), 183–200.

Bem, S. L. (1974). The measurement of psychological androgyny. *Journal of Consulting and Clinical Psychology, 42,* 155–167.

Cassels, J. (2001). *Modern apprenticeships: The way to work. The report of the Modern Apprenticeship Advisory Committee (The Cassels Review).* Sheffield: DfES.

Dale, A., Jackson, N., & Hill, N. (2005). *Women in non-traditional training and employment* (Working Paper Series no. 26). Manchester: Equal Opportunities Commission.

DfES, (2003). *21st century skills: Realising our potential: Individuals, employers, nation* (CM 5810). London: TSO.

DIUS, (2008). *World class apprenticeships: Unlocking talent, building skills for all.* London: HMSO.

Forth, J., McNabb, R., & Whitfield, K. (2003). It's Only Women's Work: A Decomposition of the Gender Pay Gap. Working Paper. http://www.cf.ac.uk/carbs/econ/mcnabb/gender_segregation.pdf.

Gottfredson, L. S., (1981). Circumscription and compromise: A developmental theory of aspirations. *Journal of Counselling Psychology, 28*(6), 545–579.

Hesketh, B., Durant, C., & Pryor, R. (1990). Career compromise: A test of Gottfredson's (1981) theory using a policy-capturing procedure. *Journal of Vocational Behaviour, 36,* 97–108.

Hurstfield, J., Miller, L., Page, R., Akroyd, K., & Willison, R. (2006). *Women in London's Economy.* IES report. http://www.employment-studies.co.uk/pdflibrary/0374gla.pdf. (Alternatively see chapter in: http://www.london.gov.uk/mayor/economic_unit/docs/womenlondoneconomy2006.pdf).

Leitch, S. (2006). *Prosperity for all in the Global Economy: World class skills.* London: TSO.

Mercer, J. (2007). Re-negotiating the self through educational development: Mature students' experiences. *Research in Post-Compulsory Education, 12*(1), 19–33.

Miller, L. (1991). *Operationalising performance judgements: Sex differences and methods of measurement.* Unpublished PhD thesis, University of Wales, Cardiff.

Miller, L., & Hayward, R. (2006). New jobs, old occupational stereotypes: Gender and jobs in the new economy. *Journal of Work and Education, 19*(1), 67–95.

Miller, L., Kellie, D., & Acutt, B. (2000a). Factors influencing the choice of initial qualifications and continuing development in Australia and Britain. *International Journal of Training and Development, 5*(3), 196–222.

Miller, L., Bilimoria, R., & Pattni, N. (2000b). Do women want new men? Cultural influences on sex-role stereotypes. *Psychology, Evolution and Gender, 2*(2), 127–150.

Miller, L., Neathey, F., Pollard, E., & Hill, D. (2004). *Gender segregation, gender gaps and skill gaps* (Working Paper No. 15). Manchester: Equal Opportunities Commission. (http://www.eoc.org.uk/PDF/occupational_segregation_ph1_report.pdf).

Miller, L., Pollard, P., Neathey, N., Hill, D., & Ritchie, H. (2005). *Gender segregation in apprenticeships* (Working Paper No. 25). Manchester: Equal Opportunities Commission. (http://www.eoc.org.uk/PDF/gender_segregation_in_apprenticeships_wp25.pdf).

Millward, L., Houston, D., Brown, D., & Barrett, M. (2006). *Young people's job perceptions and preferences*. London: DTI. (www.dti.gov.uk/files/file28575.pdf).

Newton, B., Miller L., Page R., Akroyd A., & Tuohy, S. (2006). *Equal opportunities in the young apprenticeships*. Department for Education and Skills. Brighton: Institute for Employment Studies.

Newton, B., Miller, L., Page, R., & Tuohy, S. (2007). *Building on equal opportunities in young apprenticeships*. Department for Children, Schools and Families. Brighton: Institute for Employment Studies.

Rubery, J., & Rake, K. (2000). *Gender impact assessment in the UK*. Report of the Gender and Employment Expert Group for the Equal Opportunities Unit. Employment Directorate, European Commission.

Simm, C., Page, R., & Miller, L. (2007). *Reasons for early leaving from further education and work-based learning courses*. DfES Research Report RR849, 2007.

Spence, J. T., Helmreich, R., & Stapp, J. (1974). The personal attributes questionnaire: A measure of sex-role stereotypes and masculinity-femininity. *JSAS Catalog of Selected Documents in Psychology, 4*, 43. (Ms. No. 617).

Super, D. E. (1957). *The psychology of careers: An introduction to vocational development*. New York: Harper.

Super, D. E. (1990). A life-span, life-space approach to career development. In Brown, D. & Brooks, L. (Eds.), *Career choice and development: Applying contemporary theories to practice* (2nd ed., pp.197–261). San Francisco: Jossey-Bass.

TUC. (2008). *Still more (better paid) jobs for the boys: Apprenticeships and gender segregation*. London: TUC.

Chapter 10
Where is Gender Within the Workplace Learning Agenda?

Suzanne Hyde

Introduction: Research Focus and Methodology

In this chapter, I will discuss the findings of a 32-month Higher Education European Social Fund research project where we set out to examine whether particular types of workplace learning opportunities (brokered by the Trade Union, UNISON) aimed at low-paid women workers, result in changes in self-esteem, employability, take-up of training opportunities and any associated relevant cross-cutting effects of age and ethnicity. The research was conducted between February 2004 and August 2006 with a remit to include England, Wales, Scotland and Northern Ireland. I was the sole Research Fellow on the project and was guided by a Steering Group with representation from academic colleagues and from UNISON. In outlining the research journey and findings, I refer here to 'we' or 'our' as my thoughts are as a result of dialogue with these colleagues as much as they are with the research data (although any errors are my own).

Initiated by UNISON Open College and brought to fruition by the Centre for Continuing Education at the University of Sussex, the research captured the experience of learners in their own words. UNISON describes itself as, 'Britain and Europe's biggest public sector union with more than 1.3 million members. Our members are people working in the public services, for private contractors providing public services and in the essential utilities' (2008). At the time of our research UNISON Open College was described by the Union as 'the flexible learning arm of UNISON' (2006). The types of learning opportunities captured in our sample varied but were all facilitated through partnerships between employers, employees and local/national educational providers in order to offer formal learning opportunities for employees and UNISON members.

We aimed to provide a body of stories from learners' voices that could be used to influence and inform policy makers and education providers concerning the provi-

S. Hyde (✉)
School of Education, University of Brighton, Brighton, UK

Centre for Community Engagement, University of Sussex, Brighton, UK

S. Jackson et al. (eds.), *Gendered Choices,* Lifelong Learning Book Series 15,
DOI 10.1007/978-94-007-0647-7_10, © Springer Science+Business Media B.V. 2011

sion of learning opportunities. We undertook a thematic analysis in order to identify key patterns or absences within the learning journey. Although learner stories illuminated that take-up of these formal learning opportunities had led to a rich variety of benefits and outcomes (including health and well-being, increased take-up of trade union activity and progression to higher levels of formal learning), I have chosen here to focus on learner motivations for engagement with these learning opportunities and the relationship to work-related outcomes. The reason for this focus is that I want to show that the current UK government workplace learning agenda, with its emphasis on skills, is in danger of missing the point if it wants to engage groups such as low-paid, older women workers and provide attractive opportunities that may lead to work-related benefits for individuals (especially low-paid, older women), families, communities and employers (Leitch 2006).

Research Focus and Methods

The research journey began with the collection of life stories from a variety of learners learning through UNISON-brokered courses. This included people working in all types and modes of employment and formal learning. What all respondents had in common was the study of something called a 'course' that was initiated through the workplace (as a result of a UNISON brokering role) with defined learning outcomes and formal assessment criteria.

As experienced adult educators, we were well aware of the rich and varied life and learning journeys experienced by adult learners. Sometimes these stories are articulated through reflective writing exercises or journals that form part of coursework, and personal reflections also find their way onto student feedback forms. A review of UNISON Open College research and evaluations indicated the absence of any previous attempt to conduct a national life-history project with these learners. Where student views had previously been elicited for research purposes, it appeared to be through a questionnaire, interview or focus group model (e.g. Kennedy 1995; Donaghy 2001; Darvill 2002). Learner narratives provide important insights into: the direction of government policy, gender and class differences within workplace learning, the role of the Unions in brokering learning, the conditions for enabling learning, notions of progression and the importance of outcomes for individual, families and communities; 'biographies of adult students highlight the problems that they experience as a result of government policy. Specifically, biographies powerfully reveal the contradictions within narrow, vocationally driven lifelong learning policies' (Merrill 2005, p. 139).

In 1995, Helen Kennedy undertook a national evaluation of specific UNISON/ WEA (Workers' Educational Association) learning provision, Return to Learn (R2L), a core course in their shared workplace learning package. This modular course encourages self-reflection and is social sciences and study skills orientated. Other WEA courses based on a similar model and taken by those in our sample included 'Women's Lives' and 'Women, Health and Society'. Our research sample is well represented by learners who have included one or other of these courses in their learning journey (over two-thirds).

Kennedy's evaluation of R2L provided a backdrop and a benchmark to our research. However, since the evaluation was conducted 10 years before our investigation, the economic, social and political context had shifted and the current workplace learning policy agenda had become much more firmly focused on the acquirement of work-related and basic skills. We were interested in whether learners' stories would allow us to explore the implications for a 'feminised' model of learning, (Kennedy's term), and its relationship to the current skills agenda. Our research attempted to chart the often messy, complicated and non-linear progression routes of learners, where learners often take several courses at a similar assessment level before progressing to higher-level courses (see Hyde 2006).

We collected 35 pieces of writing from learners, and conducted in-depth interviews with 52 learners; we gathered the stories of 70 learners in total. We made contact with learners in a number of ways including leaflets, web and magazine advertisements on Union and educational websites, direct contacts with tutors and class visits to WEA courses. Information packs included hints on how to write or tell your story, a consent form and a form that allowed us to collect a range of quantitative data (outlined later).

Note: Extracts from learner stories are followed by their initials in brackets throughout the rest of this chapter.

Use of a Life-History Methodology

We wanted to explore whether the personal journey and the types of personal disclosure that are possible in adult education settings are different in the workplace, accounting for individual agency in the negotiation of workplace learning opportunities. A life-history approach, with its capacity to show us individual experience, mapped against the experiences of others, helped to facilitate this. It allows us to understand what is going on, in terms of the life and learning process and how they inter-link (West 1996). We were able to capitalise on the fact that many learners are already reflecting on these issues in UNISON-brokered courses such as R2L and many express positive benefits from this opportunity. Alheit and Dausien talk about the 'biographicity' of social experience and the individual and collective rewards of telling our stories:

> If we conceive of biographical learning as a self-willed, 'autopoetic' accomplishment on the part of active subjects, in which they reflexively 'organise' their experience in such a way that they also generate personal coherence, identity, a meaning to their life-history and a communicable, socially viable life-world perspective for guiding their actions, it becomes possible to comprehend education and learning both as individual identity work and as the 'formation' of collective processes and social relations. (Alheit and Dausien 2002, p. 17)

Life-history analysis can be a powerful tool, demonstrating to learners, educators, Trade Unionists, employers and government the importance of making formal learning opportunities accessible to all. It allows us to capture the life and learning journey, with all its twists and turns, and shows the power of personal agency when activated by enabling learning:

> …biographies, importantly, illustrate the dialectics of agency and structure. Viewed from this perspective, biographical research has the potential to offer a radical and emancipatory approach to research within popular education. (Merrill 2005, p. 135)

The Policy Context

The collection of evidence for our research happened at a time of considerable change and upheaval in the adult learning sectors (2004–2006). Government policy was shifting resources towards younger learners while at the same time prioritising skills-based provision for older learners. In 1998, David Blunkett, then Secretary of State for Education and Employment, reflected the hopes and dreams of adult educationalists and Trade Unionists committed to lifelong learning, when he said in the foreword to the Government's summary of its Green Paper, The Learning Age (DfEE 1998):

> We stand on the brink of a new age…learning is the key to prosperity—for each of us as individuals, as well as for the nation as a whole…. The fostering of an enquiring mind and the love of learning are essential for our future success…. Learning enables people to play a full part in their community and strengthens the family, the neighbourhood and consequently the nation…. That is why we value learning for its own sake and are encouraging adults to enter and re-enter learning at every point of their lives as parents, at work and as citizens.

Yet despite the promises offered in the 'education, education, education' pre-election mantra by Tony Blair at the 1996 Labour Party Conference, there has been subsequent disillusionment amongst adult educationalists with New Labour policies and how they impact upon lifelong learning beyond a narrow skills-led agenda. Alan Tuckett, Director of the National Institute of Adult Continuing Education (NIACE), commented 'it needs a leap of faith now to believe the Government still wants learning that is life-wide as well as life-long' (Tuckett 2006).

The adult education sector where women are traditionally well represented, is under threat. NIACE reported in 2006 that one million learning places were threatened over the following two years and that there was already evidence of a steady decline in engagement with formal learning for the over 55s with funding cited as the biggest reason for non-engagement. However, workplace learning, where women have been traditionally under-represented, is being promoted through legislation such as the Employment Relations Act 2004 (DTI 2004). This shift in emphasis on the site and purpose of learning has implications for equity issues as there are large inequalities in who gets access to workplace training, with budgets and planning skewed towards those that already have qualifications.

> Those with the lowest levels of educational attainment are also the least likely to participate in work-related education or training. Only 11% of people employed who had no qualifica-

tions reported receiving training in the past 13 weeks compared to 42% of degree holders. (Bates et al. 2005, p. 19)

The Learning and Skills Council (2006) reports that women are overrepresented amongst those with no or few qualifications, and are significantly under-represented amongst those holding Level 3 (A level or equivalent) qualifications. Older workers are also disproportionately represented amongst those with no or few qualifications—one in four, compared to one in ten for younger members of the workforce. The survey also revealed that members of the workforce from minority ethnic communities, particularly those of Bangladeshi and Afro-Caribbean origin, are more likely to have fewer than average or no qualifications (Learning and Skills Council 2006).

New Labour emphasis on the workplace as a site of learning and the attainment of skills as the purpose of learning has included the promotion of Trade Union involvement with lifelong learning (Leitch 2006). Since 1998 there has been a marked increase in the number of people accessing learning through Union initiated activity. The Trades Union Congress claims that since 1998, 60,000 employees have signed up for Union-brokered learning and that this number is likely to increase to 250,000 by 2010 (Trades Union Congress 2004). At the same time that a skills-led workplace learning agenda was being promoted, adult educators were expressing fears that a 'skills-deficit' model was being embraced by the Unions at the expense of provision that offered workers a space and place to learn that was not tied to a narrow set of functional skills. The Leitch Review places firm emphasis on skills, 'all publicly funded adult vocational skills in England, apart from community learning, [should] go through demand led routes by 2010' (Leitch 2006, p. 138).

Tensions around Trade Union engagement with the skills agenda were in evidence in our engagement with educational providers involved in delivering Trade Union learning such as the WEA:

It is very exciting to see people previously denied opportunities changing, but the nature of the curriculum is a very important issue. Some of us in the WEA are nervous of the move by employers and Trade Unions to a skills-based NVQ curriculum—this is a qualitative shift in the wrong direction. We must avoid such a strong emphasis on skills otherwise the old liberal education agenda of learning for learning's sake will start to seem like a radical agenda. We must continue to ask ourselves—is workplace education, workers education? (Miskin 2004)

Forrester (1999, 2002, 2004, 2005) charts the role of Unions in collaborating with or challenging the New Labour rhetoric on lifelong learning and, in particular, their engagement with workplace learning agendas. He urges Unions to promote an educational framework informed by 'democratic citizenship' rather than one led by employability and/or notions of a 'skills crisis'. He is critical of the TUC (Trades Union Congress) in particular for uncritically embracing the New Labour skills-led model of workplace learning and views it as part of ' ..a widespread and contested restructuring narrative of radical, neo-liberal changes within the labour market, in the nature of work and even in the nature of capitalism itself' (2005, p. 262). He also points out that an understanding of the gender and political relationships shaping waged labour is absent from models of workplace learning linked to employability, 'the key question remains one of learning for what, in whose interests, and for what purposes' (2002, p. 53). However he singles out UNISON as one Union that is argu-ably attempting to engage with wider notions of citizenship through the promotion of lifelong learning courses.

UNISON and Brokering of Workplace Learning Partnerships

UNISON, the Union with the largest involvement in learning, launched its Open College initiative in 1994, promoting Open College Network accredited, flexible learning (Kennedy 1995; Munro et al. 1997). The current range of courses avail-able to UNISON members originated in the National Union of Public Employees (NUPE), one of the three partner Unions that formed UNISON in 1993. NUPE's members were predominantly women, mainly in low-paid, often part-time jobs and a significant number were from BME groups. According to UNISON, more than two-thirds of its members are women (2007).

Today, many learning opportunities promoted by the UNISON are as a result of partnerships brokered with employers (Munro and Rainbird 2004). During our research cycle, courses were delivered by four main educational providers—the largest was the Workers' Educational Association (WEA), Learn Direct, the Open University (OU) and the National Extension College.

Who Are the Learners?

Data supplied from the educational providers who deliver UNISON-brokered learn-ing indicated that during the academic year 2002–2003 (as defined by each pro-vider) across England there were 6,450 learners learning on courses brokered by UNISON. A total of 84% of learners were women and the average age of learners was 45. Data on the ethnic background were not available in a meaningfully com-parative format from the educational providers.

Quantitative data from our 70 research respondents indicated that 85% of re-spondents were women, 88% reported that they had left school at or before 16 with few or no qualifications, 82% reported a gross income of £15,000 per year or less, 70% reported having taken at least one non-skills-based course through UNISON and the average age of learners was 44.

As we only captured ten male respondents we felt unable to make firm sugges-tions about the comparative experience. Of those we heard from, motivations and experiences appear similar to those of female respondents. We suspect that low pay and issues related to social class may be as significant as gender in understanding motivations for engaging with some workplace learning opportunities over others; however, further research is needed to illuminate this. In this chapter, I have solely drawn upon stories from the majority of our respondents, female learners.

Motivations and Engagement of Low-Paid, Older, Part-Time Women Learners

In the research project report (Hyde 2006) we made the distinction between *engagement* and *participation* offered by Barton et al. (2005, p. 7), who point out the former is concerned with 'purposes, why people come' and the latter is defined as 'the practices they engage in while they are there'. In this section, I will focus on the motivations for engagement articulated by learners. The issue of learner motivation is important in relation to our understanding of initial engagement with formal learning as an adult, why people progress from one course to another and the type of learning perceived by learners as best suited to their needs:

> Detailed qualitative accounts of learners' lives—their identity, background and circumstances—can provide rich evidence for explaining learners' motivation, preferences and trajectories.... Students' biographical contexts and experiences can be the most important resources they bring to learning. It is therefore critical for teachers to get to know their learners as well as possible. (Quality Improvement Agency, n. d.)

Many of our respondents did not start their return to formal education through UNISON. Rather, UNISON-brokered education formed part of a complex pattern of non-linear learning, much of it self-initiated, perhaps through evening classes and often as a result of a life turning point or catalyst such as having a first child reach school age:

> The life stories told by many adult learners reveal the way in which returning to learn is used as a way of dealing with change and transition in their lives at the personal and societal level. (Lea and West 1995)

Key motivators for initial engagement pertinent to women learners in our sample were non-work-related motivations (also referred to here as 'non-instrumental') not dissimilar to those found in other adult education settings (Crossan et al. 2003; McGivney 1999; Merrill and Alheit 2004). These non-instrumental motives included: critical turning points and changes in the life cycle, perceiving the learning to be fun and pleasurable, seeking a bit of 'me' time, getting out of the house, meeting new people, seeking adult company, relieving boredom, a desire to pick up on a general education missed out on in earlier life or keeping up with children's homework. These motivations were reflected in the stories of women learning through the workplace, at a time when the government's workplace learning agenda is focused on particular job-related skills—there appears to be a disjuncture between the two.

We can see some of these non-instrumental motivations, (which reflect the majority of our sample) in the comments below:

> Originally I just went along not because I wanted to gain anything, for the fun of it really, just to see if the old grey cells were still working.... I didn't really intend to go any further than doing that course. I went into it in a light-hearted way, and I was doing it purely for fun. I didn't have any ambitions when I started doing the course. (JB)

> We [Women's Lives students] were all about the same age, and we all wanted a bit of 'me' time.... (TP)

Alheit and Dausien (2002, p. 14) report that, 'for women, continuing training is not a "neutral" instrument of career planning, but is embedded within a form of life planning that is closely tied to opportunities and perspectives in the family domain'. Even though the courses were taken in work-time or facilitated through work, in the minds of learners, the courses provided a space and stimulus away from home-life:

> At the time, because I was my ex-husband's carer, that was my couple of hours of 'me' time a week. And he knew that I was incommunicado. For those two hours, or two and a half hours, whatever it was, every other Thursday, I was out of bounds. (TP)

> The original thing was for me to do a course to meet people. I'm at work all day with little ones, and then I come home and I'm with my daughter who doesn't really talk to me much. And it's just to get out and I enjoyed the courses in the end. (NW)

The marketing of R2L and Women's Lives by the WEA and UNISON, that highlights the fun aspects of learning, may contribute to the motivations expressed by learners undertaking these courses. But this still raises questions about the attractiveness of the current skills agenda to this type of learner and the capacity to attract and retain learners traditionally least likely to take up workplace learning through promotion of an 'instrumental' skills and job aspiration model.

For many part-time women learners, even when the course was 'skills' orientated, e.g. computer skills or an NVQ (National Vocational Qualification) in Administration or Health and Social Care, the expressed motivation for engagement with the course related closely to the motivations of women learners choosing non-instrumental courses:

> I think it came down to pure boredom really. I wasn't working at the time, we'd just moved into the area and didn't know anybody. I just saw it advertised [NVQ Administration], I said, 'well, it'll get me out of the house and meeting people'. So I went along to the college, went through their interview, and started the course the following week, and it was really good. (ED)

> My daughter was going to school, she was beginning to start learning about computers, I knew absolutely nothing about computers, so I thought, well that's where I start. I...did. (SN)

Despite the emphasis in learner stories on non-instrumental motives for learning, a minority of learners (less than a third) cited work-related (or 'instrumental') motives as their primary drive for returning to learn or continuing in formal education through UNISON. In carefully examining the expressed motivations and types of provision taken-up by learners who were declaring work-related issues as a primary motive for engagement with these learning opportunities, we found different types of work-related motives for such learners.

> **Box 10.1** Less than one-third of our sample cited 'work' as the primary driver for take-up of UNISON-brokered courses. Of those that did, these motives included:
>
> 1. Taking courses that had become legislative requirements of the job, e.g. NVQ Level 2 Health and Social Care
> 2. Taking courses perceived to address specific skills for the workplace, e.g. Computing or Counselling
> 3. Taking courses on issues or topics relevant to the workplace, e.g. Death, Dying and Bereavement (an OU course popular with care workers)

For learners in the first category in Box 10.1, instrumental motivation was expressed as a fact of life in their particular job market, e.g. it was a legislative requirement or was a tacit rule of the workplace for those seeking promotion. It reminds us that motivations for learners engaging with workplace learning do not take place in a political vacuum: the growth of the 'knowledge society' is:

> ...raising the pressure on individuals to meet certain standards of skill and knowledge before they can be employed. The risks of exclusion for those who fail to meet those standards are more draconian than was ever the case.... Of course, the *logic* of exclusion is by no means new – class and gender remain the decisive indicators.... As would be expected *age* plays an increasingly significant role. (Alheit and Dausien 2002, p. 10)

Some learners talked about their individual responsibility to up-skill themselves and felt it was a requirement of the workplace that they were *seen* to be doing this by managers:

> I mean you've got to haven't you? I've been doing IT courses and 'Communicating with the Public' and I mean I enjoy them I really do but you do have to be seen to be doing them. It's important in this day and age that you are seen to be taking the initiative for your own skills. (TH)

Others reflected upon the difference between courses such as R2L and Women's Lives, which were perceived to be a matter of personal choice, as opposed to NVQ type provision, increasingly being offered as a requirement of the job and government legislation:

> I think the pressure's on. If you don't do it, you won't know your job, and if you don't know your job, it can affect your salary. If it's not on paper...it would be looked at that you're not suitable for that job. I think the way forward would be to say, 'Well OK, you can go on any course that you choose this year.' One course even that you would want to do. Flower arranging or something...we get the learning accounts through the NHS...but that's got to be linked to your development. And I think it would be nice that they say, 'right, you can go on any course you want,' ...to develop you yourself. (SE)

Some learners reflected that their first and main motivation for taking up learning through work were the needs of the job itself (category 2 in Box 10.1). These learners put themselves forward for skills-based courses as opposed to R2L/Women's Lives type provision:

> I attended this course [counselling skills] with the hopes/aims of learning how to enhance my skills at my workplace, X police station: dealing with police staff, advising UNISON members, understanding bullying and grievance procedures. I also hoped that the skills that I learnt on this course would help me in dealing with distressed and vulnerable witnesses and victims of crime, which is part of my job within the criminal justice unit with Y Constabulary. (JK)

Category 3 in Box 10.1 reflects those learners who stated that the primary attraction was course content focussed on ideas and topics relevant to the workplace such as those relating to Health and Social Care (rather than an enhancement of learners' particular skills). These work-related 'issues' courses, mainly delivered by the OU, offer an interesting counterpoint to the skills courses such as NVQ. Both attract learners because of work-related reasons, but the emphasis is arguably quite different. Where NVQ's focus on demonstrating a range of practical competencies already in use in the workplace, the OU model is closer to the reflective learning and student centred model found in adult education settings and on the R2L/ Women's Lives courses. Particularly positive comments were made about some of the OU courses that related to ideas and theories about particular client groups that learners interface with in the workplace, for example, Death, Dying and Bereavement and Health and Social Care. The content of these courses and their appeal to learners may offer an interesting way forward to bridge the divide between non-vocational courses and the workplace-related skills agenda being promoted by the government. Differentiating between what we mean by work-place skills and what we mean by vocational or non-vocational learning is as important as differentiating motives for engaging with learning. Provision which fits the third category of instrumental learner identified in our sample (see Box 10.1), those attracted by work-related 'issues', allows learners to reflect upon themselves and their practice *as well as* developing new knowledge and skills:

> [Death, Dying and Bereavement]…it just jolts you into reality and makes you think before you say and do things. Because there are a lot of things that we take for granted…somebody in the hospital, particularly older people…I won't say they're old-fashioned, but they find it very difficult to be, washed for example. And you have to know how to look after those people, how to approach them. Although I'm older and didn't have a problem broaching these subjects with them, it doesn't hurt to see what's recommended and you do remember those things when you approach them at the bedside. So, it was enormously helpful really. (MC)

In spite of the current 'employability' agenda, learners reporting instrumental reasons for wanting to return to education were in the minority. Even then, it is worth noting the differences, potentially significant, between those learners who indicate the perceived skills needs of the job was their primary motivation for uptake of workplace learning (e.g. computing or counselling), from those who emphasise the 'legislative' requirements of the job (e.g. NVQ Health and Social Care) and those that mention relevant issues of the job (e.g. becoming more knowledgeable about issues connected to their work and having a space to reflect upon issues facing clients such as dying or bereavement).

If we are to develop a constructive way forward to engage and meet the needs of so-called 'hard-to-reach' learners, such as older, low-paid, part-time women learners, it is important to understand the complexity of learner motivations for engaging with workplace learning. It is equally important to understand the complexity of the type of work-related learning possibilities and how this relates to motivations for engagement because even when learners expressed work as a primary motive for take-up of UNISON-brokered learning, these motives were far more varied and complex than merely a desire to accumulate more 'skills'.

Outcomes for Learners—the Impact of Learning

Despite the fact that the majority of women in our sample cited non-instrumental motivations for taking up part-time formal learning opportunities through the workplace, the majority also reported instrumental outcomes that they directly attributed to this formal learning.

The majority of respondents used the terms 'confidence' or 'self-esteem' to talk about the positive impact of learning, and most cited it as one of the biggest changes in their lives. This occurred without active, direct solicitation from interviewers and/or indirectly when learners were asked about 'progress' and 'impact' of learning. Some learners talked about confidence in general, whilst others related it specifically to how improvements in self-confidence have led to work-related achievements later in life. In stressing confidence gains I want to be careful not to suggest that learners are a 'blank slate', entering formal learning with no confidence in any arena of their lives:

> Research carried out by practitioners with socially excluded people suggests that a level of confidence is needed to participate in learning. Confidence can both be a pre-condition and a by-product of learning. (Quality Improvement Agency, n. d.)

Some learners actively reflected on this issues themselves:

> I feel a lot better about myself, I've got a lot more confidence. But I also realise that I could always do it, it just needed to be tapped into. But I didn't realise that until I'd got to the point where I could do it. And then, you look back on it, well, hang on a tick, I've always been able to do this, but it was just never tapped into properly. And there are a lot of people out there like that. (NW)

Learners' stories support the findings of Helen Kennedy's evaluation of 'Return to Learn' (Kennedy 1995), where she concluded that confidence was the most significant gain reported by women and low-paid workers in her sample. Many of her respondents had gained the confidence to expand their roles within work, taking on more responsibility within existing posts or applying for other/promoted posts. Both Helen Kennedy's and our own research respondents indicated that skills gained on R2L were transferable, such as learning to delegate, taking notes and being able to write reports. Learners were able to demonstrate skills to managers, and credits gained for courses were helpful in this process. Being taken more seriously and feeling more valued in the workplace were among the comments made about changes in workplace relationships. Munro et al. (1997) reached similar conclusions in their report which focused on the impact of UNISON-brokered courses from the viewpoint of all the partners/stakeholders: 'students continually commented on their own growth of confidence, their sense of the value of their own opinions and their ability to critically assess views expressed by others, be it at work, at home or from the media' (p. 24).

Many learners in our sample reflected on the impact of learning on working life, in terms of increases in skills, self-confidence at work and job satisfaction. The following learner attributed her promotion within the NHS (National Health Service), to the confidence gained from R2L:

> Actually I did change jobs.... I think probably my confidence did it. And it was another grade up, and I liked the sound of the job...it was more in-depth...talking to patients on the phone about their preparation for their X-rays. I mean the questionnaire for the patients I helped generate that, and I think that that's from the knowledge and the confidence I got from that course. (SN)

Other learners expressly link these formal learning opportunities to concrete changes in working lives:

> Out of all of us [on the course Women's Lives]...there was quite a few that went on and got different jobs...from there. Even if it was just one grade up or some went completely different from say cleaner to health care assistant. (SN)

> The auxiliaries...a lot of them went on to student nursing [from R2L]...and they went right the way through...followed the path. ...did Level 2, Level 3, then went on to go into student nursing. (LP)

> I think it's helped me get a better job.... I can now say, 'Yes I've done these courses.' I was actually part way through my course when I went to my job that I'm now doing. (TP)

Learner stories highlight that it is not just individuals who benefit from the learning opportunities taken-up. Although interviews with employers were outside the remit of this research, it is clear from the findings of earlier research such as that conducted by Munro and Rainbird (2004) that there are significant benefits for employers engaging in workplace learning partnerships. Munro et al. (1997) argue that the practice of having some learners taking courses in the workplace can lead to an overall 'culture of learning'. Kennedy's (1995) findings showed that taking a formal course at work might help to establish support networks within the workplace that could last beyond the lifespan of the course. In our sample, particular praise was forthcoming for some workplaces and their promotion of a 'culture of learning'. An evaluation of the formalised role of Union Learning Representatives demonstrates a direct link between taking courses and an increase in Trade Union activity, specifically in the promotion of learning for others in the workplace, taken-up by women employees not previously engaged in Union activism (Wood and Moore 2005). The Leitch Review also raises the issue of a 'culture of learning' but mainly in relation to an arguably narrow agenda—the promotion of a new careers service and learning accounts. An embracement of the promotion of networks of learning appears marginal or absent from much of the Leitch rhetoric (Leitch 2006, p. 140). Many learners in our sample documented that they had become Union

Learning Representatives as a result of their own take-up of learning opportunities or had informally encouraged friends, family and colleagues to pursue formal learning (Hyde 2006).

> Through my daily work now, I am far more assertive and positive. I put ideas forward. I am part of an NVQ group, helping other support workers to develop their role. (KW)

> I feel within my new post I am in the position of encouraging others to learn in a variety of ways, become [union] Learning Reps and be more active in the branch as well as being able to recruit new members. (TA)

Learners who suggest a relationship between learning, self-confidence and thirst for learning that has led them to realise childhood ambitions of becoming a nurse, social worker or teacher demonstrate that certain types of lifelong learning can remove progression barriers for low-paid, older women learners:

> I think it's great that I had this opportunity through the Union, I wouldn't be where I am today, unless I'd had that opportunity. I'm really grateful that I've had this…second chance. I can't see any way I would have been able to get into social work. I would have to be in employment to do it…. I couldn't afford to give up work and go back to university and do it through that route. So, I think I would probably just be restricted in the jobs that I would be able to do; I'd probably find a way of doing jobs that didn't require any qualification. I think it's made me much more confident about a lot of things. With my work I've now got a direction and I'm doing something that I can remember as a child I was always interested in – social work. So that's a goal I've had for a long time. And now I'm encouraging my sister to learn, the people I work with, I'm like 'why don't you do the Union Access course?' (CE)

Availability and marketing of courses to older people is equally important in relation to work-related outcomes for employers and individuals. One learner who began working for the NHS in her early 50s, after caring for children and grandchildren, reflected on the joy of returning to the work place as well as the joy of learning:

> Take some comfort in the fact that you are never too old to learn and certainly you are needed more than you realise. The NHS Trust that I work for allows you to work until you are seventy, so no early retirement for me! (TH)

Another learner who started her journey with R2L, followed by a course called Women, Work and Society and is now a tutor, organiser and manager of adult learning in the workplace comments:

> People at work asked what was the point as I was aged 53 when I graduated, what was I going to do with it? My only answer was that it had been a personal challenge but at some point I realised that I did not want to continue being a nursery nurse for the rest of my working life. It increased my confidence and belief in myself. My husband on retiring was encouraged by my success and took up training himself and is now a magistrate. We have three grandchildren and the eldest at 14 thinks its 'cool' to have had a Grandma at university. (KA)

In sum, 81% of learners in our sample reported non-work-related motivations for engaging with workplace learning opportunities brokered through UNISON whilst 87% reported some work-related benefits that they attributed to the take-up of these learning opportunities.

Conclusions

This research, which focused mainly on the learning experiences of older, low-paid women workers, came at a time when the skills-led policy agenda in workplace learning was (and is) arguably ignoring the evidence of gender differences and equalities issues in relation to patterns and sites of learning. Exciting and important relationships between gender, ageing and lifelong learning that many hoped 'The Learning Age' (Green Paper 1998) might transfer into policies aimed at promoting diversity of adult learning provision, are evident in learners' stories but arguably absent from current policy drivers (see Leitch 2006). The presence of education that is appealing and accessible to the older, low paid women workers in our sample is present in spite of the workplace skills agenda not because of it. At least 75% of learners in our sample began their return to formal learning on non-vocational courses such as R2L and Women's Lives; provision which has struggled for survival in the skills-led policy drive.

A word search of the Leitch Review reveals that gender is mentioned only once (Leitch 2006). Since the Leitch Review was published, there has been a public consultation on the equalities implications through the draft: equality Impact Assessment (NIACE 2006). This acknowledges differences within potential work-place learners and specifically acknowledges the practical barriers of childcare, travel and domestic responsibilities that often affect women learners (Edwards 1993). An acknowledgement of these issues (as long as it translates into policy and practice) is to be applauded. However, a sophisticated, nuanced and gender aware education policy also needs to recognise the more complex issues of identities, self-confidence, perception and attractiveness of different types of learning and the motivations for engaging (or not) in workplace learning that are articulated by learners themselves. If the Governments goal is an improvement in 'skills', there needs to be recognition that there is more than one way to reach this goal and lis-tening to the experiences of learners is a good starting point for understanding the relationship between motivation for engagement, types of learning and learning outcomes.

Learner stories suggest that the use of terms such as 'soft' outcomes (often re-ferred to in relation to the 'distance travelled' by learners) and 'hard' outcomes (often referred to in relation to quantifiable changes in jobs or number and level of courses taken) found in education research and practice, may impose an over-sim-plification of learners' experiences and mask a complex relationship between the two. Many learners move in and out of so-called instrumental and non-instrumental courses and use transferable skills and subject knowledge, passing from one to the other, to complement the learning journey. Alan Tuckett, Director of NIACE, re-flected on these issues:

> You don't need to denigrate learning for personal and community development to make the case for a skilled economy. Employers endlessly tell Government that 'soft skills' are what the system fails to develop. The skills of team working, communicating effectively, problem solving, working flexibly and applying creativity are at the heart of good working practice in the modern economy. Such skills can be developed in liberal education classes

at least as well as in vocational ones. And learning is not a neat business: it leaks. Skills and confidence acquired in one place apply elsewhere. Managers know this, which is why so much money is spent on executive away days building castles in the air. And, for young people and adults alike, you cannot tell the purpose of the student from the title of the course. (Tuckett 2006)

Understanding gleaned from biographies can enrich the planning and marketing of provision as it illustrates motivations through the life course. A biographical approach to researching the learner experience allows us to understand the learning process and how this relates to the wider life journey instead of just counting the outputs of learning, e.g. the number of courses taken. Life stories can be very powerful in demonstrating to learners, educators, Trade unionists, policy makers and employers the importance of the transformative possibilities of learning. This biographical approach shows the capacity of learners to overcome gender, class and age as potential barriers to learning, both in childhood and as adult learners, 'Biographies offer a tool for critiquing structural inequalities and the inadequacies and contradictions of lifelong learning and social inclusion policies' (Merrill 2005, p. 137).

Despite the emphasis from learners on non-instrumental motives for engaging with UNISON-brokered courses and the lack of an instrumental focus in much of the formal learning undertaken by older women in our sample, many learners reported positive work-related outcomes. Where work was cited as a primary motive for engagement in learning, motives were as varied as the type of workplace learning that was attractive to learners. If Unions, educational providers, employers and government want to see take-up of workplace learning and positive work-related outcomes, they need to embrace a sophisticated gender, low-pay and age-aware approach that understands the differences between types of motivations for engagement with workplace learning, differences between workplace learners and the potential to use models of workplace learning that go beyond merely an emphasis on 'skills, skills, skills'.

References

Alheit, P., & Dausien, B. (2002). The double face of lifelong learning: Two analytical perspectives on a 'silent revolution'. *Studies in the Education of Adults, 34*(1), 3–22.

Barton, D., Appleby, Y., Hodge, R., Tusting, K., & Ivanic, R. (2005). *Relating adults' lives and learning: Participation and engagement in different settings.* London: National Research and Development Centre for Adult Literacy and Numeracy. Institute of Education.

Bates, P., Hunt, W., & Hillage, J. (2005). *Learning at work: Strategies for widening adult participation in learning below Level 2 via the workplace.* London: Learning and Skills Development Agency.

Crossan, B., Field, J., Gallacher, J., & Merrill, B. (2003). Understanding participation in learning for non-traditional adult learners: Learning careers and the construction of learning identities. *British Journal of Sociology of Education, 24*(1), 55–67.

Darvill, G. (2002). *Independent evaluation report, Suffolk social services department, Ruskin college—Work-based diploma in Social Work 1999–2002.* London: UNISON.

DfEE (Department for Education and Employment. Great Britain). (1998). *The learning age: A renaissance for a new Britain* (Summary of the Green Paper). London: HMSO.

Donaghy, P. (2001). *Work based learning in Northern Ireland, Empowerment through lifelong Learning. The threat of a good example*. Belfast: UNISON.

DTI (Department of Trade and Industry. Great Britain). (2004). *The Employment Relations Act 2004*. London: HMSO.

Edwards, R. (1993). *Mature women students*. London: Taylor and Francis.

Forrester, K. (1999). Ambiguous agendas: The development of 'Employee Development Schemes' in the 1990's. *Adult education and the labour market (V)*. Roskilde University, ESREA.

Forrester, K. (2002). Work-related learning and the struggle for employee commitment. *Studies in the Education of Adults, 34*(1), 42–55.

Forrester, K. (2004). The quiet revolution? Trade union learning and renewal strategies. *Work, Employment and Society, 18*(2), 413–420.

Forrester, K. (2005). Learning for revival; British trade unions and workplace learning. *Studies in Continuing Education, 27*(3), 257–270.

Hyde, S. (2006). *Women and work: Progression through learning*. Sussex: University of Sussex.

Kennedy, H. (1995). *Return to learn: UNISON's fresh approach to trade union education*. London: UNISON.

Lea, M., & West, L. (1995). On biographies and institutions: changing selves, fragmentation and the struggle for meaning. In P. Alheit, A. Bron-Wojciechowska, E. Brugger, & P. Dominice (Eds.), *The biographical approach in European adult education*. Vienna: Verband Wiener Volksbildung. (Published for ESREA).

Learning and Skills Council. (2006). *Skills in England 2005* (Vols. 1 and 2).

Leitch Review. (2006). *Prosperity for all in the global economy—world class skills*. London: DfES.

McGivney, V. (1999). *Informal learning in the community: A trigger for change and development*. Leicester: NIACE.

Merrill, B. (2005). Biographical research: Reasserting collective experience. In J. Crowther, V. Galloway, & I. Martin (Eds.), *Popular education: Engaging the academy international perspectives*. Leicester: NIACE.

Merrill, B., & Alheit, P. (2004). Biography and narratives: Adult returners to learning. In M. Osbourne, J. Gallacher, & B. Crossan, *Widening access to lifelong learning: Issues and approaches in international research*. London: Routledge.

Miskin, J. (2004) *ESREA Conference*. Northern College, Yorkshire.

Munro, A., & Rainbird, H. (2004). Opening doors as well as banging on tables: An assessment of UNISON/employer partnerships on learning in the UK public sector. *Industrial Relations Journal, 35*(5).

Munro, A., Rainbird, H., & Holly, L. (1997). *Partners in workplace learning: A report on UNISON/employer learning and development programme*. London: UNISON.

NIACE. (2006). The big conversation. www.niace.org.uk.

Quality Improvement Agency. (n. d.). *Skills for life quality initiative. Motivation and persistence*.

Trades Union Congress. (2004). *Empowerment through equality*. London: Congress House.

Tuckett, A. (2006). *Creative workers come at a price*. Times Educational Supplement.

West, L. (1996). *Beyond fragments: Adults, motivation and higher education—A biographical analysis*. London: Taylor and Francis.

Wood, H., & Moore S. (2005). *An evaluation of the UK union learning fund— its impact on unions and employers*. London: Working Lives Research Institute, London Metropolitan University.

Chapter 11
An Opportunity to Widen Participation Through Work-Based Learning? The Impact of Gender

Anita Walsh

This chapter will consider the extension of higher-level learning opportunities into the workplace, and examine the effect that gender has on workers' ability to take advantage of such opportunities. Drawing a distinction between the young 'novice' learners inside the university and those more mature, more experienced learners in the workplace, the chapter will consider both the gendered nature of the labour market, and the effect this has on restricting women's access to the educational opportunities which are developing through work-based learning. Consideration will be given to both formal and informal structuring of the constraints which are experienced by women workers, and proposals will be put forward relating to how work-based learning could be used to help women overcome the occupational barriers they face.

In recent years, there has been a strong policy emphasis in the United Kingdom (UK) on widening participation in higher education, and on ensuring that under-represented groups are encouraged to progress from school into higher-level learning. Considerable resources have been devoted to supporting both the attraction and retention of such students—for example, in the allocation of the 'post code premium' (additional funding allocated to institutions for students who are recruited from areas with little experience of higher education) and the setting up of Lifelong Learning Networks whose role is to support the transition into higher education of those learners with vocational qualifications. These initiatives are intended to address the higher educational needs of specific social groupings, and do not focus on gender. Overall, girls and women are well represented in both compulsory and post-compulsory education. For example, 39% of girls get two or more passes at 'A'/Scottish Higher level, compared to 31% of boys, and there are more female than male undergraduate students (Hibbett 2003, p. 507). However, these figures reflect the current situation and, for people who are already in the workforce, 'women as a group are still more likely than men to have no qualifications, due to the fact that older women are much less likely than older men to have any qualifications' (Hibbett 2003, p. 507).

A. Walsh (✉)
Department of Social Policy and Education, Birkbeck, University of London, London, UK

S. Jackson et al. (eds.), *Gendered Choices,* Lifelong Learning Book Series 15,
DOI 10.1007/978-94-007-0647-7_11, © Springer Science+Business Media B.V. 2011

In addition to the social justice element of widening participation which has long been part of the higher education debate but which, as previously stated, does not explicitly address gender as an issue, a strong economic case is also being made for greater access to university. Not just in the UK but also in the countries covered by the proposed European Higher Education Area, it is argued that higher-level skills are fundamental in supporting the competitiveness of the economy. In the recent consultation on higher-level skills being undertaken by the Department for Innovation, Universities and Skills (DIUS), the argument is put forward that:

> High level skills—the skills associated with higher education—are good for the individuals who acquire them and good for the economy. They help individuals unlock their talent and aspire to change their life for the better. They help businesses and public services innovate and prosper. They help towns and cities thrive by creating jobs, helping businesses to become more competitive and driving economic regeneration. High level skills add value for us all. (DIUS 2008, p. 3)

This confidence in the social and economic benefits that higher-level skills development can bring has led to a focus on what are often referred to as 'employability skills'. Higher education institutions are increasingly encouraged to embed programmes to develop employability skills into the undergraduate curriculum. The requirement to embed such skills is explicitly to provide full-time undergraduates (who are assumed to be young and at the beginning of their working life) in developing the generic skills which are valued by employers at the same time as they acquire more specific academic skills. Interestingly, the two sets of skills (employability skills and academic skills) are usually treated as distinct, and there is a requirement for institutions to indicate where in a programme employability skills are developed. Such an approach is in contrast to that taken by higher education pre-widening participation, when an Honours degree of any sort was perceived to integrate the necessary 'graduate skills' and was seen as effective preparation for the graduate employment market.

As will be apparent from the discussion of the importance of developing skills that make young people employable, much of the emphasis in current widening participation policies has been on the 'traditional' student who is assumed to be studying before entering the labour market. The mainstream policies and activities adopted under the umbrella of widening participation are therefore directed at someone who is relatively young (under 30 years of age), and are designed to encourage them to enter into conventional higher education. The assumption is that such learners will enter university straight from school or from a college course to take a full-time Honours degree programme which is designed to equip them to enter the graduate labour market. As mentioned earlier there are more female undergraduates than males in full-time study, most of whom are young women at the beginning of their working lives. Yet, the gender-pay gap is higher among those workers with degrees—'women with no qualifications earn 85% of male equivalent earnings for full-time work, and this falls to 79% for women with a degree or equivalent' (Hibbett 2003, p. 507).

In addition, there is one group of learners whose needs are not explicitly addressed by current widening participation policies. For potential learners who may wish to undertake higher-level study but who have already entered employment or undertaken domestic responsibilities of various sorts, the requirement to set aside these responsibilities in order to enter full-time higher education is an unrealistic one. For example, Reay (2003, p. 309) outlines the difficulties for women with children who were taking an Access course to prepare them for higher education, and who found themselves 'caught up in a constant balancing act between wanting to study, meeting domestic responsibilities, [and] needing to earn money'.

For these women, and other mature students with similar responsibilities, being a student in higher education means something 'entirely different from the conceptions and experiences of younger students' (Reay 2003, p. 309). The idea of student life 'with its combination of independence, dependence, leisure and academic work, was totally alien' to the mature female students who were often sacrificing limited leisure time in order to take the programme (Reay 2003, p. 309).

Moreover, although it is not immediately apparent from their widening participation policies, the Government does recognise that getting more young learners into higher education will not be enough to address future skills needs. They are aware that 'around three-quarters of the 2020 workforce have already left compulsory education' (DIUS 2008, p. 6), and acknowledge that people already in the workforce will need to gain higher-level skills. Skills development for those adults already in the workforce cannot be achieved using the conventional model of full-time higher education, and many potential learners who are already fully employed would not wish to become full-time students. In addition, they have often developed a level of professional competence and a range of life skills which causes them to resist becoming a novice in an educational context. Such learners are seeking a different response from higher education than young students for whom full-time higher education is part of their move towards maturity. They need a response that is more inclusive and responsive to their particular needs, for example, in terms of flexible timing and structuring of programme delivery and assessment.

Developments which support such a response are already taking place in higher education. At the same time, as policies have been developed to encourage more learners to enter mainstream higher education there has been an increasing recognition that people learn in a far broader range of contexts than the purely formal learning which takes place in schools and colleges. There is now an established academic debate which engages with the recognition of this wider range of learning, and which considers pedagogic practice relating to learning outside the lecture theatre (Chaiklin and Lave 1993; Tynjala 1999; Boud and Solomon 2001). As Skule (2004, p. 8) states, 'It is only during the last 30 years that the public policy debate on lifelong learning has moved from a unilateral focus on institutionalised education, into recognition that learning is "lifewide", taking place at work and elsewhere.' The contrast being made here is between an approach to lifelong learning which assumed that the learners would need to attend educational institutions in order to learn, and the approach which integrates informal learning from life and work experience with formal learning in the lifelong learning debate. Such an approach broadens the range of contexts in which learning can occur and affords recognition to incidental informal learning in the workplace. Skule (2004, p. 9) points out that,

'In terms of European policies, informal learning is defined broadly as "learning resulting from daily life activities related to work, family or leisure."' He states that often such learning is unintended learning, in that it takes place when the learner is involved in a formal or personal project of their own choosing.

Such learning is often implicit and occurs in the course of an individual working to achieve particular outcomes, and is 'hidden', in that the focus on the outcomes obscures awareness of the learning achieved through undertaking the process. Learning of this kind offers a real contrast to the intentional learning which is consciously undertaken when one enrols for a course at an educational institution, and the integration of such learning into academic awards requires a different 'skillset' to that commonly used in higher education pedagogy. Informal learning also provides a challenge to the model of education which is widely established, which is based on cognitive theory and which locates learning in educational institutions. In cognitive theory, it is assumed that learning is an entirely intellectual activity and that the learning mind needs to be separated from the distractions of the activities of the 'real world' (Chaiklin and Lave 1993; Tynjala 1999; Walsh 2007).

In contrast to seeing the 'real world' as a distraction, recognition of informal learning draws on 'The widening acceptance of learning as an inter-psychological process (i.e. between individuals and social sources of knowledge) [and] now prompts a consideration of learning as engagement with the social world' (Billett 2002, p. 57). From such a perspective there is an emphasis on the 'sociality of knowledge' which 'rejects the view that knowledge is either intrinsically "in the mind" (idealism) or in the world (materialism) or in any sense given; all knowledge, it asserts, in that it is produced by human beings, is inescapably social in origin' (Young 2004, p. 192). Knowledge and learning is therefore produced through social practices, and 'Workplaces, like homes, community settings and educational institutions are generative of social practices in which learning occurs through participation in those practices' (Billett 2004, p. 111).

This means that, in contrast to the traditional approach to teaching and learning which assumes that valid knowledge is created in the academy, and disseminated from there (hence the need for teaching), learning takes places in a wide range of contexts, and occurs through the undertaking of activities which are new to us. As Engestrom (2004, p. 150) points out, 'In important transformations of our personal lives and organizational practices, we must learn new forms of activity which are not yet there. They are literally learned as they are being created. There is no teacher. Standard learning theories have little to offer if one wants to understand these processes.' This focus on the necessary link between the construction of meaning, activity and learning means that new educational practices must develop, because current practice cannot effectively support such learning. Tynjala (1999, p. 359) points out that, 'Traditional teaching is claimed to produce inert knowledge in students, knowledge that can be used in educational settings such as preparing for tests and examinations, but cannot be transferred into real life situations.'

The organisation of knowledge within the university focuses very much on the importance of disciplinary subject content, and on abstract theoretical knowledge. Yet educational practitioners are aware of the importance of the experience-based learning which is acquired through general life activities. As Evans et al. (2004, p. 222) point out, 'The part played by tacit skills and knowledge in work performance is well recognised but not well understood. It is one of the central tenets of adult education that adults draw on life experience to good effect in learning programmes.' This statement emphasises the recognised value of informal learning in supporting formal learning, but it is increasingly argued that informal learning is the most valuable form of learning. For example, Skule (2004, p. 9) quotes Eraut et al. in claiming that, 'Learning from other people and the challenge of work itself proved to be the most important dimension of learning for the people we interviewed. Although some reported significant learning from formal education and training, this was by no means universal, and often only of secondary importance.'

It is perhaps worth reminding ourselves that most standard learning theories relate to the learning of children and young people, and therefore place the teacher in a position of authority. However, those academic practitioners who engage with adult learners and are developing new practices to accommodate experience-based learning argue that, 'the pedagogic model [which] permits the teacher to take full responsibility for decisions about what is to be learned, how it is to be learned, when it is to be learned and if it has been learned' is an inappropriate response to the learning needs of experienced adults (Laycock 1993, p. 4) In contrast to pedagogy, Laycock advocates the adoption of an approach based on Knowles' concept of andragogy, which is defined as 'the art and science of helping adults learn' (Laycock 1993, p. 4). Such an approach involves the recognition that these learners are competent adults, who have developed a range of capabilities and who are capable of managing their own learning with appropriate support.

As indicated, the recognition of the importance of an experience base for learning in context and the advocacy of a more egalitarian approach to working with adult learners has a strong academic rationale and pedagogic underpinning. However, the introduction of pedagogic practice to support experience-based adult learning in the workplace and elsewhere has not been entirely straightforward. As Laycock (1993, p. 129) points out, 'No practitioner, however adaptive, would ever doubt the political complexity of introducing such an innovation into…conventional practice. In all work-based learning there is a serious challenge to the dominant discourse of higher education, to what counts as a legitimate site of learning, to what counts as legitimate knowledge.' This is because, historically, the structuring and organisation of higher education has been based on academic disciplines, and on the importance of subject content. The knowledge produced through experience-based learning in the workplace and elsewhere does not take the form of the abstract theory with which the academic disciplines are familiar. Until recently, therefore, there was no mechanism through which such learning could be awarded academic recognition.

Evans argues that it was the introduction of the higher education credit framework which introduced the possibility that such learning could be recognised, claiming that, 'In 1986 CNAA [Council for National Academic Awards] established a Credit Accumulation and Transfer Registry. Before that, work-based learning for academic credit in higher education was off limits, beyond thought even' (quoted in Walsh 2007, p. 502). The principle underlying the credit framework introduced by the CNAA was that appropriate learning which was assessed should be recognised, wherever it occurred. The intention with the framework was to support students with professional and experience based learning to demonstrate the equivalence of their learning to that contained in academic awards. The term 'equivalence' is an important one, in that there was no attempt to demonstrate identity with the kind of learning found inside the academy. Rather the intention was to show that the sophistication of the learning was equivalent, i.e. that the nature of the learning was similar even thought the content and context of the learning was different.

The credit framework includes a number of levels which are consistent with the qualifications levels in the Framework for Higher Education Qualifications, and for which there are credit levels descriptors. These descriptors indicate the generic characteristics for a learning experience at a given level, and can accommodate a much broader range of learning than that conventionally recognised by higher education. A major advantage of credit levels in terms of the recognition of work-based learning was that, in contrast to vocational awards such as National Vocational Qualifications whose vocational framework is 'functional, non-aspirational...[and] concerned principally with performance to an agreed standard' (Robertson 1994, p. 155), the credit framework is concerned with recognising learning achievement. As Gosling (2001, p. 282) points out, 'The concept of level in credit frameworks emphasises the importance of epistemological, curricular and personal development.' In addition, because the specification/explication of the characteristics of learning required to meet the demand integral to a particular level was set out, it 'enable[s] any given programme of learning to be identified as being at a given level, regardless of whether it takes place inside or outside the university' (Gosling 2001, p. 282). Credit therefore facilitated the full integration of experience-based learning to academic awards, enabling work-based higher education awards to 'do more...than attest occupational competence...[to] set out to cultivate broader intellectual abilities' (Higher Education Quality Council quoted in Brennan and Little 1996, p. 13).

There therefore exists a mechanism whereby academic recognition of experience-based learning can be fully integrated into higher education awards. Such a development is fundamental to being able to effectively reach out and respond to the needs of mature learners in the workplace. This represents an important aspect of widening participation, as it provides the access to university to those whose personal circumstances mean they cannot access full-time higher education. In addition, as Billett (2002, p. 57) points out, 'For many workers, perhaps most, the workplace represents the only or most viable location to...further develop their vocational practice.' The opportunity to gain academic recognition of workplace learning can be of particular value to those workers who under-achieved at school, or to those workers who have been either out of the labour market for some time, or, as is the case with many women, who are working part-time to accommodate other life responsibilities. This is of considerable benefit in the current context. The facility to acquire formal academic qualifications without taking time out for formal study, helps people develop themselves in a situation where 'personal experience and socio-economic change have become deeply entwined in recent years,...[as]

illustrated by the growing importance of participation in formal education and the attainment of qualifications for young and older workers' (Fuller 2003, p. 2). In addition, as Billett (2002, p. 57) points out, keeping one's personal and professional development is perceived to be an individual requirement as 'the transfer of responsibility for maintaining the currency of vocational practice [is] now being increasingly passed to workers in the current reformulation of lifelong learning policies and practices'.

The academic recognition of experience-based learning in the workplace therefore represents a very real extension of learning opportunities, which has the potential to be of real personal and professional benefit to a range of workers. Given current government policies, it could be argued that this is a model of higher education which will be used increasingly, both for initial undergraduate education and for the postgraduate professional qualifications which can be obtained through Continuing Professional Development (CPD). It is therefore important that such opportunities are made available as widely as possible, and to both men and women. The intention here is to explore the likely effect of gender on access to this new availability of recognition of experience-based learning in the workplace.

If we briefly consider the current situation regarding gender and formal qualifications it is widely recognised that, at school and university, girls/young women are out-performing boys/young men (Hibbett 2003, p. 507). However, Charles (2002, p. 17) argues that, 'relatively better educational achievement for girls than boys will not necessarily mean that the gendering of paid employment is going to be transformed in women's favour'. It appears that, despite the existence of a National Curriculum which is designed to be gender neutral and to be delivered to boys and girls together, the 'hidden curriculum' which directs girls towards 'feminine' subjects and occupations is still in existence. Charles (2002, p. 106) points out that, 'even in the 1990s teachers were on record as saying that jobs were not as important for women as for men', because women will have domestic and childcare responsibilities. In addition, as soon as students can choose their subjects free from the constraints of the National Curriculum, a clear gender bias emerges. For example, at A level, 70% of English Literature and Social Studies students are female, and only 24% of Physics students are girls (EOC 2005, p. 4). In vocationally related subjects the bias is even stronger, and in education provided by Further Education Colleges, 91% of Hairdressing and Beauty Therapy students are female, whereas 90% of Engineering, Technology and Manufacturing students and 94% of Construction students are male (EOC 2005, p. 6).

Moving on to consider employment, those young women whose highest educational qualification on entering the workforce is the General Certificate of Secondary Education (GCSE) enter the lower levels of the labour market, and occupations here are strongly gendered. Kerfoot and Korcynski (2005, p. 388) claim that, 'Gender stereotypes about women's "proper" place in relation to paid work and their presumed attachment to so-called "softer" skills…act to reinforce and reproduce gender divisions in the workplace.' Statistics appear to support these claims, as the following employment areas (all of which are associated with personal and/or customer care of some sort) are female dominated: receptionists, educational assistants, care assistants and home carers, general office assistants and clerks, cleaners and domestics, retail cashiers and check-out operators and customer care (EOC 2005, p. 11). Charles (2002, p. 31) argues, 'Women's jobs…are associated with low pay… low grade, low status, involve subservience, and are jobs that men would not like to do. They are associated with "feminine" qualities of caring, being good with people and dexterity.' The roles in the list above would appear to support her contention.

The wider availability of work-based academic qualifications has real implications for women in these roles. Purely vocational qualifications such as National Vocational Qualifications (NVQs) and Modern Apprenticeships are designed to provide qualifications with a direct link to a particular type of employment. They are designed to develop workplace competence in particular workforce roles, and to respond to particular workforce development needs. Given the gendered nature of the lower levels of the labour market, this means that any formal work-based qualifications at lower levels are more likely to confine workers to the occupational areas they already occupy. In other words, workforce qualifications such as NVQs are likely to confirm women's employment status, and help confine them to the low grade and low status jobs previously referred to.

With regard to vocational qualifications in higher education, the introduction of the Foundation degree (FD), a higher education award where programme designers are required to integrate both work based learning and the award of academic credit for experience-based learning into the course, potentially offered a real opportunity to extend participation in higher education (Jackson and Ward 2004, p. 433). The distinctive nature of the award, linked with the fact that often it prepares learners for a specific occupational sector and is often delivered locally, has meant that it is attractive to many 'widening participation' learners. The number of students taking FDs is growing quickly, and national policy envisages that growth in student numbers in higher education will be predominantly in this area. It is, therefore, interesting to consider the gender patterns which are emerging here.

FDs can be taken either full time or part time, and there are clear differences between the types of student opting for the different routes. Full time students on these programmes were mainly 25 years old or younger; in contrast, 85% of students enrolled on part time programmes were over 25 years of age (Quality Assurance Agency (QAA) 2004, p. 13). About two thirds of the students enrolling on FDs were female, but only 38% of female students studied full-time, compared to 74% of male students (QAA 2004, p. 14). In addition, 'the programmes reviewed reflect the significant gender differences between subjects that are also seen at national level. Women are a significant majority in FDs (sic) in education and social policy, administration and social work. The subjects with most male students are computing, design and business studies' (QAA 2004, p. 15). The gender balance in this new vocational award is therefore consistent with established patterns of gendered employment and education. And again, since the vast majority of part-time students are over 25 and female, it is likely that the FD will operate to confirm women's confinement to particular areas of employment, many of which are low pay and low status. Therefore, although offering part-time workers access to higher education via a vocational route, at the same time the awards are likely to reinforce the gendered nature of employment to the disadvantage of female workers.

As indicated above, in addition to the introduction of FDs into higher education, a more learner-centred approach to work-based learning has been developed by a number of institutions. This gives learners the opportunity to take academic programmes which enable them to use their experience-based learning in the workplace as 'raw material' for their studies. Such workplace programmes can lead to either undergraduate or postgraduate awards, depending on the level of performance involved. The availability of these programmes is limited at the moment, but there is a great deal of interest in this area and practice here is developing rapidly. As outlined earlier, such programmes introduce an important degree of responsiveness into academic programmes designed for work-based learners, and, in recognition that work/life experience is not neatly organised into academic disciplines, the programmes are designed to recognise any learning at an appropriate level of demand. This requirement for learning to be at a level equivalent to that of other awards in the UK Framework for Higher Education Qualifications (FHEQ) is an important aspect of the maintenance of academic standards. However, it does have very real implications for learners in the workplace who might wish to take such programmes. For example, in order for a workplace learner to demonstrate achievement equivalent to that at Honours level of undergraduate study, they would have to be in a context where they could demonstrate the following skills:

- The exercise of initiative and personal responsibility
- Decision-making in complex and unpredictable contexts
- The learning ability needed to undertake appropriate further training of a professional or equivalent nature (QAA Qualification Descriptor for an Honours Degree)

They would therefore need to be in an occupational situation which afforded them an appropriate degree of flexibility and autonomy in their work role, in order to be in a context which afforded the opportunity for the demonstration of such skills.

When considering the workplace as a site of higher-level learning, Skule (2004, p. 14) points out that opportunities for learning in the workplace are not uniformly distributed, and distinguishes between what he terms 'learning intensive' jobs and 'learning deprived' jobs. He lists the conditions for learning intensive jobs as being: a high degree of exposure to change, a high degree of exposure to demands from 'customers', managerial responsibilities, extensive professional contacts, superior feedback, management support for learning and the rewarding of job proficiency via salary increases, promotion etc. Given the range of opportunities contained in such jobs, these will be at higher levels in organisations, and could fall into the 'graduate entry' category. Certainly Skule says that a good education (by which he means the achievement of high-level formal qualifications) is the route into learning intensive work. However, he also outlines his finding that 'For all levels of education, men had more learning intensive jobs than women...' (Skule 2004, p. 12). This highlights the gender variation in returns to the investment in human capital individuals make when they undertake higher education.

It is worth emphasising here that Skule was not distinguishing between organisations offering learning intensive jobs and organisations offering learning deprived jobs, but was considering the distribution of jobs within the organisations he studied. He was therefore observing what Billett would consider to be the outcome of the power plays within organisations. While recognising that workplaces are sites of significant learning, Billett also points out that workplaces can 'have significant limitations in terms of opportunities for learning, the prospects of securing effective learning experiences and the issue of recognition of that learning...' (Billett et al. 2005, p. 219). This is because, in contrast to the bureaucratic discourse which presents the functioning of organisations as neutral, the distribution of 'Access to activities and guidance through work can render learning opportunities either rich or poor. The...factors that can make available and distribute these opportunities are not benign' (Billett 2002, p. 65). In other words, the distribution of learning intensive roles will be affected by factors such as 'seniority in workplaces...and work demarcations...Workplace cliques, affiliations, gender, race, language or employment standing' (Billett 2002, p. 62). Billett argues that such organisational practices 'may well be organised to maintain the status and standing of one group of workers (e.g. full-time workers) at the expense of another (e.g. part-time workers)' (Billett 2002, p. 62).

When considering gender the impact of such practices is clear. Charles states that, 'At the beginning of the twenty-first century, processes within organisations and, particularly, informal cultural practices, have been identified as reinforcing gendered boundaries and gender identities.' (Charles 2002, p. 43). As mentioned earlier, lower-level jobs are clearly segregated by gender, but there is some evidence that there are 'more permeable boundaries in some middle class jobs' (Charles 2002, p. 26). However, the professions are the only area where women are 'making inroads' into mainly male employment, for example 61% of teaching professionals are female (Charles 2002, p. 26). In addition, attitudes which attribute gender to personal characteristics still operate and 'qualities such as aggression, ambition, an ability to exercise authority and cope with stress, a national affinity with machines and superior intelligence' are associated with men, which may help explain why there are so few women in positions of real power (Charles 2002, p. 31). Even in female dominated professions, for example, in primary school teaching where 86% of teachers are female, what Lupton (2006, p. 105) terms the 'glass escalator' operates to elevate men to positions of authority. Fourty-one percent of head teachers of primary schools are male.

As the Equality and Human Rights Commission (formerly the Equal Opportunities Commission) points out, 'The lack of women at the top is all the more striking given that girls now outperform boys at school, women account for nearly half the workforce, more women than men are entering higher education and high-flying professions like the law' (EOC 2006, p. 2). However, in implicit recognition of the lower returns to formal qualifications experienced by women, and of the importance of informal interactions in the workplace, they go on to state that, 'Of those women who have made it to the top, it is still too often the result of their exceptional strength of character and drive to achieve despite significant barriers' (2006, p. 2).

In addition, in their discussion of women's place in the workforce, the Commission appears to overlook the fact that a vast proportion of the increase in female employment during recent years has been in part-time 'female' jobs, which are low status and low pay (Charles 2002, p. 22).

The foregoing consideration of the gendered employment structure indicates the extent to which women, particularly those in occupations outside the established professions, are likely to find themselves disadvantaged in their access to learning intensive working environments and thus to workplace learning. In professional occupations, employees are likely to undertake continuing professional development to further develop their professional practice, indeed they are often required to do so. It is therefore career women in the professions who benefit from equal employment policies, 'rather than women in the routine, more working class jobs' (Charles 2002, p. 37). This supports Skule's claim that formal qualifications are the way to access learning intensive work environments. It also means that those women for whom workplace learning is most accessible are those women who entered employment with formal qualifications. The consequence of that is that, in spite of the increasing range of workplace learning which can be recognised at all levels, it is those who enter the workplace with low-level qualifications who also lose out in terms of opportunities for the kind of workplace learning which can noticeably enhance their employment opportunities. Women who have left school early and/or without many formal qualifications are consistently disadvantaged, with no opportunity afforded to them to make up for their lack of formal learning. Therefore it is currently apparent that, 'This means that the workplace does not substitute efficiently as an alternative to school-based learning for early school leavers' (Skule 2004, p. 12). In addition, even at higher levels of employment, women can find it difficult to reach positions whereby they can enhance their qualifications through, for example, postgraduate workplace learning.

In light of the foregoing, a high proportion of working women will be unable to take advantage of the facility to get their professional learning and performance recognised academically, because they will not be in a position to do so. The large proportion of women who are in gender-segregated occupations are frequently located low on the occupational ladder, and their work roles do not allow the exercise of sufficient autonomy to allow them to build on this for high-level learning. It appears highly likely, therefore, that the wider academic recognition of workplace learning will serve to reinforce existing gendered divisions in the workplace, rather than providing opportunities for wider participation in higher education. But does that need to be the case, or could the availability of workplace learning respond more effectively to the needs of women in the workplace? In considering this question, it is helpful to look at the main impediments to women's advancement in the workplace, which are the predominance of part-time work and the effect of organisational structures and cultures. Hibbett (2003, p. 505) points out that women are more likely to work part-time if they have a child aged under five—67% of women with small children work part-time, compared with only 32% of women with no dependent children.

Women make up the majority of part-time workers, and in the academic debate relating to women and part-time work, Hakim's 'preference theory' has been extremely influential. This puts forward the argument that full time women workers and part time women workers have different attitudes to employment, and that part time work is the result of different personal priorities (Walters 2005, p. 193). The perceived advantage of Hakim's theory is that it presents women as agents making positive choices relating to their level of engagement with the labour market, rather than being passively pushed into a particular segment of that market. However, Walters argues that Hakim understates the structural constraints that child care places on the choices made by women, particularly those in lower income groups (Walters 2005, p. 196). In the report of a study she has undertaken which explores women's attitudes to part time employment, Walters emphasises the influence that the structure of welfare provision and social attitudes towards gender roles can have on women's participation in employment. Walters' study focuses on part-time employment in the low status, low pay section of the labour market and the women she interviews are all employed as check-out operators and general assistants in the retail sector. This study offers a valuable insight into the workforce experience of women who lack the high salaries which accompany professional status, and who therefore are unable to buy surrogate care for their children.

Walters (2005, p. 196) points out that, 'Despite the introduction of "family friendly" policies in April, 2003, Britain remains a strong male-breadwinner state' and that this places particular constraints on labour market choices for many women with children. This emphasis on the male as breadwinner is accompanied by an assumption that the female is carer, of both the breadwinner and any children of the family. The availability of help with childcare is limited, as the EOC (2005, p. 16) points out, 'Since there are almost 4.7 million under eights in England and just over a million places with childminders, in full day care or in out of school clubs, there are four children for each place in these types of provision.' Given the assumed roles, this puts particular pressure on women who are trying to combine work and family responsibilities. In Walters' study many of the women were 'satisficing'. Satisficing is an economic term which indicates that, rather than maximising one's interests in a particular area, one is having to balance conflicting demands without being able to maximise returns in any one area. Walters (2005, p. 209) uses the term to indicate that the women were trying to balance family requirements and their own working goals, without being able to maximise either. Many of the women recognised the limitations of their current job, but felt that, while their children were small, they had no alternative but to work in part time jobs requiring low levels of expertise.

In the longer term, when their children had grown and become more independent, a majority of the women intended to move to more challenging employment, and some planned to return to education to gain qualifications which would help them get a better job (Walters 2005, p. 205). However, evidence is that such part-time workers can become 'trapped' in low-level part-time employment, because they have lost any human capital they had previously accrued due to the low level of their current role. In addition, they do not have access to training so that they can meet up to date job criteria (e.g. familiarity with particular computer packages) (Walters 2005, p. 209). The emphasis on pre-labour market entry education and qualifications neglects to address this issue that the organisation of employment is such that many fewer educational opportunities are available for part-time female employees, or that women outside the professions may need access to educational opportunities at different points through life.

The current widening participation policy focus on 19–30-year-olds disadvantages many mature workers, but the requirement for women to balance childcare and career development in the absence of alternatives causes this group particular problems. The wider availability of workplace education/training (e.g. through the activities of UnionLearn) is a positive development, and does provide some women workers with opportunities to develop their skills and education. However, scale of organisation is an important factor in terms of access to such provision, and many smaller organisations do not participate in such schemes. An alternative approach would be the provision of funds for childcare in order to allow women to undertake such training outside the workplace. This would be of real benefit to part-time female learners, provided it was offered in a flexible way. It would also enable those women who have left school with few or no qualifications, the opportunity to explore their personal and professional development from a standpoint of greater maturity. Given the ageing nature of the workforce, and the current concerns that this generates, it appears highly desirable to encourage further development of mature workers at all levels of the economy. However, there is currently no indication that the government intends to recognise the demands of this group of workers, and the focus of the 'work–life' balance debate appears firmly on the professional family.

Within this debate the discourse tends to highlight shared family responsibilities, with gender neutral terminology (e.g. parental leave) and it is easy to gain the impression that, in professional employment, women have gained equality. It is, of course, illegal to discriminate in employment on the basis of gender, but there is clear evidence, not least from the requirement for the inclusion of gender in the Equality Act 2006, that the passing of equality legislation during the 1970s has not been effective in achieving either equal pay or equal opportunities for women in the workplace. This situation can be extremely frustrating for women, in that they are aware of the 'glass ceiling', and with regard to women's effective access to higher-level workplace learning, it is informative to consider the nature of organisational structures and cultures.

Charles (2002, p. 37) claims 'there is evidence that the cultures of many organisations are masculine…practices [exist which] convey a message that women are out of place and studies have shown that women receive this message loud and clear'. However, even in organisations where such a strong masculine culture is not evident, women often find themselves in more junior positions than their male colleagues. Martin (2006, p. 255) has undertaken an interesting exploration which offers insight into the perpetuation of the disadvantages experienced by women in the workplace. She argues that, by considering what she terms 'non-reflexivity' relating to the practice of gender, it is possible to understand 'why well-intentioned "good people" practise gender in ways that do harm'. Her work offers an explanation of the way in which gender inequalities are still both tolerated and perpetuated. Martin points out that the practice of gender is well established, and 'Like many other social dynamics, the practising of gender is informed by tacit knowledge. Tacit knowledge is associated with liminal consciousness; knowledge that is below the level of full consciousness' (Martin 2006, p. 261). She claims that, because this is the case, many people act in gendered ways without really thinking about it as they follow established organisational patterns. It is the non-reflexive nature of these acts which perpetuates gender disadvantage, as this means it is acted out through unintended informal processes. Martin (2006, p. 268) points out that, 'When men call women "girls", they infantilize them and call into question women's competence and authority' and engage in a practice which appears trivial, but is in reality undermining. In this context it is interesting to note that, when standing for election as Speaker in the House of Commons recently, it was reported that John Bercow claimed, 'he would clamp down on "sexual remarks uttered sotte voce"' (Stratton and Perkins 2009).

For Martin the answer to the problem is to develop reflexivity with regard to gender interactions. She argues that, 'Reflexivity requires individuals to consider carefully or meditate on their actions and their likely effects prior to behaving. To be reflexive about gender entails the thoughtful consideration of one's options...' (2006, p. 260). In her view well-intentioned 'good people' who took this approach to their own behaviour would moderate the way they practised gender. Interestingly, this approach has strong echoes of the kind of reflective learning required of 'reflective practitioners'. This model requires professionals to analyse and evaluate their practice, and is a model which is widely used in the pedagogy of both experiential and workplace learning. It is, however, a practice which learners can find extremely difficult to develop, even when they are supported by educational professionals. This makes it difficult to envisage how the practice of reflexivity could easily be applied to social dynamics in the workplace. The consideration of gender dynamics, which 'routinely elude researchers' efforts to capture them', could pose a particular problem for such an approach (Martin 2006, p. 268).

It could be argued, therefore, that, although practices are developing which do support the recognition of workplace learning at all levels, and thus help widen participation in higher education, female workers will continue to be disadvantaged. Given the gendered structures and cultures of most organisations, wider availability of workplace learning and qualifications is likely to help reinforce existing gendered arrangements, if only through the unreflexive adoption of gender-based practices. However, there is no reason why this should be the case. A different set of policies would enable the wider recognition of workplace learning to start to address gender disadvantages which women currently experience in their working lives. This could be achieved in a number of ways. The transdisciplinary approach and the experience base which are integral to work-based learning provide specific elements which could address the professional development needs of women at many levels of the workplace.

For those women whose skills are losing/have lost currency because they have been forced by domestic circumstance to undertake low skill part-time work, the possibility of developing generic skills could enhance both their confidence and their skill set, facilitating their move to more responsible work roles when their domestic circumstances permit. The facility to base such learning directly on workplace activities, and thus to make development activities directly relevant to the organisation, provides a strong incentive for employers to support such learning. In addition, it would be possible to focus current learning policies on employees who are conventionally excluded from workplace training and development.

For professional women who are being told they are equal, yet who cannot pass the 'glass ceiling' through their own efforts, work-based learning offers an insight into the organisational dynamics which are constraining them. It does this through the use of critical reflection on practice to achieve what Argyris and Schon call 'double loop' learning. Such a process requires professionals to evaluate not just their activities, but also the implicit assumptions underlying these activities. Once assumptions are made explicit, they can be analysed and evaluated, and then challenged and changed if necessary. Reflective practice can, therefore, provide women with a way of identifying the mechanisms of their disadvantage, and with the confidence to challenge these.

The factors affecting many female workers, whether in low pay, low skill sectors of the economy or not, are likely to mean that the wider availability of work-based learning will not automatically lead to greater opportunities for women. However, a situation now exists where it would be entirely possible to actively address the disadvantages experienced, and to develop a model of pedagogy which 'is concerned with the inherent connectivity between learning, social actions and socially just futures' (Wagner and Childs 2001, p. 551).

References

Billett, S. (2002). Critiquing workplace learning discourses: Participation and continuity at work. *Studies in the Education of Adults, 34*(1), 56–67.

Billett, S. (2004). Learning through work—workplace participatory practices. In H. Rainbird, A. Fuller, & A. Munro (Eds.), *Workplace learning in context*. London: Routledge.

Billett, S., Smith, R., & Barker, M. (2005). Understanding work, learning and the remaking of cultural practices. *Studies in Continuing Education, 27*(3), 219–237.

Boud, D., & Solomon, N. (Eds.). (2001). *Work-based learning: A new higher education?* Buckingham: Society for Research into Higher Education and Open University Press.

Brennan, J., & Little, B. (1996). *A review of work-based learning in higher education*. London: Department for Education and Employment.

Chaiklin, S., & Lave, J. (Eds.). (1993). *Understanding practice: Perspectives on activity and context*. Cambridge: Cambridge University Press.

Charles, N. (2002). *Gender in modern Britain*. Oxford: Oxford University Press.

Department for Innovation, Universities and Skills (DIUS). (2008). *Higher Education at Work— High skills: High value*. Consultation document, Department for Innovation, Universities and Skills.

Engestrom, Y. (2004). The new generation of expertise: seven theses. In H. Rainbird, A. Fuller, & A. Munro (Eds.), *Workplace learning in context*. London: Routledge.

Equal Opportunities Commission (EOC) (2005). *Facts About Women and Men in Great Britain*.

Equal Opportunities Commission (EOC). (2006). *Sex and Power: Who Runs Britain?*

Evans, K., Kersh, N., & Sakamoto, A. (2004). Learner biographies: Exploring tacit dimensions of knowledge and skills. In H. Rainbird, A. Fuller, & A. Munro (Eds.), *Workplace learning in context*. London: Routledge.

Fuller, A. (2003). *Participative learning through the work-based route: From apprenticeship to part-time higher education* (pp. 27–30). Paper presented at the European Association for Research into Learning and Instruction conference.

Gosling, D. (2001). Lost opportunity: What a credit framework would have added to the national qualification framework. *Higher Education Quarterly, 55*(3), 270–284.

Hibbett, A. (2003). Key indicators of women's position in Britain. *Labour Market Trends, 2003*(October), 503–511.

Jackson, N., & Ward, R. (2004). A fresh perspective on progress files—A way of reporting complex learning and achievement of students in higher education. *Assessment and Evaluation in Higher Education, 29*(4), 423–449.

Kerfoot, D., & Korcynski, M. (2005). Gender and service: New directions for the study of 'frontline' service work. *Gender, Work and Organization, 12*(5), 387–399.

Laycock, M. (1993). Enterprise in higher education and learner-managed-learning: The use of learning contracts. In N. Graves (Ed.), *Learner managed learning: Practice, theory and policy*. Leeds: Higher Education for Capability.

Lupton, B. (2006). Explaining men's entry into female-concentrated occupations: Issues of masculinity and social class. *Gender, Work and Organization, 13*(2), 103–128.

Martin, P. Y. (2006). Practising gender at work: Further thoughts on reflexivity. *Gender, Work and Organization, 13*(3), 254–276.

Quality Assurance Agency (QAA). (2004). *Report of a Survey to Follow Up Foundation Degree. Reviews Carried Out in 2002–03*. Gloucester: Quality Assurance Agency.

Reay, D. (2003). A risky business? Mature working class women student and access to higher education. *Gender and Education, 15*(3), 301–315.

Robertson, D. (1994). *Choosing to change: Extending access, choice and mobility in higher education*. The report of the HEQC CAT Development Project. London: Higher Education Quality Council.

Skule, S. (2004). Learning conditions at work: A framework to understand and assess informal learning in the workplace. *International Journal of Training and Development, 8*(1), 8–20.

Stratton, A., & Perkins, A. (16 June 2009). Speaker candidates call for end to prime minister's questions. *The Guardian*.

Tynjala, P. (1999). Towards expert knowledge? A comparison between a constructivist and a traditional learning environment in the university. *International Journal of Educational Research, 31*(5), 357–442.

Wagner, R., & Childs, M. (2001). Work-based learning as critical social pedagogy. *Australian Journal of Adult Learning, 41*(3), 314–334.

Walsh, A. (2007). Engendering debate: Credit recognition of project-based workplace research. *Journal of Workplace Learning, 19*(8), 497–510.

Walters, S. (2005). Making the best of a bad job? Female part-timers' orientations and attitudes to Work. *Gender, Work and Organization, 12*(3), 193–216.

Young, M. (2004). Conceptualizing vocational knowledge: Some theoretical considerations. In H. Rainbird, A. Fuller, & A. Munro (Eds.), *Workplace learning in context*. London: Routledge.

Chapter 12
Educated Women in the Labour Market of Iran: Changing Worlds and New Solutions

Narjes Mehdizadeh and Gill Scott

Introduction

Women's access to education and training, as well as to measures supporting labour market insertion, can be key factors in increasing the role that women play in the socio-economic growth and development of any society. It is a role that is well recognised in Europe where increasing numbers of economists argue that rising rates of female employment represent a major driving force of growth in the past two decades (Finance and economics 2006). Outside the EU, research has also shown that women can be key players in economic development particularly if their economic involvement is combined with increased access to education and training (Murthy et al. 2008). Realising that potential, however, is not easy, particularly in the region that is the focus of this chapter—the Middle East (ME). Labour force statistics show, for example, that women's employment rates in the Middle East and North Africa (MENA) are amongst the lowest in the world, despite marked increases in the levels of education achieved by women. In Iran, one of the most powerful countries of the ME, the overall increase in women's participation in education, particularly since the 1990s, has been outstanding (Bahramitash 2003) but the rise of women's employment has been much slower and limited. So, whereas a number of studies indicate a close relationship between education/training and employment (Shanahan et al. 2002), in Iran, where there has been a dramatic increase in the number of educated women, this relationship does not fully appear to apply. Higher rates of educational achievement have simply not been matched by a similar rise in participation in the labour market. Statistics indicate, for example, that 58.6% of university entrances in 2006 were women but only 12.4% of women were economically active in the same year, compared to 65.6% of men (Statistics Centre of Iran 2007). This chapter will attempt to explore some of the reasons behind this paradox and why it is a paradox most keenly experienced by graduate mothers.

N. Mehdizadeh (✉)
School of Law & Social Sciences, Glasgow Caledonian University, Glasgow, UK
e-mail: narjes.mehdizadeh@gcal.ac.uk

S. Jackson et al. (eds.), *Gendered Choices*, Lifelong Learning Book Series 15,   145
DOI 10.1007/978-94-007-0647-7_12, © Springer Science+Business Media B.V. 2011

Women, Development and Citizenship

Before exploring the specific experience of Iran it is worthwhile examining in a little more depth the importance of the "gender debate" in development and why attention to both women's education and employment is important. While earlier arguments often stressed the unfavourable impact of development on women, Rogers (1980) stressed the adverse influence of women's exclusion on development. In view of the growing economic crisis in the developing countries, she recommended that constant neglect of women's productivity was a costly mistake that planners could no longer afford to make. 'The issue was not so much that women needed development, but that development needed women' (Kabeer 1994, p. 25). In order to achieve this Afshari (1996) argues that, in the first instance, economic policies should focus on human development strategies that include changes in beliefs and education: she sees education as a means to increase the participation of all strata of society. Consequently, changes of attitude towards women and also the removal of sex discrimination are needed if the gendered values dominant in MENA societies for centuries are not to limit human development.

Economist Sen (1999) goes further in arguing that such development should be based on the expansion of human freedom (including access to education, public facilities and social care for its own sake) as well as narrow concepts of economic development. His arguments contrast with general accounts that consider development more narrowly in terms of income or Gross National Product (GNP), industrialisation, or technological advance. Sen argues that working outside the home and earning an independent income are not just necessary for a nation's economic development but also because it can have a clear influence on the social standing of women in a society and household. He suggests that:

> The extensive reach of *women's agency* is one of the more neglected areas of development studies, and most urgently in need of correction. Nothing, arguably, is as important today in the political economy of development as an adequate recognition of political, economic and social participation and leadership of women. This is indeed a crucial aspect of development as freedom. (Sen 1999, p. 203)

It is not only in development theory that we see attention being paid to a more gendered analysis. Gender and citizenship is a critical issue for social policy. According to Lister (2003) citizenship involves political, economic and social dimensions. Whilst she recognises that economic independence, particularly the right to work, is central to women's claims for full citizenship and is always a precondition of women's liberation she rightly points out that too often such rights reflect male education and employment patterns. Her argument is that women's participation is limited by their care responsibilities and by societal beliefs about their role in society. It is these that will prevent women achieving full citizenship. It is a widespread argument within debates about women, care and citizenship in the developed world: it takes for granted women's now well established access to education and sees access to care and men and women's equal involvement in parenting as the key variable affecting economic citizenship. It is an area, though, that needs a more nuanced analysis in the ME.

It seems, then, that development theorists have recognised that changes in women's lives are critical to economic and social development in a society but debates on citizenship in recent European social policy have highlighted the additional need to examine more fully the factors limiting women's economic participation if women and society are to benefit. In this chapter the limits on women's economic participation in Iran rather than Europe are examined and the reasons why education that has been opened up to Iranian women has not proved as economically liberating as many would hope are explored. Education is seen as a key area to explore because in many societies the exit point of education is the entry point to employment for women as well as men, but also because the content of education, its connection with the world of work and the possibility of work-based learning are key factors affecting personal and social growth.

Education, Women and Work in Iran

The education system of Iran that provides the basis for women's increased involvement in employment was developed in two different eras: during the Pahlavi era (before the Islamic Revolution 1979) and under the Islamic Republic state. Before the Revolution in 1979 the Pahlavi regime used the education system to modernise and secularise Iran and was seen as key to opening up employment opportunities for women. Post-1979 the Islamic Republic focused on inspiring Islamic culture and values (Babran 2005) with routes into higher education initially squeezed in the some fields of study for women, only to be opened up again in the 1990s. In many ways the situation of women's access to education and employment in Iran is a historically fluctuating one and one that is not always connected to improving human capital for the economy. In the next few paragraphs these fluctuations are outlined.

Prior to the Islamic Revolution in 1979 the highest percentage of women's participation in higher education was reported as 32% (Farasatkhah 2000) which mostly included the elite and middle class women in urban areas and was accompanied by rising employment. Between 1979 and 1990, however, both education and employment became more difficult to access for women. Post-1979, the Cultural Revolution that led to the closing of universities,[1] and the lack of experience in decision-making, plus migration from war regions, the increase in the fertility rate and social and economic problems of families impacted strongly on education as well as women's economic position (Alaedini and Razavi 2005). Women's access to education declined at this time despite equal opportunities being presented as one of the ideals that the government pursued in their plan for the expansion of education for women (Mehran 1999; Shavarini 2005). The result was a highly gendered inequality in the labour force supply in 1989, a deterioration from the situation in 1979. This was further compounded by an increasing stress on traditional culture

---

[1] In 1980 for three years universities were closed for fundamental and structural changes and Islamization.

and customs that demanded a secondary and peripheral gender role for girls and women socially. These patterns overshadowed families' and parents' educational preferences and even women's own attitudes, behaviours and tendencies. Traditional norms, culturally and politically enforced, produced a domestic role for women (as wives and mothers), and girls themselves learned that some fields of study, jobs and activities were not suitable for them (Bouzari 2002). At the same time as this, shifts were occurring in higher education under the approved laws of the Cultural Revolution Headquarters. These laws were responsible for determining "gender standards" and limitations for women in the fields of agriculture and technical/ engineering (Farasatkhah and Mokhtari 2001). Separate quotas were often determined for men and women who wanted to enter the universities and in some fields, women's quotas were only 10–20% (Bouzari 2002). Indeed, they were reduced further when quotas for combatants and handicapped persons and the members of the Revolutionist Institutions were approved in 1982. Statistics show that these trends resulted in further gender inequality in the supply of an educated workforce. Farasatkhah's (2000) study shows, inter alia, that:

- Women's share in the university student community fell below the previous low of 32% in 1979 to 28.6% in 1989.
- The percentage of women students in the agriculture and veterinary medicine groups dropped from 18.4% in 1979 to 4.1% in 1989.
- Female students' share in the medical group dropped from 53.8% in 1979 to 42.5% in 1989.
- Women in M.A./MSc and PhD courses were 28.8 and 25.4% respectively in 1979 and 1989.

Since 1990, however, the situation in Iran has changed. In contrast to the 1980s, a phenomenon of the 1990s was women's tremendous speed in closing the gender gap in higher education (Shavarini 2005, p. 332). The restrictions of 1979 to 1990 began to wane, women's demands became greater and economic growth replaced the stagnation for women of the post-war economy. This was reflected in women's gross registration rate in high school education increasing from 69.1% in 1988 to 90.9% in 1997 (Management and Planning Organization 1999). As a result, the proportion of women graduates in high school education and pre-university period reached 57.6% and 59.8%, respectively, in 1997–1998, more than that of men (Statistics Centre of Iran 2002). It is in higher education, though, that we see the biggest change. Partly reflecting demands from women, the education system was reformed, allowing women greater participation in previously restricted fields of study. Direct limitation of the regulations relating to women's higher education were removed by the decision of the Ministry of Science in 1993 because of women's ever-increasing awareness and change of discourse in favour of their citizenship rights (Bouzari 2002). The regulations forbidding females to study a number of subjects were modified, creating more opportunities for women to work in different fields. A significant consequence of these changes was an increase in women's demands for continuing their studies in the universities and other higher education institutes. By 1997 49.36% of people applying for university admission were women; by 2002

Table 12.1 Women's acceptance into universities with educational subjects. (Source: Technical and Statistical Analyzing Office 2002)

| Year | Frequency rate of women's acceptance into universities compared to total acceptance (%) | | | | | |
	Total subjects	Math-ematical & technical	Experimental sciences	Human sciences	Art	Foreign languages
1995	40.2	23	56.2	41	44	51.6
1996	47.8	29.1	60.2	50.7	56	60.6
1997	49.4	28.7	61.3	54.6	57.8	62
1998	52	32.4	61.8	56.6	57.8	64.9
1999	57.2	38.5	68.2	60.6	59	73
2000	59.9	41.9	69.1	63.3	63.9	76.7
2001	61.6	43.7	71.3	66	64.5	77.6
2002	62.7	46	73	68	69.5	73

women represented 59.7% of applicants and by 2007 the figure was 62.8% (Technical and Statistical Analyzing Office 2008). Given this trend, it was natural that the rate of women's acceptance into the universities would exceed that of men's. In fact by 1997 49.4% of students were women and this rose to 62.7% by 2002 (Technical and Statistical Analyzing Office 2002). (See Table 12.1 for further details.) Many scholars such as Shavarini (2005) argue that:

> One of the most commonly cited reasons for women's progress in entering institutions of higher education is the solid and strong Islamic identity that Iranian universities have established. It is an atmosphere that has secured the trust of traditional religious families, who compose the majority of the Iranian population. (p. 335)

Given the gross fluctuations in educational opportunities outlined above it is worthwhile asking what the position of women in education today is and how it is likely to develop. Statistical prediction indicates that women's participation in higher education will reach over 70% in future (Technical and Statistical Analyzing Office 2002). There can be little doubt that in recent years considerable changes have taken place in regard to women's position generally and higher education specifically. For example, in 2007–2008 female students represented 64% of applicants to universities (Statistics Centre of Iran 2008). Ballard (MP) (2002) even observed:

> Women in Iran are in many ways among the most assertive and socially independent women I have met. Women can and do work; more women take engineering degrees in Iran than in the UK; there are more female university vice-chancellors than in the UK; and more women in parliament than, for example, in Germany. (p. 2)

The picture from the 1990s, however, is not quite as positive as it appears at first sight. In the universities and higher education institutes other than Islamic Azad universities[2] women's share in Masters' degrees in 2002 was only 28.34% and their share in specialized PhDs is only 23.53% (Statistics Centre of Iran 2002). Even

[2] Islamic Azad University is a type of private university whose numbers have grown. By 1982 there were 73 such universities.

Table 12.2 Unemployment and employment rate of graduates according to sex in 1997–2002.
(Source: Statistics Centre of Iran 2002)

Year	Unemployment rate in total			Unemployment rate among graduates			Employment rate among graduates		
	Total	Male	Female	Total	Male	Female	Total	Male	Female
1997	13.1	12.8	14.9	6.5	5.7	8.6	93.5	94	91.4
1998	12.5	12.2	13.7	9.3	8	13	90.7	92	87
1999	13.5	13.5	13.6	11.1	9.6	15	88.9	90.4	85
2000	14.2	13.8	16.5	12	10	17	88	90	83
2001	14.2	13.2	19.8	13.8	10	22.5	86.2	90	77.5
2002	13	11.2	22.4	13	9	21.5	87	91	78.5

more important is the fact that despite an increase in the number and statistical growth of female university students recently, difficulties in translating such educational shifts into employment remain.

It is certainly the case that labour market entry for educated women is not commensurate with their improved position in education. Unemployment figures amongst educated women as a whole suggest that demand for the specific skills of educated women is more limited than for those of educated men.

As Table 12.2 shows, the employment rate of female graduates has declined from 91.4% in 1997 to 78.5% in 2002 and recent figures from the 2006 census show a continuing decline to 56% in 2006 (Bahramitash and Salehi-Esfahani 2009). Overall, the decline in the employment rate could be due to the economic condition of the country as a whole and the shortage of job opportunities for men and women. However, a mismatch between education and current labour market needs and practical skills, as well as lack of information about labour market needs are more important reasons for unemployment among educated women in Iran. (Alafar 2003; Salehi 2002). Salehi-Isfahani (2005) argues that this is not due to bad choices on the part of women but arises because a poor connection exists between what students learn in the Iranian education system and what they need if they are to be hired later. He argues that, in a situation where the economy is largely controlled by the state and job protection rather than job creation has been a priority, education is not contributing to economic growth and cannot provide a wide-ranging route to employment for educated women. Per capita growth fluctuates with oil prices, not education, and whilst education provides a route to a good wage and secure public sector employment for some women, it is not currently providing the skills necessary for entry into private sector employment for many others or indeed providing the basis for the national economic growth necessary for job creation.

It is certainly the case that where educated women are employed it is predominantly in limited types of jobs in the public sector: in 2001 84% of women and 55% of men with secondary schooling or above were in government employment, suggesting that the skills they do acquire in education may be of limited applicability. The statistics of 2004 show that amongst employed graduates, 65% of women were working in the educational sector, 14.6% in health and social work sector and only 20.4% in other sectors while 28.8% of graduate men were working in the educational sector, 6.1% in the health and social work sector and the remaining 65% work in other sectors. Whilst these limitations in the type of jobs available to educated women can be explained by the types of education and curriculum they engage in, traditional cultural patterns and powerful structures rooted in patriarchy also cut women off from the possibility of varying their fields of economic participation. Consequently, women have encountered a much higher rate of unemployment than men, even though they have developed their access to higher education. The rate of unemployment for female graduates had reached 21% by 2002, a much higher rate than that of men under the same conditions (Centre of Research and Women Studies 2003).

So if, to reiterate an earlier point, there is no obvious limitation for women's success from the viewpoint of the Constitutional Law in Iran or no obvious barrier to accessing higher education, how can we explain the higher rates of unemployment for women, the more limited job opportunities and their lack of success at senior levels? Perhaps even more important, what is the likelihood of change? Addressing the limited and non-work related curriculum is one aspect, but the development of clear government guidelines for change, redressing poor access to vocational and enterprise training before and in work and exploring the need for childcare and changed gendered divisions of labour within the home are others to be explored below. These are important areas to explore as the economic and social position of women continues to change in Iran and, whilst there are problems, women's education in recent decades has shown it can play a very important role in transforming women's role in the labour market of Iran (Bahramitash and Kazemipour 2006; Taleb and Goodarzi 2004). If Iran is to benefit from women's clearly established capacity to benefit from higher education in a way that benefits the economy and women themselves there is a need to explore whether trends do exist for further change.

Shaditalab (2005) in her article "Iranian Women: Raising Expectations" argues that: 'Iranian women who have rising expectations are an accelerating force for change in Iran' (p. 54).

Can such expectations be realised?

The question of whether further change can occur and the disparity between educational and employment opportunities for educated women be reduced is a significant one if Iran continues to enjoy increased economic growth. In this section of the chapter recent and possible changes in government plans are examined to assess whether the changes identified in education for women are likely to impact on employment and what factors continue to limit progress.

Government Plans

A major question here is whether there is an effective orientation and plan for gender balance in the country. A positive answer may come by analyzing the contents of development plans in Iran. An analysis of the Third Economic and Socio-Cultural

Development Plan 2000–2004 (TESCDP), however, shows that the government did not undertake the necessary tasks for removing discrimination, inequality and gender imbalances even though there was, in theory, an emphasis on and specification of a goal of equality. Indeed, the most important article concerning women in the TESCDP, i.e. article 158, merely put a stress on family reinforcement instead of considering the basic development of structural changes and providing women with more employment-relevant support such as childcare. The result was that traditional roles of man and woman in the family remained major obstacles for the development of women's participation (Management and Planning Organization 2001).

Nevertheless, in the most recent economic plans in Iran the top priority is women's employment. Thus, in comparison to the TESCDP there has been some progress; the Fourth Economic and Socio-Cultural Development Plan 2005–2009 (FESCDP) includes an emphasis on the necessity of the development of women's participation. It is also apparent that attention is now being paid to the presence of inequality, discrimination and lack of gender balance. For example, the government particularly pays attention in article 111[3] of the FESCDP to the gender composition of the workforce and this could be a very important point for the resolution of unemployment of educated women. Other regulations in Iran, such as the Charter of Women's Rights and Responsibilities (CWRR), have strengthened this with attempts at the multilateral promotion of women's employment and by offering general guidelines. At the same time, however, the government emphasizes the strength of the family institution and promotes a particular view of "correct" family behaviour without fully taking into the account women's need for work-related welfare/support policies (Mehdizadeh 2009).

Examining the government's role in relation to education for work related skills is probably even more important. In Iran, it has been easier to invest in physical rather than human capital. Oil revenues have provided significant income and the state has been concerned with using that to develop services such as education and health and to provide security through government jobs, particularly in those sectors. The involvement of the state in encouraging new directions in education and training relevant to the private sector has largely been limited to regulating private employers in a way that gives security to those in employment rather than engagement in economic development activity such as enterprise creation, work-based training and subsidy for new types of employers. The result is that instead of

---

[3] Article 111 of FESCDP 2004–2009:165–166:

With the objective of strengthening the role of women in the society and development of opportunities and enhancement of the level of their participation in the country, government is charged with taking the following actions:

A. compilation, approval and implementation of the comprehensive plan for development of women participation, including re-examination of the laws and regulations, especially the civil law, strengthening women's skills in line with the needs of the society and technological transformations, identification and increase of the investment entities in the employment-generating opportunities, with attention be paid to the gender composition of the supply of the manpower, enhancement of the quality of life of women, as well as promoting public convictions towards their worthiness.

investing in an education system that focuses on economically productive human resources and matching skills to productive activity there has been an extension of education that suits the public sector more than the private. There has been a concentration on physical infrastructural development and maintenance of a rigid but safe labour market. This limits demand for the educated workforce, especially for women whose skills and knowledge are more relevant to the public sector (Farjadi 2003). At the same time global developments in information technology and the advent of new information services provide evidence of economic change that could be developed in Iran and provide a possibility for the development of employment opportunities for graduate women if their education was made more relevant to such sectors. If guidelines could be created for the country for a "knowledge-based economy" things might change. Education or human investment could play a more primary role in the formation of the labour force and economic growth.

Focusing for the moment on the knowledge economy it could be argued that the government could produce change. Governmental economic policies and their interactions with the non-governmental sectors, and universities' promotion of the contribution of a higher education focused on knowledge and information technology could allow female graduates to contribute to the country's economic production capabilities more effectively. But a new curriculum and better work-related support for women are essential preconditions for this. Developing access to the subjects that constitute the basis for a "knowledge-based economy" is critical for the country and could draw on women's capacity for education. Furthermore, it could help to promote women's citizenship. Marrying the two, however, would seem to demand a focus on the specific barriers to women's employment. They could be as follows:

- Development of periods of apprenticeship in the field of information technology for women if they are to be key players in a "knowledge-based economy"
- Supporting educated women in entrepreneurship and investment through granting facilities and bank credits, tax exemptions and duty-frees, discounts in insurance in order to enable women to play a leading role in a "knowledge-based economy"
- Providing more institutional resources for supporting women in domestic duties such as childcare.

Vocational and Workplace Training in Iran

This idea of the need for a more employment relevant curriculum, including subjects relevant to the knowledge economy, in Iran is supported by a recent International Labour Organisation report (ILO 2005) which comments,

> Skills development is critical for employability and overall labour market flexibility to allow workers in making transitions as the economy enters into a new, competitive environment. Iran is faced with a large number of graduates and dropouts from educational institutions without requisite skills for employment. (ILO 2005, p. 23)

Table 12.3 Potential demand for skills development at different educational levels, 1996–2011 (in '000). (Source: ILO Report 2005, p. 23)

	1996	2001	2006	2011
Non-formal skills training at VET	208	271	192.7	164.7
VET at secondary level	327.1	709.5	1,150.5	1,163.5
Applicants to AA/AS courses	613.6	840.6	1,043.7	1,197.0
Total	1,148.7	1,821.1	2,386.9	2,525.2

In 2001, over 1.8 million probable jobseekers were estimated to require skills training from vocational education training (VET) services. Potential total demand for skills has been predicted to increase to about 2.5 million by 2011 (see Table 12.3).

The ILO report is based on discussions in Iran from the end of 2002 to the end of 2003 with various government officials, employers and workers' organizations and NGOs as well as on thematic background papers prepared by ILO officials, national academics and experts in the areas of the macro economy, labour market information, skills development, small enterprise development, social security, social dialogue and gender equity. It highlights the need for skills development. Unfortunately, it also reports that whilst vocational education and training are given importance at the secondary level in Iran the academic stream predominates in higher education and where vocational training has developed that might address the skills gap for educated women it has tended to be poorly funded and of poor quality.

Nevertheless, some programmes in the area of work-based learning/training and continuing professional development do exist and open up some hope for improving women's situation in the labour market. For instance, recruitment rules have been drawn up by the government that specify training sessions for employees in relation to skills development such as ICT, statistic, ethics, management and planning as well as subject specific training. Agreements also exist amongst some public and private sector employers to collaborate bilaterally with international bodies in running training and skill development programmes for staff and they are usually the same for women and men already employed in the organisations. For example, after a visit to Iran by high ranking German Technical Cooperation (GTZ) company members and other delegates in June 2008, an agreement was set up to run training for women and disabled people as well as in ITC, entrepreneurship and new and advanced technology. The number of vocational training centres for women has been increased, from 31 in 1996 to 160 in 2006. Graduates have appeared in plans: for example the Ministry of Industries and Mines apprenticeship programmes for university graduates was launched 3 years ago in order to ease their entry into the employment. According to this plan university graduates volunteer and receive a subsidy for 11 months to work in industry and mining units. This programme receives financial help from the Mines & Mining Industries Development & Renovation Organization of Iran (Iran Technical and Vocational Training Organizations Report 2008).

Funding for such programmes, however, remains problematic. The principal means of financing technical training until 2003 was through a payroll tax on employers with more than 10 employees but, since 2003 and the abolition of the payroll tax, employer-related funding has declined. The Ministry of Finance has become the major source of funding for the Technical and Vocational Training Organisation (TVTO). One of the unfortunate consequences of that change has been that industry needs have not been incorporated fully into training courses even though the vocational and training system has expanded and is popular with young women as well as men. Courses have often been too short, and their quality according to one ILO report is often questionable. Such training has not automatically resulted in increased employment for trainees, has not been favoured by employers or parents and is certainly poorly connected to both graduate and employer needs. There are too many providers, too many state sub-sidised centres competing with one another and too little direct connection with industry. The ILO's conclusion was that a partnership of providers, employers and workers' organisations is needed in order to meet market demands more effectively.

Changing the skills of job seekers is one thing, but the supply of skilled work-ers alone is seldom sufficient for the generation of employment. And thinking of the particular group that has been focused on in this chapter—female graduates—it has to be asked whether better vocational training could realistically change the picture of a small number of female graduates being employed in government and a greater number of educated women remaining unemployed. As was observed above supporting educated women in entrepreneurship and investment through granting facilities and bank credits, tax exemptions and duty-frees could help educated women play a greater role in the non-governmental sectors. The limited potential for employment generation for educated women in what are capital-intensive large enterprises in Iran also provides a case for supporting small and medium sized enterprises (SMEs) in which educated women could play a larger part and for developing more business start up and enterprise courses for women. European research suggests that graduate unemployment in a rigid labour market is best approached by developing new "stepping stones" to employment and that the development and support of entrepreneurial skills can assist in the expansion of SMEs which would provide such a route to employment. This is an argument which has been used in parts of Europe where female graduate under-employment has occurred (Schomburg and Teichler 2006; Webster 2007). It is a case which has also received some support from the government in Iran. The TESCDP and the FESCDP both emphasised the need to encourage SMEs and there are some programmes and incentives in place that could create the good quality jobs that educated women want. According to the ILO report referred to above, however, numerous biases in the policy and regulatory environment exist that place limita-tions on women's abilities to take advantage of existing incentives and further steps to reduce taxes and fees as well as increase incentives and SME-based train-ing are still needed.

Childcare and the Future of Graduate Women's Employment

Whether it is possible to take advantage of work based and other opportunities for vocational and professional development after university is not something that has been explored much by those researching education and work in Iran: their focus has been on the type of course that could be developed to open up the labour market rather than address the barriers to the uptake of vocational and continuing education and to work itself. Nevertheless for women it is essential that specific barriers after graduation be examined as they significantly affect the contribution they could make to a changing economy. As discussed earlier, compared to the Pahlavi era, post revolutionary Iran saw women gain equal rights with men in education and a number of other social and religious activities, albeit within an Islamic doctrine. However, as with most Middle Eastern cultures, there is a tendency for women in Iran to adopt and be expected to adopt a role that prioritises family above all else. The result is that childcare responsibilities as well as education and the labour market significantly affect the economic behaviour of women as they enter or contemplate motherhood. Since motherhood tends to be entered into shortly after graduation this is highly significant for the picture of female graduate unemployment. There are, undoubtedly, clear maternity rights that employed women have in Iran but there is little childcare available and the lack of childcare for school age children and other work–family balance strategies has a particularly strong impact on women (Mehdizadeh 2009). This is true for employed mothers but even more so for those who have not yet entered employment. The average age at which educated women have children is at the point of graduation, adding to the barriers to employment that graduates experience in the country. Providing more institutional resources for women with family responsibilities becomes highly significant if the transition to employment from education is to be made possible (Mehdizadeh and Scott 2008). Developing the skills and the enterprises of a modern economy is crucial to Iran's long-term success but educated women's involvement in a modern economy depends as much on their access to childcare as their capacity to enter the new sectors of the economy and possibly develop a knowledge based industry that could make a difference to economic growth. Childcare for working mothers in Iran is not well developed; its development mirrors the expansion and contraction of education for women. The purpose of contemporary day care and preschool establishments is aimed more at pedagogy than in allowing more women to enter the labour market. This has not always been the case: in 1975 all government organizations were given responsibility to establish day care centres for women employees and for the welfare of mothers and children. The result was that different ministries established nurseries run by the Women's Organization and during the oil boom years of 1973–1978, before the revolution, there was a rise in interest in day care and pre-school education, mostly attached to places of employment of women (Salehi-Esfahani and Kamel 2006, p. 12). From 1980, however, occurring at the same time as the reduction in access to university education for women, these centres were all closed and their functions were synthesised under a new format, the State Welfare Organization (SWO)[4]. In 1980, with ratification of a bill by the Ministry Committee, every factory was given responsibility to establish a nursery if women employees have a minimum total of 10 children. Although according to labour law (Article 78) employers are now obliged to provide childcare for working mothers, this law still remains more of a theory than actual practice, because employers consider it is the government's responsibility to fill this gap (Mehdizadeh 2009). Shortages of job opportunities could be one factor that limits the implementation of this law and the other reality which should be accepted is that employers have the right to choose the employee. Given the importance of the state in directing the economy the views of one senior government official, interviewed as part of a study of policy makers' attitudes to women and employment, is indicative of low expectations of change,

> At the moment the demand for jobs is high compared to the number of vacancies and unemployment is high for men and women. When men and women go for the same job, although they have equal abilities, a private company manager may decide on the man rather than comply with the maternity period, feeding babies and other facilities that are needed for women. Therefore, managers and owners of the company will decide on men. The regulation should be such that the employer considers not the loss but the benefits that women can bring to the business, and this should be implemented through the government. (Mehdizadeh 2009, Mothers' interview reports, no. 4)

According to a report of the Ministry of Education (2007), the number of pre-school children more than doubled from about 259,000 to 550,000 between 1979 and 1990. There are, however, not so much childcare as pre-school units. Their hours are short, they have not been expanded to meet the needs of working mothers and we know little about whether they enable a balance between work and home to be met by the newly educated women of Iran. Thus although gender equality in education is strengthening women's citizenship in Iran, the gap between education and employment is made worse by a lack of childcare and this makes women's citizenship vulnerable. Therefore, there is an urgent need for the government to pay attention to this issue. According to one report, a key linkage that needs to be made if the gender balance in the labour market is to be improved is that between the care economy and paid work,

> The care economy includes most of women's unpaid work as well as the public and private provision of social services. Women are hampered in finding paid jobs because of their family responsibilities. (ILO 2005, p. 42)

Thus, it can be argued that if employment policy in Iran wants a smoother transformation of women's role in the labour market and a better way to meet the demands of educated women, expansion of childcare as well as work-related support (Mehdizadeh 2009) and training strategies would be key.

One study to examine this issue in some detail is research carried out into childcare and work amongst 547 mothers living in Shiraz, a large city in Iran, who were

---

[4] The SWO's main purpose was to fulfil the welfare commitments of Articles of 3; 21 and 29 of the Constitution Law.

educated to at least High School Diploma Level (Mehdizadeh 2009). The research found that some 35.5% of the educated mother respondents who were not working felt that "difficulty in childcare arrangements" was the major reason for not working and a further 17.8% of the respondents said "restriction by husband" was the main problem. Despite high rates of unemployment, only 16.5% of the respondents believed that "shortage of job opportunities" was the reason for them for not working. The majority of non-working mothers (80%) believed that availability of childcare influenced their decision whether to work or not. In addition, the most common reasons, as cited by the respondents, for leaving or changing their jobs, were looking after children and family responsibilities. The majority of respondents indicated that they had thought about leaving their job because of concern for the care of their children. The major reason mothers reported for not working was difficulty concerning childcare arrangements. It is not only access to work that is seen as affected by childcare; 45.5% of working mothers in the same study reported that they had thought of leaving their job because of childcare difficulties. As one mother puts it, hours of work and career prospects are affected by childcare responsibility:

> I prefer to work in an education authority because of their hours of work and holidays. I was working in the Ministry of Health; I had to work during summer holidays too. I also had to work until 2.30pm every day. ... for the sake of my children I changed my work to the education authority. (Mehdizadeh 2009, Mothers' interview reports, no. 3)

Is it possible to begin to address the lack of childcare? In the main, it has to be said, that the same research showed conflicting views exist of the best route to take when it comes to the balance between family and work for educated women. One senior NGO policy analyst, for example, said, 'this is a duty of the government - for the welfare of all and to create employment for women, appropriate childcare facilities should be established at low cost and near the work place.' (Mehdizadeh 2009, NGO interview reports, Policymakers, no. 6)

Whilst another senior government official felt in contrast to that:

> In our views of training and rearing we don't want mothers to get far from children.... Expenses of that should be paid by the future generation. We want women to go as early as possible to be beside their children. In the short term mothers think of the gain in income. But in the long term their children are deprived of motherly affection and kindness. (Mehdizadeh 2009, GO interview reports, Policymakers, no. 3)

In such a situation it is unlikely that the needs of educated mothers will be met easily, and without a clear strategy mothers, children and the society may lose out on the contribution that such mothers can make, development will remain subject to changes in the political and economic context of mothers' work and childcare policies.

Conclusion

This chapter has highlighted the lack of a close relationship between higher education and employment. It has focused on Iran, where there has been a dramatic increase in the number of educated women but where higher rates of educational achievement have simply not been matched by a similar rise in participation in the labour market. The problem has been presented as one that not only prevents economic growth within the country but also contributes to a reduced experience of citizenship amongst women, particularly amongst graduate mothers.

Interactions between economic and ideological change as well as increased gender consciousness are significant in explaining the increased levels of female employment and education: far higher now under the Islamic state than at the height of modernisation in the 1960s and 1970s, but there is no doubt a problem remains. Key factors producing the paradoxical situation of high numbers of female graduates combined with a low rate of female graduate employment were seen to lie not so much in traditional patriarchal attitudes or Islamization (Bahramitash and Salehi-Esfahani 2009) but in a fluctuation of state support of women's education and employment following political and economic change, a lack of flexibility in the curriculum that women can pursue, a lack of opportunities and work based learning for women to make the most of their talents outside the public domain and finally a lack of childcare and work-related welfare/support policies that fit with working mothers' needs and preferences for reconciliation work and care.

The conclusion must be that curriculum change to allow greater flexibility when entering the labour market, more continuing education that opens up entrepreneurial possibilities and better links between universities and employers are possibilities that should be exploited if the potential for a state-dominated economy such as Iran to effect such policy change is to be achieved. Such changes would improve the prospects for all graduates, but for women the additional burden of childcare needs to be addressed and incorporated into economic development policy. The potential for change will clearly be affected by the direction of both the local and global economy but state ideology towards women and children, as well as existing gender relations, will continue to be of great importance for the young women who look to education as a route to a more equal citizenship and national economic development.

References

Afshari, Z. (1996). *Zanan va toseeye ensani (Woman and human development)*. Conference paper. Tehran: Alzahra University.

Alaedini, P., & Razavi, M. R. (2005). Women's participation and employment in Iran: A critical examination. *Critique: Critical Middle Eastern Studies, 14*(1), 57–73.

Alafar, E. (2003). *Barrasi avamel moasser bar eshteghal zanan fareghotahsil daneshgahi (A study of effective factors on employment of graduated women)*. Tehran: Ministry of Labour and Social Affair.

Babran, S. (2005). Zanan dar amoozesh ali keshvar, hozoor kammi ya kaifi? (Women in higher education of Iran, quantity or quality presence?). *Payam Zan, 13*(12), 208–219.

Bahramitash, R. (2003). Islamic fundamentalism and women's economic role: The case of Iran. *International Journal of Politics, Culture and Society, 16*(4), 551–568.

Bahramitash, R., & Kazemipour, S. (2006). Myths and realities of the impact of Islam on women: Changing marital status in Iran. *Critique: Critical Middle Eastern Studies, 15*(2), 111–128.

Bahramitash, R., & Salehi Esfahani, H. (2009). Nimble fingers no longer! Women's employment in Iran. In A. Gheissari (Ed.), *Contemporary Iran: Economy, society, policies* (pp. 77–122). Oxford: Oxford University Press.

Ballard, J. (2002, January 7). Another kind of freedom. *Guardian.* http://www.guardian.co.uk/world/2002/jan/07/gender.uk. Accessed 21 June 2007.

Bouzari, S. (2002). *Jaygah zanan dar faleyathay pejouheshi keshvar (Women status in research activities in Iran).* Tehran: Institute of Research and Planning of Higher Education.

Centre of Research and Women's Studies. (2003). *Abaad jenseyati bazar kar va vijegihay eshteghal dar Iran (Gender dimensions of labour market and employment characteristics in Iran).* Tehran: Tehran University.

Farasatkhah, M. (2000). *Barrasi marahel tahavvol daneshgah dar Iran (A study on developmental stages of university in Iran)* (2nd ed.). Tehran: Institute of Research and Planning of Higher Education.

Farasatkhah, M., & Mokhtari, M. (2001). *Barrasi va arzyabi amalkard Shoray Ali Enghelab Farhangi (A study and evaluation of the function Supreme Council of Cultural Revolution)* (3rd ed.). Tehran: Supreme Council of Cultural Revolution Office.

Farjadi, G. (2003). *Barnamerizi nirooy ensani: barrasi doreh doktora amouzesh ali (Planning for human force: A study on PhD education).* Tehran: Shahid Beheshti University and Institute of Research and Planning of Higher Education.

Finance and economics: A guide to womenomics; women and the world economy. (2006, April 15). *Economist, 379*(8473), 80.

Fourth Economic, Social and Cultural Development Plan of the Islamic Republic of Iran, 2005–2009. (2004). Management and Planning Organization Law. Tehran.

ILO (International Labour Organization). (2005). *An employment strategy for the Islamic Republic of Iran.* New Delhi: Sub-Regional Office for South Asia, ILO.

Iran Technical and Vocational Training Organizations Report. (2008). http://tvto-itc.ir/tabid/36/Default.aspx?PageContentID=29. Accessed 19 Apr 2009.

Kabeer, N. (1994). *Reversed realities: Gender hierarchies in development thought.* London: Verso.

Lister, R. (2003). *Citizenship: Feminist perspectives.* Houndmills: Palgrave Macmillan.

Management and Planning Organization. (1999). Qozareshe melie toseyeh ensani gomhori eslami Iran (National Report of Human Development of Islamic Republic of Iran), Tehran.

Management and Planning Organization. (2001). Ghanone barnemeh sevome eghtesadi, ejtemai and farhangi (Third Economic, Social and Cultural Development Plan), Tehran.

Mehdizadeh, N. (2009). *Women, children and state: Analysis of childcare policies related to women's employment in Iran.* Unpublished PhD thesis, Glasgow Caledonian University, Glasgow.

Mehdizadeh, N., & Scott, G. (2008). *Educated mothers in Iran: Work, welfare and childcare.* 42nd Social Policy Association Annual Conference, 23–35 June 2008, University of Edinburgh, Scotland.

Mehran, G. (1999). Lifelong learning: New opportunities for women in a Muslim country (Iran). *Comparative Education, 35*(2), 201–215.

Ministry of Education. (2007). Enghelab va amoozesh va parvaresh, moroori bar barkhi az mohemtarin dastavardhay amoozesh va parvaresh (Revolution and education, review on some important education achievements). Parto Enghelab Eslami. http://medu.ir/IranEduThms/medu/cntntpge.php?pgid=99&rcid=2#kh2. Accessed 21 May 2007.

Murthy, R., Sagayam, K., Rengalakshmi, J., & Sudha, N. (2008). Gender, efficiency, poverty reduction, and empowerment: Reflections from an agriculture and credit programme in Tamil. *Gender & Development, 16*(1), 134–156.

Rogers, B. (1980). *The domestication of women: Discrimination in developing societies.* London: Kogan Page.

Salehi, E. (2002). *Barrasi vazeyat eshteghal danesh amookhtegan zan: Mored barrasi: Daneshgah Mazanderan (An investigation on the situation of graduated women: Case study, Mazanderan University).* Working paper, University of Mazanderan, Iran.

Salehi-Esfahani, D., & Kamel, H. (2006). *Demographic swings and early childhood education in Iran.* Working paper, Department of Economics, Virgin Tech.

Salehi-Isfahani, D. (2005). Human resources in Iran: Potentials and challenges. *Iranian Studies, 38*(1), 117–147.

Schomburg, H., & Teichler, U. (2006). *Higher education and graduate employment in Europe: Results from graduate surveys from twelve countries.* London: Springer.

Sen, A. (1999). *Development as a freedom.* Oxford: Oxford University Press.

Shaditalab, J. (2005). Iranian women: Rising expectations. *Critique: Critical Middle Eastern Studies, 14*(1), 35–55.

Shanahan, M. J., Mortimer, J. T., & Hannes, K. (2002). Adolescence and adult work in the twenty-first century. *Journal of Research on Adolescence, 12*(1), 99–120.

Shavarini, M. K. (2005). The feminisation of Iranian higher education. *International Review of Education, 5*(14), 329–347.

Statistics Centre of Iran (SCI). (2002). Salnameh amari keshvar (Annual statistics of Iran). Tehran, Iran.

Statistics Centre of Iran (SCI). (2007). Salnameh amari keshvar (Annual statistics of Iran). Tehran, Iran.

Statistics Centre of Iran (SCI). (2008). Salnameh amari keshvar (Annual statistics of Iran). Tehran, Iran.

Taleb, M., & Goodarzi, M. (2004). Ethnincity and gender: A study of ethnic groups in Sistan and Baluchestan. *A Quarterly Journal of the Centre for Women's Studies, 2*(1), 2–48.

Technical and Statistical Analyzing Office. (2002). *Barrasi vazeyat paziresh dar konkoor sarasari salhay 1374 ta 1381 be tafkik jens (A study on university admission in national exam during 1995–2002 by gender).* Tehran: Evaluation of Education Organization.

Technical and Statistical Analyzing Office. (2008). *Barrasi vazeyat paziresh dar konkoor sarasari salhay 1386–1387 be tafkik jens (A study on university admission in national exam during 2007–2008 by gender).* Tehran: Evaluation of Education Organization.

Webster, J. (2007). *Changing European gender relations: Gender equality policy concerning employment and the labour market.* Brussels: European Commission.

Chapter 13
Part II: Conclusion

Kate Thomas, Sue Jackson and Irene Malcolm

Part II has built upon the insights offered in Part I in exploring gendered choices and pathways into and within work. For example, Chap. 12's reporting of limitations placed on Iranian women's employment choices within specific sectors, including technical and engineering industries, provides an interesting international reflection of the underrepresentation of women in SET careers outlined by Herman et al. in Chap. 5. Each chapter in this section has also continued the exploration, begun in Part I, of the interaction of policy and experience and the way these interactions are crosscut by gender class and race. In different ways, from different cultural perspectives and using different methodological approaches, the authors have addressed the implications of differential access to lifelong learning opportunities in the form of work-based learning for the way in which women's economic participation is constructed and valued. All the authors have stressed the need for the work-based learning and skills agendas, and the funding regimes attached to them, to be responsive to the changing requirements and circumstances of women throughout their lives.

In discussing the ways in which work-based learning is shaped by and shapes identity, the chapters in Part II also anticipate the focus on gendered identities in Part III. Graduate mothers in Iran, low-paid female UNISON members, NVQ learners in the care professions—all of these are gendered identities which inform choices in lifelong learning. The next section takes up this theme in detail.

K. Thomas (✉)
Schools and Colleges Partnership Service, University of the West of England,
Frenchay Campus, Coldharbour Lane, BS16 1QD Bristol, UK
e-mail: kate2.thomas@uwe.ac.uk

S. Jackson et al. (eds.), *Gendered Choices*, Lifelong Learning Book Series 15,
DOI 10.1007/978-94-007-0647-7_13, © Springer Science+Business Media B.V. 2011

Part III
Identity, Intimacy and In/Formal Pathways

Chapter 14
Part III: Introduction

Sue Jackson, Irene Malcolm and Kate Thomas

The previous section considered gendered experiences of learning and the workplace, including the choices or lack of choices women feel are available to them, and ways in which 'choice' is exercised. This section moves on to explore the ways in which our gendered identities impact on 'choice', which itself is gendered. The authors in this final section consider aspects of women's gendered identities which inform the formal and informal lifelong learning pathways they take. They explore ways in which identities are developed by and through learning, work and intimate family and other networks. Common to all four chapters is the development of greater understandings of the gendered choices and constraints that impact upon women's lives, building and developing themes which have been interwoven throughout the book.

All four chapters in this section draw on empirical research to extend and develop arguments about ways in which gendered identities impact onto the choices that are made by women trying to access lifelong learning, as well as the real or perceived lack of choices. The research takes place in three countries (England, Wales and Canada) but the findings have a far greater reach, highlighting themes and issues that are relevant to a wider readership. For example, all chapters are concerned with the gendered nature of learning. The first two chapters are interested in vocational learning and its links to career and employment choices, including through the vocational degrees which have been developed within the knowledge economies of the developed world (Webb et al. 2006; Spring 2009); whilst the second two chapters are concerned with informal learning: Chap. 17 with the informal learning which takes place in (feminist) not-for-profit organisations, and Chap. 18 with informal learning in the (not so feminist) women's institutes. What all four chapters have in common is the exploration of gendered informal learning which is also constructed through differences of social class (Jackson 2003; Reay et al. 2005), and age. Whilst none of the chapters are explicitly concerned with race, it

S. Jackson (✉)
Birkbeck Institute for Lifelong Learning, Birkbeck University of London,
26 Russell Square, WC1B 5DQ London, UK
e-mail: s.jackson@bbk.ac.uk

S. Jackson et al. (eds.), *Gendered Choices*, Lifelong Learning Book Series 15,
DOI 10.1007/978-94-007-0647-7_14, © Springer Science+Business Media B.V. 2011

is of course the case that race structures the experiences of black and ethnicised women in places of learning (Mirza 2008) as does gender, social class and age.

The chapters all engage in a debate about the emotional labour which women undertake (Reay 2004) and the networks in which they participate (see in particular Chaps. 16 and 18). Emotional labour is about the management and display of feelings which will support the emotional wellbeing of others (Hochschild 1983), very evident here in the work undertaken by the early years workforce (see Chaps. 15 and 16). Whilst the accumulation of emotional capital that emotional labour requires can occur in the intimate networks described in Chap. 16, as Chaps. 15 and 17 show it is also accumulated in the workplace and within sites of formal and informal learning. Women arrive at the workplace and at their site of learning with a pool of emotional capital which is spent to the benefit of others (Burke and Jackson 2007). Diane Reay (2002) suggests that emotional capital is not just gendered but also classed although, as Chap. 18 indicates, in many ways middle-class women undertake emotional labour in similar ways to working-class women.

Both Chaps. 16 and 18 are concerned with the networks of intimacy within which women not only engage in emotional labour but also construct and reconstruct their identities. What is clear from the chapters in this section is that women require safe spaces where they can learn to re/construct their identities, including through vocational education and training (Chaps. 15 and 16) and through women-centred work and informal spaces (Chaps. 17 and 18). It is through the construction of identities that educational and career choices (or lack of choices) come about. As all the chapters in this section show, women—often bound into the work of emotional labour—can find it difficult to develop professional identities that are not embedded in constructions of gender and social class, as well as age. It has been argued that the meaning, significance and consequences of gender in the workplace varies according to the power differences which arise from the sex composition within an organisation's hierarchy. Nevertheless, this was not necessarily the case for the women represented in these chapters.

Forming a link between the previous section and this one, Chap. 15 examines work-based learning and transitions in professional identity through empirical research which investigates women in the early years workforce. In particular, Carrie Cable and Gill Goodliff explore the impact for women studying for a Foundation degree in early years education. In doing so, they explore some of the complexities for women who are engaged in work that is both gendered and classed. The women who undertake the Foundation degree are employed in a range of low-paid, low-status and often insecure early years work (Colley et al. 2003; Osgood 2006), including childminding, learning support assistants and teaching assistants. However, in addition to the physical labour of early years work, it also involves emotional labour (Colley 2006) and constructions of gender and class combine with vocational education and training, carrying high costs to those involved. As Colley (2006) demonstrates, emotional labour carries costs for those involved in early years work not just because children consume emotional resources, but because the emotional labour of early years workers is often controlled and exploited for profit by employers.

In their empirical work which considers gendered identities through early years education and labour; however, Cable and Goodliff show that engagement in vocational training can enhance gendered and classed identities, developing confidence in a new professional identity. Participants are able to draw on their programme of study, their work experience and, for many of those involved in this study, their experiences as mothers to enhance practice. Although the work in which they engage—both in their employment and as mothers—remains highly gendered, the women themselves feel a stronger sense of a positive identity which can transform their engagement with others.

Chapter 16 extends the discussion by considering gendered educational and career decision-making in networks of intimacy. Like the authors of the previous section, Alison Fuller, Ros Foskett, Brenda Johnson and Karen Paton also draw on empirical research which is concerned with the under-representation of significant parts of the population in higher education, both in the UK and internationally. Their concern is with the ways in which 'networks of intimacy', made up of family and friends, provides a critical context within which thinking about higher education is embedded and constructed. In doing so, they expose some of the assumptions which underpin much of the policy discourse on lifelong learning and educational 'choice'. They show how conflicting feelings of ambivalence may be explained in relation to gendered and classed norms and argue that having access to the different types of social capital available through networks of intimacy is relevant to understanding (gendered and classed) educational and career choices.

This chapter explores the complexities of women's lives as expressed through interpersonal ties and intimate network cultures. The authors challenge the notion of decision-making as an individualised process, and illuminate understandings of gendered choices. In particular, they disclose the normative discourses associated with female and male caring and economic roles, and the significance of these to educational and career decision-making. In doing so they draw attention to the ways in which women's (and men's) lives and choices are revealed through gendered roles and network cultures.

In Chap. 17, Leona English moves the debate from formal to informal learning, arguing that the informal learning sphere has been both under-funded and neglected. However, she shows that informal routes to lifelong learning have been, and remain, attractive to many women. In recent times, feminist non-profit organisations have become popular and public learning spaces for women, and have enabled women to engage with and actively pursue an effective social change agenda. The author argues that informal venues deserve closer attention in the lifelong learning policy agenda although, in doing so, she also shows that they are complex and contradictory sites of power, knowledge and resistances.

The author draws on a Foucauldian post-structuralism (see, e.g., Nicholson 1992; Ramazanoglu 1993; Weedon 1997) to look at the intersections of power and knowledge in the ways in which women engage in learning in particular sites of practice: feminist not-for-profit organisations. She shows how becoming part of a feminist community unit enables women to learn informally how collective voices may achieve social justice, opening up previously unimagined choices. Feminist pedagogic practices (Jackson 2004) enable new ways of knowing to be developed (Belenky et al. 1986), allowing ascribed identities to be resisted and new (feminist) identities to be constructed. The chapter concludes by arguing that women's choices and the re/constructions of their identities are affected by geography, social class and gender and by the interplay of power and resistances to power. The informal learning that is developed through the feminist not-for-profit organisations outlined in this research shows how central it is for safe spaces of informal learning to be developed for women in order to actively create and recreate subject re/positionings.

The final chapter of this section develops the theme of informal learning and safe spaces for women by examining the learning opportunities available to older women and the barriers they face in accessing learning in later years. It discusses older women's learning aspirations and shows that, even in retirement, choices for women are influenced by family responsibilities and expectations of the wider communities in which they live. In exploring these issues, the authors draw on detailed empirical research undertaken for an Economic and Social Research Council (ESRC)-funded project researching the National Federation of Women's Institutes in England and Wales. Jan Etienne and Sue Jackson illustrate the nature, type of learning and participation in later years as well as the choices open to women, although they also question the reality of 'choice', even for a group of seemingly more privileged women. They demonstrate how gendered identities are also differently determined by social class and by age, arguing that there is a clear indication that older women suffer a loss of identity due to changing roles in the family, retirement and to societal perceptions of older women.

Older women are often rendered invisible in a gendered society that additionally values youth over age, and one way to claim back an identity is through informal involvements and social network ties (MacRae 1990). The learning that takes place in the informal and safe social spaces of the women's institutes involves the re/construction of identities. The project of becoming (Burke and Jackson 2007) and the impact of developing confidence can be considerable for some women. In particular, the authors conclude that women-only spaces enable the development of emotional and learning spaces which are highly valued and which give women the ability to resist power relations elsewhere.

References

Belenky, M., Clinchy, B., Goldnerger, N., & Tarule, J. (1986). *Women's ways of knowing: The development of self, voice and mind.* New York: Basic Books.

Burke, P., & Jackson, S. (2007). *Reconceptualising lifelong learning: Feminist interventions.* London: Routledge.

Colley, H. (2006). Learning to labour with feeling: Class, gender and emotion in childcare education and training. *Contemporary Issues in Early Childhood, 7*(1), 15–29.

Colley, H., James, D., Tedder, M., & Diment, K. (2003). Learning as becoming in vocational education and training: Class, gender and the role of vocational habitus. *Journal of Vocational Education and Training, 55*(2), 471–496.

Hochschild, A. (1983). *The managed heart: Commercialization of human feeling.* Berkeley: University of California Press.

Jackson, S. (2003). Lifelong earning: Lifelong learning and working-class women. *Gender and Education, 15*(4), 365–376.

Jackson, S. (2004). *Differently academic? Developing lifelong learning for women in higher education.* Dordrecht: Kluwer.

Osgood, J. (2006). Professionalism and performativity: The feminist challenge facing early years practitioners. *Early Years, 26*(2), 187–199.

MacRae, H. (1990). Older women and identity maintenance in later life. *Canadian Journal on Aging, 9*(3), 248–267.

Mirza, H. (2008). *Race, gender and educational desire: Why black women succeed and fail.* London: Routledge.

Nicholson, L. (1992). Feminism and the politics of postmodernism. *Boundary, 19*(2), 53–69.

Ramazanoglu, C. (1993). *Up against Foucault: Explorations of some tensions between Foucault and feminism.* New York: Routledge.

Reay, D. (2002). Gendering Bourdieu's concept of capitals?: Emotional capital, women and social class. Paper presented at *Feminists Evaluate Bourdieu Conference*, Manchester University, October 11.

Reay, D. (2004). Gendering Bourdieu's concept of capitals?: Emotional capital, women and social class. In L. Adkins & B. Skeggs (Eds.). *Feminism after Bourdieu.* Oxford: Blackwell.

Reay, D., David, M., & Ball, S. (2005). *Degrees of choice: Social class, race and gender in higher education.* Staffs: Trentham.

Spring, J. (2009). *Globalization of education.* New York: Routledge.

Webb, S., Brine, J., & Jackson, S. (2006). Foundation degrees and the knowledge economy. *Journal of Vocational Education and Training: Special Issue on Gender Matters. Perspectives on Women, Work and Training, 58*(4), 563–576.

Weedon, C. (1997). *Feminist practice and poststructuralist theory* (2nd ed.). Oxford: Blackwell.

Chapter 15
Transitions in Professional Identity: Women in the Early Years Workforce

Carrie Cable and Gill Goodliff

Introduction

This chapter explores the impact of Foundation degree study on the changing professional identities of women, who comprise the majority of workers in the early years workforce. Historically, the care of young children has been seen as the (natural) preserve of women and as one that needs little knowledge and few, if any, formal qualifications save those gained through the experience of motherhood. The professionalisation of the early years workforce is seen as a key element in the English government's reform agenda for the early years and we consider some of the challenges early years students face in becoming reflective and reflexive practitioners within a strongly regulated environment.

Drawing on qualitative data from students, tutors and students' work, we examine the role that work-based learning plays in students' learning and transitions in their professional identities. In our study we were keen to explore students' and tutors' perceptions of the impact which studying the Open University (OU) Foundation degree in Early Years (FDEY)—and in particular studying the work-based learning modules—had on their academic and professional identity and practice. As part of an internally funded research study we surveyed the first cohort of students to study and complete the OU FDEY. This study followed up an earlier scrutiny and textual analysis of a sample of reflective accounts written by this cohort as the final assignment for the first work-based learning module during the academic year 2005 (Cable et al. 2007). Forty-eight students were sent a questionnaire, which could be completed anonymously, and there was a 50% return rate. We interviewed ten students who volunteered through their responses to the questionnaires. Students were also invited to submit postings to an electronic asynchronous course evaluation forum after they had completed the final assignment. There were 13 contributions to this forum; four contributions were from students who had also agreed to be interviewed. Overall we felt this was a good response rate although we acknowledge the possibility of bias insofar as respondents' views may not be fully

C. Cable (✉)
Department of Education, The Open University, Milton Keynes, UK
e-mail: c.e.cable@open.ac.uk

S. Jackson et al. (eds.), *Gendered Choices*, Lifelong Learning Book Series 15,
DOI 10.1007/978-94-007-0647-7_15, © Springer Science+Business Media B.V. 2011

representative of all students in the cohort. We also interviewed the four associate lecturers involved in tutoring the module.

In the following discussion we draw on commentaries relating to the development of students' professional identities and in particular their relationships with colleagues in their settings, other colleagues they come into contact with as part of their professional practice and their fellow students. However, we begin by providing an overview of the development in the United Kingdom (UK) of Foundation degrees, which have a strong vocational orientation and relationship with the aims of widening participation in higher education, an element of lifelong learning. We focus, in particular, on the introduction of FDEY for practitioners working with young children from birth to 7 years and describe the key features, learning experiences and expectations of the two work-based learning modules (an integral feature of all Foundation degrees) in the OU FDEY.

Foundation degrees and Work-Based Learning

Foundation degrees are vocational qualifications (and embrace a number of professions within study disciplines), designed to integrate academic study with work-based learning. Located within the Intermediate level of the Framework for Higher Education Qualifications (FHEQ), they were introduced in England, Wales and Northern Ireland in 2001 with the aim of enabling adults to continue working while studying for a higher-level qualification. Foundation degrees are recognised as an award equivalent to level 5 (of 8) within the National Qualification Framework (QCA 2009). They are equivalent to the first two years of higher education study. A shared feature of all Foundation degrees includes a clearly articulated progression route that offers students the opportunity to 'top-up' with additional study and assessment in order to achieve a bachelors degree with honours. It is this latter award that in Europe, under the terms of the Bologna declaration, Bergen (2005) would represent the end of the first cycle of higher education qualifications.

The reviews of Foundation degrees in England, carried out in 2004–2005 (Quality Assurance Agency for Higher Education 2005), have shown that since 2002 the provision of Foundation degree programmes has increased. There has also been significant growth in applications and enrolments and clear evidence that students who were being recruited to these programmes were those 'who might not otherwise enter HE' (p. 8). The introduction by the Department for Education and Skills (DfES) of the Early Years Sector-Endorsed Foundation degrees (DfES 2001), that included the incentive of a financial support package, is cited as being a contributory factor for 'Education Studies' being the subject area with the largest number of enrolled students. The expectation was that participants would be 'returners' to learning and have competing commitments beyond their employment that required them to 'juggle responsibilities' (at home and in the workplace) with their studies (DfES 2001, p. 11). A longitudinal study evaluating Early Years Sector Endorsed Foundation degrees (see for example Mowlam et al. 2003; Knight et al. 2006;

Snape et al. 2007) found that the majority of students were female, over 25 years, and perceived work-based learning as attractive and a valuable component of the degree.

Work-based learning is not a new phenomenon, especially within initial training and continuing professional development programmes for practitioners working with children and young people. However the integration of work-based learning into higher education courses for early years practitioners in the UK context has previously been associated with the training of teachers, especially through Early Childhood or Bachelor of Education degrees, and has often been referred to as teaching practice/practicum with the underlying assumption that student teachers are putting into practice what they have learnt somewhere else.

The new FDEYs are not aimed primarily at teachers or those who wish to enter teaching but at the wide variety of other practitioners who support children's learning and development from birth to 5 years: they form part of a government agenda to develop a 'professional' workforce in the early years (CWDC 2006; DfES 2006) and are now seen as a key element in the progression route to the graduate Early Years Professional Status (EYP) (CWDC 2006). Higher education work-based learning courses do not, therefore, form part of initial training but at the same time they are not exactly continuing professional development. Boud et al. (2001) describe them as 'a class of university programmes that bring together universities and work organisations to create new learning in workplaces' (p. 4).

However, there is at least another element involved in work-based learning that forms part of Foundation degree study in the early years. The government workforce reform agenda includes competency frameworks developed for those studying FDEYs (DfES 2001) and for those wishing to achieve (EYP) (CWDC 2006). The associated assessment requirements influence both the content and structure of work-based learning modules, the relationships that universities have with workplace settings and student relationships with those they work with on a day-to-day basis. The challenge for course providers is to ensure that the tenets of higher education—including enabling the development of thinking, questioning individuals—are not subjugated to the acquisition of a set of externally derived and culturally and historically situated attributes.

Views about children and childhood are not static or universal and policy, procedures and practice are constantly emerging and subject to change and contestation (Moss 2008; Waller 2005; Woodhead 2008). The challenge for students is to develop the ability to balance the messages they receive relating to policy and practice through government documents, leaders in the workplace and established workplace cultures, with the demands of their study which is encouraging them to reflect, question and explore their own ideas, values, behaviours and practices. Such a critically reflective position 'is inevitably risky—people who take this position risk alienating others and being alienated from them' (MacNaughton 2005, p. 202).

In work-based learning, learners and learning are viewed as inseparable from workplace settings. Students are not in the traditional higher education situation (for professionally related courses of study) of applying a developing understanding of theory and research to practical situations (although students will be involved in doing this) but rather relating their knowledge and understanding of practice, and their own practice in their own setting in particular, to their developing understanding of theoretical frameworks and perspectives and research findings. These courses attract students who are already experienced practitioners and who have developed their practice through their everyday work and relationships with more experienced others through an apprenticeship model of learning (Wenger 1998). Some have pursued training courses but many have not. Most of the students on the FDEY are women and mothers who draw on their experience of being women and mothers in their practice. Many draw on their mostly implicit knowledge, beliefs and understandings but lack confidence in their ability to articulate their views or understandings of why they do the things they do in the way that they do them.

The Early Years Foundation degree at the Open University

The OU Sector-Endorsed FDEY commenced in 2003. It is offered part-time by supported distance learning. Students are drawn from practitioners working in a diverse range of early years settings including home-based (self-employed) child-minders, nursery and pre-school staff, learning support assistants (LSAs), teaching assistants (TAs) and higher level teaching assistants (HLTAs) in schools, and practitioners working in the new multi-disciplinary Children's Centres.[1] There are no entry requirements for OU study so students also come with a varied experience of prior study and training and from across the UK. Students study two 30-credit, knowledge-based modules and one 60-credit, work-based learning module at (Certificate) Level 4. At Level 5 (Intermediate), students choose from a number of optional modules and take a second compulsory 60-credit, work-based learning module. Both work-based learning modules require students to participate in online discussion forums and to carry out personal research in their workplaces as well as other activities.

The aims of the OU FDEY are twofold: to develop and enhance in students the intellectual and practical skills required for working as senior practitioners in the early years and to prepare them to engage with further study and enquiry through developing skills of critical questioning and reflection. As with other Foundation degrees for early years practitioners, the OU Foundation degree 'enables students to learn by examining attitudes, perceptions and realities relating to their own practice in the workplace' (O'Keefe and Tait 2004, p. 28). For students this is a journey with different starting and end points. The position of many of those working in the early years field, traditionally a low-paid, low-status and gender-stereotyped (Colley et al. 2003; Osgood 2004) occupation where individuals have limited autonomy,

---

[1] There are a number of job titles for adults working in early years contexts in England. Some commentators would refer to these as 'para-professional' roles.

can mean that students pass through a number of different transitions, both personal and professional during their journey.

In developing work-based learning materials, and providing support for students studying at a distance, we[2] have sought to enable students to explore international perspectives on learning, child development and professionalism and to develop their understanding of the historical, social and cultural influences on developments in the UK. Our modules are also informed by socio-cultural perspectives that view learning and meaning making as situated in a process of social participation. Learning is thus relational and found in daily conversations and interactions with others. Through situated learning (Lave and Wenger 1991) in the workplace and the online discussion forums students can find that their values, beliefs, views and practices are confirmed and validated but more often they find they are in a position where they are challenged and where they need to accommodate new understandings and apply these to their practice and relationships with children and adults. The active participation and process of reflection that work-based learning offers has the potential to transform students' personal and professional learning. Lave and Wenger (1991) highlight this by stating that thinking and learning is situated in participation in communities of practice where '…it [learning] is mediated by differences of perspective amongst co-participants' (p. 15).

Learning involves social participation and work-based learning provides opportunities for social interaction. Wenger (1998, p. 5) identifies four components in this process of learning:

1. Meaning: a way of talking about our changing ability—individually and collectively—to experience our life and the world as meaningful.
2. Practice: a way of talking about the shared historical and cultural resources, frameworks, and perspectives that can sustain mutual engagement in action.
3. Community: a way of talking about the social configurations in which our enterprises are defined as worth pursuing and our participation is recognised as competence.
4. Identity: a way of talking about how learning changes who we are and creates personal histories of becoming in the context of our communities.

Work-based learning modules thus can empower students to review their participation in their 'community of practice'—be it an early years classroom, children's centre or childminding setting—to co-construct (together with the children and colleagues within and beyond their setting) meanings and new knowledge about themselves and the activities they engage in. Rogoff (2003, p. 285) argues that 'mutual understanding occurs *between* people in interaction'. The process of participation with others is thus agentive for the learners. We will return to this later on in the chapter in discussions relating to transitions in students' professional identity.

---

[2] The OU FDEY academic team.

Developing Reflection

The first two 30-credit, work-related modules focus on building knowledge, understanding and skills to support practitioners to reflect on their role in working with and supporting young children. Students are introduced to Schön's (1983) work and encouraged to explore the distinction between 'reflection-in-action'—thinking on your feet and 'reflection-on-action'—thinking after the event (Craft and Paige-Smith 2007). These early modules are explicitly designed for students entering higher education and academic study either for the first time or after a long period away from study. When students progress to the first work-based learning module they are expected to use the acquired underpinning knowledge and skills—such as the analysis of theoretical concepts, the organisation and articulation of opinions and arguments, reflecting on their own and others' values, and taking account of appropriate conventions for academic writing—as the basis for developing their practice and documenting and presenting evidence. Work-based learning involves continuing interaction between their academic study and their professional practice in the workplace. As part of the assessment process students are required to document and present evidence against 12 core learning outcomes set out in the Statement of Requirement (DfES 2001). These are externally ascribed competences designed to create a standardised notion of professionalism for early years practitioners.

The course materials aim to build on the notion of 'reflective practice' to describe a way of approaching their work that involves questioning why and how they do something while they are actually doing it; the students are introduced to a structured, four stage, Reflective Practice Cycle (RPC). Designed to support them as they think about and question different aspects of their practice (including working with parents and other professionals; promoting children's learning and development; and promoting children's rights and child protection) the four stages of the Reflective Practice Cycle cover:

- Thinking about my practice
- Exploring my practice
- Reflecting on my practice
- Documenting evidence of my practice

One student considered that there were pivotal points or points of transition in her study particularly in terms both of her relationships with parents and other professionals, and in how she viewed herself:

> I think there have been huge changes, particularly [in the first work based learning module] we had a questionnaire on communication with parents and other professionals and that was a huge sort of turning point for me, I approached the reception class teacher and the preschool leader and asked questions about how we communicate and how it can be improved and I find that we have a much more professional understanding of each other now. I am quite happy to speak to anyone involved with the children on a higher level than I was before, so I feel more knowledgeable now. (Student 5, Childminder)

Childminders often position themselves as having lower status than others working with young children (Griffin 2008). We would argue therefore that this quote from a childminder illustrates how early years practitioners can view their own knowledge developed through experience and practice in the home as less significant than that learnt through formal study. It suggests that membership of the work-based learning community endowed this childminder with a newly negotiated professional identity (Osgood 2006b).

In working through the Reflective Practice Cycle three times students explore, and are encouraged to begin to articulate, the 'hidden' values and beliefs that underpin their professional practice. Students are also introduced to a Three Layer Model of Professional Practice. Like the metaphor of the iceberg which Goodfellow (2004) employs (drawing on Fish 1998), this was developed to enable students to visualise the moving interactions between their day-to-day practice and how their knowledge, values and beliefs influence the ways they work and their interactions with children and other adults. It is the hidden knowledge that is not readily articulated—comprising values and beliefs, hidden assumptions and ideas about child development, culture and society—that it is hoped students will be able to expose and begin to articulate with colleagues in the workplace, with fellow students in the online forum and tutorials and in assignments submitted for assessment. As Goodfellow (2004, p. 68) suggests: 'It is important to address hidden qualities and dimensions of our professional practice if we are to improve our way of being professional.' The first three stages of the reflective practice cycle—thinking about, exploring and analysing their practice—provides the framework for writing reflective accounts of the process of investigation. The fourth stage in our RPC, which involves documenting evidence in a Practice Evidence File, also provides a source of material for the students' analytical writing. Goodfellow (2004, p. 64) suggests: 'Professional portfolios provide a way of not only getting inside practice but interrogating those practices through gaining insight into one's thinking and professional decision making.'

The second work-based learning module, and final module in the FDEY, is designed to support students in further developing their academic and professional identities. It aims to encourage greater critical reflection about children's care and education and their role. The following comment clearly describes a transition from the way the student positions herself based on her perceptions that others view her ('just as someone who works with the children') to a view of herself as an active member of a team—as someone who can contribute to discussions with other professionals about support for children's learning. It can also be argued that academic study has contributed to the individual empowerment this student feels.

> Again I think it is—because I am more confident now in my role and having confidence in understanding of theories behind things, I feel more competent and more able to talk to other colleagues, other professionals, especially external professionals and I have been involved with the educational psychologist and also more recently with a speech and language therapist for a child in the class that I work and I think its given me more of a partnership place with them rather than just somebody who worked with the children and perhaps threw a few ideas at them, I now feel that we work together more on a team basis. (Student 9, HLTA)

Refining skills of 'reflection-on-action' (Schön 1987) remain critical but the focus in this second work-based learning course is the process of researching practice. By undertaking the role of a researcher, practitioners investigate the 'voices' of children in their settings. Developing a reflexive approach is nurtured throughout the course to enable the students to become increasingly aware of their own influence on the children, the environments they provide and their relationships with colleagues and parents. Evaluating leadership skills and exploring and responding to change—two crucial facets of the professional role and responsibilities of a senior practitioner form the lens for these reflective investigations:

> My childminding setting is now run in almost equal partnership with the children. I am able to share my knowledge with other childminders, pre-school, school and other agencies. I am better able to support, [and share] experience and ideas with my supported childminders. (Student 5, Childminder)

> In the middle of a discussion with a Practitioner recently I realised that I was describing Bronfenbrenner's theory and actually understood what I was talking about. ...As a Manager I have always had to lead the setting and the course has enabled me to be more reflective and hopefully a more leaderful leader. (Student 10 in the online evaluation forum)

In this second work-based learning module students use research tools drawn from the Mosaic approach (Clark and Moss, 2001) to investigate the lived experience of children in their settings. This approach to researching and listening to children's views encourages practitioners to view children as active participants in their own learning and environments. Students gather data from four small-scale studies in their setting that focus on the following features of provision and practice:

- Children's environments for care, learning and development
- Support for children's personal, social and emotional development
- Co-ordinating and evaluating the curriculum for children's care, learning and development
- Promoting participation and inclusion

Again the emphasis is on students using the same framework to repeat an investigation in their workplace with a requirement to share their findings with colleagues and critically evaluate both their findings and their colleagues' responses. Students are expected to utilise the analysis of their data from each of the investigations in four critical written evaluations of their professional practice that they submit for assessment during the course. An extended written account that synthesises the evaluations of their professional development as they have researched the views of children in their setting is submitted as an end of course assignment together with separate explanations of the evidence they have documented against the learning outcomes in their portfolios. Five students mentioned the significant impact that the Mosaic approach had on their ability to initiate discussions and bring about change. One said

> It has been the single most significant aspect of the course for me. The use of Mosaic tools and the theoretical approaches have formed the basis for discussions with my colleagues in

bringing about changes to my setting from the child's perspective. (Student 11 in the online evaluation forum)

The module is organised in six study blocks. Each block explores theoretical perspectives and wider empirical research associated with the practice features that the students research in their workplace. During each of their four investigations all students are expected to participate in and contribute to, time-limited, asynchronous online, tutor group discussions and also broader 'route' discussions. Students select a 'route' to follow through the course based on the age of the children they work with and their role in the workplace. The tutor group forums are facilitated by the students themselves, whilst the 'route' forums are moderated by tutors. Student commentaries suggest that these online forums offer a valuable opportunity to engage with, and be challenged by, different ideas and perspectives (Goodliff and Twining 2008), thus contributing to transitions in their confidence and professional identities. MacNaughton (2005, p. 201) highlights the 'transformative' nature of 'learning with others to link knowledge and practice' and to change 'how we think and act'.

Developing the Confidence to Act

The following postings to an online forum where students were invited to evaluate the module contain many references to an increase in confidence particularly in terms of students' ability to reflect on their practice, articulate ideas and communicate these to others. For example, one student said 'the course has developed my confidence on looking at my practice more reflectively, and through the eyes of the child' whilst another student said she was 'able to articulate and support my ideas much better and with greater confidence'. Another student mentioned that she had 'become more confident as I have travelled through the FDEY and find myself speaking up if I think I need to, being in a more knowledgeable frame of mind' and another student claimed that 'reflective practice is such an eye opener…I have definitely gained in confidence and am much more confident in my approach to fellow practitioners and other professionals'.

Participating in online forums also contributes to the acquisition of ICT skills, another important aspect of students' development in terms of both of their academic study and their professional practice. It is an area where many (although not all) students feel they have developed knowledge, skills and confidence:

I think I am a lot more confident now in addressing ICT. I don't shy away from it. Before I shied away from any kind of ICT skills, in the classroom as well I would always say, 'oh no I can't do ICT' and I would actually think—'oh don't ask me', but I think now I am a lot more confident,…and I hope I pass that on to the children who I work with that it is alright to have a go, it doesn't matter if you get it wrong and I think that's most important… sometimes things do go wrong and sometimes you don't know how to work things and it is alright to do so. (Student 12, Teaching Assistant)

Tutor comments acknowledge students' developing confidence in articulating their growing knowledge and understanding, showing how the process of articulation gives the women strength and endorses emerging views of themselves as professionals. Adopting a critical reflective position that questions and dares to challenge prevailing 'truths' relating to children's development and learning and their professional role requires confidence (Osgood 2006b; MacNaughton 2005). One tutor described how she saw some of her students enacting this in their relationships with colleagues.

> I think their confidence there has really come up, because about, I should say it's about six of them I can think of, who've actually said to me I can actually contribute to this conversation now, at the planning meeting and not feel as if I might be out talked by another member of staff, or that they feel their opinion, that they can actually contribute to a decent discussion at training meetings...some of their schools they're at are very hierarchical, you know qualified NVQ teaching assistants are still called Welfare, the Welfare, the Welfare Team or something so that, those students in particular it's really helped them to say no, no I'm a qualified member of staff and I do know what I'm talking about and I can offer a discussion.

Developing confidence in their own ability to engage with others from a secure knowledge base and through reflection on their own practice and the practice of others enables practitioners to develop or enhance their professional identities. Having the confidence to engage with others also involves taking the initiative to make spaces for their voices to be heard and a willingness to take risks. As students begin to recognise their own agency they can become informed active participants in decision making and contribute to change.

Professional Identity

Defining what 'professionalism' looks like in the early years is the subject of much debate in the UK and elsewhere. The diverse profile of early years practitioners, the variety of workplace settings, roles, resources and regulation that cover the age range (Blenkin and Yue 1994; Moss and Penn 1996) has made it difficult for agreement to be reached on what should constitute a corpus of professional knowledge. Osgood (2006a, p. 192) argues that the notion of professionalism being promoted through the reform agenda in early years in the UK context is 'highly problematic and politicised' and that 'the increased demands to demonstrate competence mean that professional judgement is subordinated to the requirements of performativity'. Moss (2003) argues that the training and assessment routes for the Senior Practitioner role associated with the FDEY and subsequently the Early Years Professional role, reflect a 'technician' model of training, in that they are based on a standards framework and have nationally prescribed outcomes.

However, being a professional in the early years (and in a number of other contexts) encompasses more than just professional knowledge or a set of competences; it also includes skills, dispositions, values and beliefs, the 'tools' of a profession and notions of professional expertise. As Osgood (2006a, p. 191, drawing on Katz

1995) notes, 'It is widely acknowledged that the nature of early years work demands strong feelings towards protecting and supporting children and engaging empathetically with a child's wider family and community.' While feelings and emotion and even passion (Moyles 2001) are generally acknowledged as important elements within the field of early years they do not feature highly within the masculinised constructions of professionalism which favour competences and performativity and seek to limit both autonomy and personal agency.

Moyles (2001, p. 89) suggests that 'professionalism' is related to thinking about facets of one's role and that 'it requires high levels of professional knowledge coupled with self-esteem and self-confidence'. The ability to reflect on practice is an important component in developing professional and pedagogical knowledge, understanding and practice (see Menmuir and Hughes 2004; Dahlberg et al. 1999). Developing students' ability to reflect on their practice is a critical element in transforming personal and professional views of self.

> On a personal level I feel every aspect of my practice has been enhanced. I feel well informed and far more up-to-date with developments in the early years than many of my colleagues. (Student 10, Teaching Assistant)

> I do feel that I am much more professional now in my attitude to my work...I am the one that does all the reading and updating everybody on changes in policy, or any news that is about to do with early years, that is kind of my job now at meetings and I will be running our group soon as well and I am hoping to encourage people to develop their practice more. (Student 6, Childminder)

Oberheumer (2005) suggests that informed professional action requires a willingness to reflect on one's own taken for granted beliefs and an understanding that knowledge is contestable. The responses of the students we surveyed suggest an increased sense of their ability to communicate their understanding of theory and research through discussions and presentations. A tutor talked about the importance of supporting students in developing their ability to discuss, articulate, reflect and share their developing knowledge and understanding. The ability to communicate understanding is an important aspect of professional identity formation and through doing so students make learning their own. The following quote illustrates this transition in professional identity:

> But when we get further into it, because the language that they use is completely different... the level of the language demonstrates more understanding, more knowledge and I think the way that I supported that is by encouraging them to discuss, to have the confidence to share, to share, not only on conference, but when they have been in tutor group...but during the tutorials we've managed to get some really good work done that gives me evidence of their, of their development of their practice and knowledge.

The questionnaire returns in our survey indicate that 92% of students felt that their study had enhanced their underpinning knowledge of relevant theory and research to a significant or considerable extent and 71% of students felt that their study had enabled them to communicate ideas more effectively to a significant or considerable extent. The following comment illustrates one student's feelings about her own personal and professional growth and the recognition of this by others:

> I think because my confidence and because of the activities and things that I did on this course, they seem to listen to me more and come to me more for advice. I mean obviously I was offered this new job and that's because of the qualification and the work that I have done on this course and I think they listen to me more now rather than just someone working within the setting, they actually you know actually think that I have got something to say! (Student 18, LSA)

As we showed above, the concept of community is important in understanding how early years practitioners move through and move to understanding. Seeing development as 'a transformation of participation of people engaged in shared endeavours avoids the idea that the social world is external to the individual and that development consists of acquiring knowledge and skills' (Rogoff 1998, p. 691). Women undertaking work-based learning are already part of various communities and their study, together with opportunities to share understandings with peers and tutors, and to observe and imitate the practices of others, enables them to participate in and become members of broader communities and to construct for themselves a professional identity within their own community.

> The person is defined by, as well as defining, these relations. Learning thus implies becoming a different person with respect to the possibilities enabled by these systems of relations. To ignore this aspect is to overlook the fact that learning involves the construction of identities. (Lave and Wenger 1991, p. 53)

Conclusion

We acknowledge that the data we draw on in this chapter represent the voices of a small number of students following a particular form of higher education study—work-based learning through distance learning. The data do not represent the whole current student group on our Foundation degree or even the whole cohort of first 'graduates'. These are the comments of students who continued through to the last course, a minority of those who began their studies on the Foundation degree. It is likely that those who chose to participate in our research were those who felt they had gained most from their studies. Students were also asked about the challenges they faced and these included carrying out tasks in the workplace; the difficulties they had in collecting and documenting evidence of their practice; their powerlessness in bringing about change in their settings; and the difficulties they experienced grappling with new ideas and in preparing assignments. As women they were involved in the juggling act that many women with family and domestic responsibilities who work outside the home carry out when they choose to engage in study. In talking about the difficulties and challenges they faced, most students also talked about how they overcame them and demonstrated great persistence and resolve—including developing the confidence to ask for and give help to their fellow students. Many mentioned the support their families provided as well as support from tutors and course materials. The data have provided us with much to reflect on in terms of how we support students who are new to higher education or returning to study after a long period of absence, who lack confidence in terms of their professional role and knowledge base as well as their ability to engage in study at HE level and who are working in a profession which is still viewed by many as 'women's work' and an extension of the natural mothering role.

Our study suggests that the content of the work-based learning modules and the journey that we support students through has the potential to enable many of them to develop a professional identity by the end of the Foundation degree—an identity that is based on a strong specialist knowledge base in terms of theoretical understanding and the achievement of the externally recognised learning outcomes but also, and significantly, the ability to relate and reflect on this learning and knowledge in terms of their practice. The notion of a developing community of practice is useful in considering what we aim to achieve through supported work-based learning:

> A community of practice is not merely a community of interest. It brings together practitioners who are involved in doing something. Over time, they accumulate practical knowledge in their domain, which makes a difference to their ability to act individually and collectively. (Wenger 2004, p. 3)

Many students in our survey talked about the development of their confidence in communicating with their colleagues and underpinning this were feelings that they are more knowledgeable, are able to contribute more, are more respected by colleagues and feel themselves to be more professional. This has impacted on their working relationships and in some cases transformed the way they see themselves and the way others see them. We would argue that until students have developed their own 'voice' they are unable to bring about changes in their own practice (through rationalisation of the reasons for the change) and in the practice in their settings (through the ability to communicate the reasons to others).

The development of students' confidence in their ability to communicate their new knowledge and understanding to colleagues in the workplace and to their tutors in face-to-face sessions, electronic forums and in their essays reflects the transitions and journey students have made. It could be argued that for these students it is about contesting, questioning and developing a critical attitude and about opening up space to think about how it might be possible to do things differently—giving them the confidence to push against their own boundaries and boundaries in their workplaces. For some students this increase in confidence has enabled them to move from a position where they want to give up or change jobs—from feeling disempowered—to a position where they recognise their own agency and how they might bring about change in their own practice and relationships (the ability to act individually) and even make a contribution to change in their own settings (the ability to act collectively).

> I think *my colleagues now understand that,* you know because I have studied, that *perhaps I have a greater insight* into what it is that affects children's learning and perhaps, although I am a non teaching staff member, *I still have a knowledge* and because I have studied recently that *perhaps I have newer insights than they have,* there is something that I can give that they can't give, but also they recognise now that as I have studied and I have that knowledge of theory base if you like, that *perhaps things that I can give to them can enhance what they do* and *I feel I have become a better team member for that.* (Student 9, HLTA) (italics added)

For many women working in the early years (and we would argue elsewhere), developing confidence is a fundamental part of developing a professional identity and opens up the possibilities of acting collectively to define what professionalism in the early years should entail.

References

Bergen Conference of European Ministers Responsible for Higher Education. (19–20 May 2005). http://www.bolognabergen2005.no/EN/BASIC/050520_Framework_qualifications.pdf. Accessed 3 May 2008.
Blenkin, G. M., & Yue, N. Y. L. (1994). Profiling early years practitioners: Some first impressions from a national survey. *Early Years, 15*(1), 13–22.
Boud, D., Solomon, N., & Symes, C. (2001). New practices for new times. In D. Boud & N. Solomon (Eds.), *Work-based learning: A new higher education?* Buckingham: Open University Press.
Cable, C., Goodliff, G., & Miller, L. (2007). Developing reflective early years practitioners within a regulatory framework. *Malaysian Journal of Distance Education, 9*(2), 1–20.
Children's Workforce Development Council (CWDC). (2006). *Early year professional prospectus.* Leeds: CWDC.
Clark, A., & Moss, P. (2001). *Listening to young children: The mosaic approach.* London: National Children's Bureau and Joseph Rowntree Foundation.
Colley, H., James, D. J., Tedder, M., & Diment, K. (2003). Learning as becoming in vocational education and training: Class, gender and the role of vocational habitus. *Journal of Vocational Education and Training, 55*(4), 471–496.
Craft, A., & Paige-Smith, A. (2007). Reflective practice. In L. Miller & C. Cable (Eds.), *Professionalism in the early years* (pp. 87–97). London: Hodder.
Dahlberg, G., Moss, P., & Pence, A. (1999). *Beyond quality in early childhood education and care.* London: Falmer.
Department for Education and Skills (DfES). (2001). *Statement of requirement: Early years sector-endorsed foundation degree.* Nottingham: DfES.
Department for Education and Skills (DfES). (2006). *Children's workforce strategy: Building a word-class workforce for children, young people and families: The Government's response to the consultation.* Nottingham: DfES.
Fish, D. (1998). *Appreciating practice in the caring professions: Refocusing professional development and practitioner research.* Oxford: Butterworth Heinemann.
Goodfellow, J. (2004). Documenting professional practice through the use of a professional portfolio. *Early Years, 24*(1), 63–74.
Goodliff, G., & Twining, P. (2008). Computer mediated communication: Using e-learning to support professional development. In L. Miller & C. Cable (Eds.), *Professionalism in the early years* (pp. 98–108). London: Hodder.
Griffin, S. (2008). The 'P' word and home-based child carers. In L. Miller & C. Cable (Eds.), *Professionalism in the early years* (pp. 65–74). London: Hodder.
Knight, T., Tennant, R., Dillon, L., & Weddell, E. (2006). Evaluating the early years sector endorsed foundation degree—a qualitative study of students' views and experiences. London, National Centre for Social Research for the DfES, Research Briefing RB751.
Lave, J., & Wenger, E. (1991). *Situated learning: Legitimate peripheral participation.* Cambridge: Cambridge University Press.
MacNaughton, G. (2005). *Doing Foucault in early childhood studies: Applying poststructural ideas.* London: Routledge.
Menmuir, J., & Hughes, A. (2004). Early education and childcare: The developing professional. *European Early Childhood Education Research Journal, 12*(2), 33–41.

Moss, P. (2003). Structures, understandings and discourses: Possibilities for reenvisioning the early childhood worker. *Contemporary Issues in Early Childhood, 7*(1), 30–41.

Moss, P. (2008). The democratic and reflective professional: Rethinking and reforming the early years workforce. In L. Miller & C. Cable (Eds.), *Professionalism in the early years* (pp. 121–130). London: Hodder.

Moss, P., & Penn, H. (1996). *Transforming nursery education*. London: Paul Chapman.

Mowlam A., Murphy M., & Arthur S. (2003). Evaluating the introduction of the early years foundation degree. London: National Centre for Social Research (NATCEN).

Moyles, J. (2001). Passion, paradox and professionalism in early years education. *Early Years, 21*(2), 81–95.

Oberheumer, P. (2005). Conceptualising the early childhood pedagogue: Policy approaches and issues of professionalism. *European Early Childhood Education Research Journal, 13*(1), 5–15.

O'Keefe, J., & Tait, K. (2004). An examination of the UK Early Years Foundation Degree and the evolution of senior practitioners—Enhancing work-based learning by engaging in reflective and critical thinking. *International Journal of Early Years Education, 12*(1), 25–41.

Osgood, J. (2004). Time to get down to business? The responses of early years practitioners to entrepreneurial approaches to professionalism. *Journal of Early Childhood Research, 2*, 5–24.

Osgood, J. (2006a). Professionalism and performativity: The feminist challenge facing early years practitioners. *Early Years, 26*(2), 187–199.

Osgood, J. (2006b). Deconstructing professionalism in early childhood education: Resisting the regulatory gaze. *Contemporary Issues in Early Childhood, 7*(1), 5–14.

Quality Assurance Agency for Higher Education. (2005). *Learning from reviews of Foundation Degrees in England carried out in 2004–05*. Gloucester: QAA. (Also available online www.qaa.ac.uk).

Quality Assurance Agency for Higher Education. (2009). Qualifications can cross boundaries—A rough guide to comparing qualifications in the UK and Ireland. http://www.qaa.ac.uk/standardsandquality/otherrefpoints/Qualsboundaries09.pdf. Accessed 27 May 2009.

Rogoff, B. (1998). Cognition as a collaborative process. In E. Damon et al. (Ed.), *Handbook of child psychology* (5th ed., Vol. 2). New York: Wiley.

Rogoff, B. (2003). *The cultural nature of human development*. New York: Oxford University Press.

Schön, D. (1983). *The reflective practitioner: How professionals think in action*. New York: Basic Books.

Schön, D. (1987). *Educating the reflective practitioner*. San Francisco: Jossey-Bass.

Snape, D., Parfrement, J., Finch, S., & National Centre for Social Research. (2007). *Evaluation of the early years sector endorsed Foundation Degree: Findings from the final student survey*. London: DfES.

Waller, T. (2005). Modern childhood: Contemporary theories and children's lives. T. Waller (Ed.), *An introduction to early childhood. A multidisciplinary approach*. London: Paul Chapman.

Wenger, E. (1998). *Communities of practice; Learning, meaning and identity*. Cambridge: Cambridge University Press.

Wenger, E. (2004). Knowledge management as a doughnut. Shaping your knowledge strategy through communities of practice. *Ivy Business Journal, January/February*: http://www.itu.dk/people/petero/speciale/Wenger%20knowledge%20management.pdf (last accessed 7th February 2012).

Woodhead, M. (2008). Promoting young children's development: Implications of the UN convention on the rights of the child. In L. Miller & C. Cable (Eds.), *Professionlism in the early years* (pp. 154–156). London: Hodder.

Chapter 16
'Getting by' or 'Getting Ahead'? Gendered Educational and Career Decision-Making in Networks of Intimacy

Alison Fuller, Rosalind Foskett, Brenda Johnston and Karen Paton

Introduction

In social network analysis it is social relationships rather than individuals that form the unit of analysis. A key strength of this approach is that it prevents decisions and behaviour being viewed as either individually or structurally determined. This chapter draws on research[1] that is examining the potential of network data to help explain educational decision-making, with a specific focus on Higher Education (HE) in the United Kingdom. The study is designed to explore the ways in which 'networks of intimacy' (Heath and Cleaver 2003) made up of family and friends may provide a critical context within which thinking about HE is embedded and co-constructed. The following discussion represents an early attempt to explore the network of intimacy as the unit of analysis for understanding decisions about education, including the decision to participate, or not, in HE. For the purposes of this chapter, we are focusing on one network which we suggest is illustrative of (among other issues) the gendered nature of educational 'choices' and transitions.

In focusing on the interpersonal ties between family and friends, we aim to avoid the assumptions which underpin much of the policy discourse on lifelong learning (LLL) and educational 'choice' and which, for example, have been exposed by critical feminist theorists (*inter alia* Brine 1999; Jackson 2007; Burke and Jackson 2007; Leathwood and Francis 2006). These include treating identity as fluid and flexible (*inter alia* Bradley 1997; Halford and Leonard 2006); the individual in isolation from gender, class and race, and decision-making as individualised:

---

[1] The research is funded under the UK's Economic and Social Research Council's Teaching and Learning Research Programme under the title 'Non-participation in Higher Education: decision-making as an embedded social practice' (award number: RES 139-25-0232).

A. Fuller (✉)
Lifelong and Work-Related Learning Research Centre, University of Southampton, Southampton, UK
e-mail: a.fuller@soton.ac.uk

S. Jackson et al. (eds.), *Gendered Choices*, Lifelong Learning Book Series 15,
DOI 10.1007/978-94-007-0647-7_16, © Springer Science+Business Media B.V. 2011

Learners are conceptualised outside of social structures, without identities or subject positionings, and are seen as highly individualised beings within a neo-liberal model based on
deficit. (Burke and Jackson 2007, p. 14)

There is also the unhelpful and persistent policymaker error of using qualifications
as proxies for skills, knowledge and understanding, which leads to the 'read across'
that those with few or low formal qualifications are inevitably poorly skilled (Keep
et al. 2006). In a period where (particular forms of) LLL are being exhorted in the
policy discourse (e.g. DfEE 1998), there is also the danger that those not heeding
the call to engage as 'responsible learners' can be constructed as falling short as
citizens (Webb and Warren 2007).

In order to explore what new insights in educational decision-making and participation can be gleaned by focusing on networks of intimacy rather than 'the
individual', we are drawing on concepts associated with social network analysis,
such as the strength and nature of inter-personal ties (*inter alia* Granovetter 1973;
Bott 1957), and types of social capital (*inter alia* Putnam 2000; Woolcock 1998;
Quinn 2005). We are also examining the extent to which structural groups, including
gender and class, underpin and are relevant to making sense of network data in relation to patterns of participation in education and work. Such categories are particularly relevant given that non-participants are more likely than participants in HE to
follow traditional gendered and classed pathways into 'early adulthood' and work.

In relation to gender, we know that females outnumber male enrolments in
HE (e.g. Gilchrist et al. 2003). However, it is also known that the type of post-
compulsory provision, subjects and vocational areas in which males and females
enrol is highly gendered in Britain and internationally (*inter alia* Reay et al. 2005;
Fuller et al. 2005; Macleod and Lambe 2007; Peter and Horn 2005). In addition,
there is evidence that the pay gap between males and females persists (see, for
example, Olsen and Walby 2004). In relation to class, Gilchrist et al. (2003), for
example, show that nearly all those from social classes I and II with HE level entry
qualifications at age 21 have achieved HE qualifications by the time they are 30,
whereas the proportion of those from class III (non-manual and manual) to V ranges
from just over a third down to under a fifth of the group.

The chapter is organised in five sections. The first section provides a brief review
of the research context to our study. We then outline our focus on social networks
and discuss the relevance of insights deriving from the literature on social capital
(Sect. 2). The third section describes our methodology and data collection, and introduces one of our networks of intimacy. The empirical part of the chapter, the
fourth section, explores a variety of themes raised by the network, including the
extent to which the data are revealing normative discourses associated with female
and male caring and economic roles, and the significance of these to educational
and career decision-making. The final section offers a range of concluding remarks.
Overall, we suggest that evidence collected from social networks can challenge the
notion of decision-making as an individualised process and suggests the potential
of using this unit of analysis to augment existing understandings of females' and
males' educational 'choices' and transitions. We argue that a key way the data do
this is by drawing attention to the linked and conjoined nature of people's lives as

expressed through interpersonal ties and revealed in gendered roles, network cultures, discourses and the structural positions of members.

Research Context

Our research is set within a policy context which is demanding new insights into, and remedies for, the continuing under-representation of significant parts of the population in HE in the UK (e.g. HEFCE 2004, p. 34) and internationally (David 2007; Thomas and Quinn 2007). Our project starts from two premises (a) that empirical research and related debates in widening participation in HE have been too narrowly focused on transitions at 18 and on the individual, and (b) that participation should not automatically be conceived as 'a good thing'. In this latter regard, we are in agreement with writers who challenge the 'deficit model' of non-participation (for example, Jones and Thomas 2005). Research in this area has mainly focused on those who actually enter or at least apply to HE (Ball et al. 2000; Brooks 2005; Forsyth and Furlong 2003; Pugsley 1998; Reay 2003; Reay et al. 2005). Much less attention has fallen on non-participants (Archer and Hutchings 2000 provide an exception) and those adults, particularly aged 30 plus, who fall outside conventional age-related educational transitions, and recent UK government policy directed at increasing participation in HE of 18 to 30 year olds (Fuller and Paton 2008).

At the level of individual choice, the literature across the social sciences has drawn primarily on data at school and individual level. Various models have been used to explain choice in such analyses, and while each provides some insightful perspectives all have limitations on their applicability. Structuralist models (Ryrie 1981; Roberts 1984; Gambetta 1996) explain choice and decision making in education and training as being largely constrained by socio-economic and environmental factors, resulting in significant reproduction of social, economic and cultural capital (Bourdieu 1986). However, recent research on educational choice has provided some support for the idea that some groups exercise agency in their post-16/18 educational decisions (Ball et al. 2000; Brooks 2005; Archer et al. 2003).

Approaches, such as Phil Hodkinson and colleagues' careership model (1996), emphasise the situatedness of individuals within family, institutional, socio-economic and 'lived' contexts. Here, the role of young people's 'pragmatic rationality' is highlighted with choice being conceptualised as a path of least resistance for the chooser based on changing and sometimes contradictory information (Hodkinson et al. 1996). Foskett and Helmsley-Brown (2001) argue for an integrative approach that acknowledges the dynamic nature of individual decision making in a changing environment and the relevance of multiple sources of influence, including from: peers (Brooks 2005); careers education and guidance activities (Morris 2004); school organisation and ethos (Foskett et al. 2004); as well as how race, gender, class and 'institutional habitus' persist in shaping individual choices (e.g. Reay et al. 2005). Recent cross-national research indicates the importance of parental education on first-generation entry to HE (Thomas and Quinn 2007).

Social Network Approach

The aim of our research is to use a social network approach to build conceptually and methodologically on the extant literature on understanding individuals' participation decisions. Our empirical work involves interviews with social groups involving an individual (who has the qualifications to enter HE), our 'entry point' and also interviews with members of her or his friends and family (network of intimacy). In this regard, our methodology differs from studies on educational decision-making which mainly collect data from individuals or parents and children, by acknowledging the potential influence of broader 'networks of intimacy' (embracing a diverse range of 'family-like' connections and friendships) on educational decision-making amongst older as well as younger adults. This strategy allows us to explore decision-making as an aspect of inter- and intra-generational networks of intimacy. In addition, it foregrounds the notion of life-stage and the factors in people's lives (e.g. family and work responsibilities) which are perceived as differentially constraining or enabling males and females transitions (Heath and Johnston 2006). Underlying our interest in networks of intimacy is the idea that the relationships, and contacts they entail, have 'value' and can shed light on the social context in which educational and decision-making are embedded. Including network members as interviewees affords the opportunity to gain a deeper understanding of the nature of network influences (Fuller et al. 2011).

The notion of 'network value' has been explored extensively: for example, the economic sociologist Mark Granovetter discusses the nature of inter-personal ties identifying the strength of the tie as depending on factors such as, 'emotional intensity', 'mutual confiding' and 'reciprocal services' (1973). He suggests that a focus on 'strong ties' is associated with analyses of bounded small groups characterised primarily by the density of relationships (who knows who) and relative lack of weaker ties to other groups and communities. Granovetter draws on empirical data on how people find jobs to argue that it is the weaker ties which 'bridge' people's contacts to other groups and that this facilitates access to new opportunities (in this case jobs). Schuller et al. (2000) point out that identifying (the degree of) 'connectedness' as the key characteristic of social networks was the central finding of Elizabeth Bott's (1957) earlier study of family and social networks. She found that the stronger the intra-group connections, the stronger the imposition of norms and role expectations of members. This insight helped her interpret the way conjugal roles were organised in different families: a sharper division of labour (into 'his' and 'hers' activities) was associated with strongly connected networks:

> The norms – or the culture…of conjugal segregation are appropriate to families in close-knit networks. If the family moves, or if for any other reason their network becomes loose-knit, a new culture becomes appropriate. (Bott 1957, p. 219)

Fifty years on from Bott's study, debates continue about how far traditionally gendered divisions of labour in domestic and work settings have been overcome (Crompton and Mann 1986; Bonney 2007). This is despite contemporary theorising about social change which implies that trends such as 'individualisation', 'detraditionalisation' and the disembedding of social relations can reduce normative gendered and classed identities and role relations (Giddens 1990, 1991; Beck 1992; Beck et al. 1994). It is the inter-connections between these micro level and macro level ideas which we are able to explore through a research design that focuses on social networks and the reflexive and mutually constitutive relationships to which they give access.

Ideas about the relevance, workings and implications of social networks for social organisation and behaviour have, of course, been developed and discussed in detail in recent years, and perhaps most notably in terms of social capital (*inter alia* Coleman 1994; Bourdieu 1984; Putnam 1996[2]). In his book *Bowling Alone*, Robert Putnam defines social capital as 'connections among individuals—social networks and the norms of reciprocity and trustworthiness that arise from them' (2000, p. 19). He goes on to draw attention to the by now well-known distinction between 'bonding' and 'bridging' social capital. The former refers to the values of solidarity, mutual reinforcement, support and specific forms of reciprocation associated with homogeneous groups. The latter refers to more diffuse and indirect forms of linkage and reciprocation between and within groups: 'bonding social capital constitutes a kind of sociological superglue, whereas bridging social capital provides a sociological WD-40' (2000, p. 23). For de Souza Briggs (1998), bonding social capital facilitates 'getting by' while 'getting ahead' requires bridging social capital (cited in Putnam 2000, p. 23).

Bourdieu and Passeron (1977) focus on the role educational qualifications play in reproducing families' existing social capital and socio-economic status. Field's (2000) more recent analysis of LLL, links increases in adult participation in 'organised learning' in North America, the UK and other European countries to increases in opportunity and uncertainty that characterise the contemporary period. Liz Thomas and Jocey Quinn, through their focus on first generation entrants to HE, suggest that contemporary policy and social conditions have created 'spaces' for 'non-traditional' groups to penetrate new social networks through new forms of participation. Hence, in addition to bridging and bonding forms of social capital they draw attention to the relevance of two other forms of social capital, 'linking' (Woolcock 1998) and 'imagined' (Quinn 2005) for explaining changing patterns of educational participation. The former refers to 'the ability to access resources from formal institutions' (Thomas and Quinn 2007, p. 60). Such institutional resources would, as the authors suggest, include the HE sector. They would also include other educational, employment and intermediary sectors, including careers advice and guidance services. Imagined social capital refers to 'the benefit produced by imagined and symbolic networks which people create to re-imagine themselves and their lives' (ibid). As we shall see from the network evidence presented below, having access to different types of social capital is relevant to understanding our entry point's ongoing educational and career decision-making.

---

[2] For an excellent review of the 'genealogy' and development of the concept of social capital, and an analysis of its strengths and weaknesses, see Schuller et al. (2000).

Given that the networks involved in our research are populated by individuals nominated by our initial interviewee as people they feel close to and who they feel are influential in their educational and career decision-making, we can also expect the groups, in general, to be close-knit. Important issues for us to explore, then, are the adequacy of notions of connectedness, social capital and structural categories to explaining and understanding the collective context for educational and career decision-making, including the making and remaking of network norms and discourses over time.

We are also working with the sociological concept of ambivalence which has been developed by Kurt Luscher for understanding intergenerational relationships: 'that is, the observable forms of intergenerational relations among adults can be socio-scientifically interpreted as the expression of ambivalences, and as efforts to manage and negotiate these fundamental ambivalences' (Luscher 1999). Applying the concept to family ties, Connidis and McMullin define 'ambivalence' as 'simultaneously held opposing feelings or emotions that are due in part to countervailing expectations about how individuals should act' (2002, p. 558). They discuss how 'ambivalence' helps them to make sense of the conflicting emotions experienced by male and female partners in relation to work and family spheres.

From the perspective of our study, and the network discussed below, we are exploring the relevance of the concept of ambivalence for explaining conflicting feelings in relation to work, family and gender roles and also educational spheres, and how these might relate to gendered and classed norms (Heath et al. 2008). Bonney (2007) also reminds us from his review of the quantitative data sets that social class (as defined by the occupation of the main earner, which in the UK is still usually a male) explains differences in patterns of male and female partners' employment following the birth of children. This finding is also likely to be relevant to understanding decision-making and patterns of male and female educational participation.

The Empirical Research

The project is employing a multi-level methodology involving two overlapping and interacting phases. In phase one, desk research has been used to analyse existing quantitative data and to review empirical, conceptual, methodological and policy literatures (Johnston and Heath 2007; Maringe and Fuller 2006; Staetsky 2008). In phase two, we are conducting primary qualitative research in the South of England and involving: (a) interviews with 32 key informants representing a range of national, regional and local organisations with policy and practice interests in HE participation and ranging from the creation of policy through to its implementation and delivery; (b) interviews with an 'entry point' sample[3] of 16 individuals aged over 21 who are 'potentially recruitable' to HE, defined for the purposes of our research

---

[3] See Johnston and Heath (2006, 2007) for a detailed discussion of our sampling strategy and decision-making.

as those whose current highest level of qualification is at Level 3[4] or equivalent and who have subsequently neither participated in HE nor are currently applying to do so. As part of this phase, we have also interviewed members of an entry point's network including family, usually across generations, and friends with a variety of qualifications (or none), and who have a variety of educational, social and economic backgrounds. Each network consists of around six interviews, which has generated a total sample of 107 respondents. The interviews have lasted approximately 90 minutes and explore the personal background, educational and career experiences of participants and invite them to reflect on the extent to which they believe they might have influenced, and in return been influenced by, others in their network.

Introducing Joanna's Network

The entry point to this network is Joanna[5], who is aged 32 years. Her father is a mechanic and her mother a shop-worker. Joanna is married to Peter. The couple have two sons aged six and three, one of whom is autistic[6]. They live in a small town in an isolated part of the county. Joanna works as a part-time administrator in the health service. She left school at 16 with several GCSEs at grade C and went to college where she studied to become a medical secretary and gained a Diploma in Secretarial Studies (level 3). More recently she has gained an NVQ level 3 in Business Administration through her employment. Joanna nominated six members of her network for interview.

The chart maps out the network and the characteristics of its members. In summary the network has the following gender, age, social class, employment, educational and life-stage characteristics:

- There are five females and two males aged between 29 and 50 years old.
- The network comprises family members (Joanna's older brother, her husband and sister-in-law) from one generation. and three of Joanna's female friends.
- In terms of social class, two members described themselves as 'working class', one as 'lower middle', one as 'middle', one as 'just normal' and two said they 'didn't know'. Using parental occupation as an indicator of social class, reveals that all members of the network would be classified (using the NS-SEC 2001 classification) as class 3 or below. Using respondents' current occupation as an

---

[4] In the UK level 3 includes a variety of academic and vocational qualifications including A levels, BTEC national certificates and diplomas and National Vocational Qualifications (NVQ3).

[5] We are using pseudonyms to help protect confidentiality.

[6] It was interesting that Joanna did not suggest that having an autistic son had had a strong influence in her educational and career decision-making. There was no evidence to suggest that having a child with this condition had influenced the gendered division of labour in the family any more than having children *per se*. We have therefore decided not to foreground the son's autism in this analysis of the gendered nature of decision-making in this network.

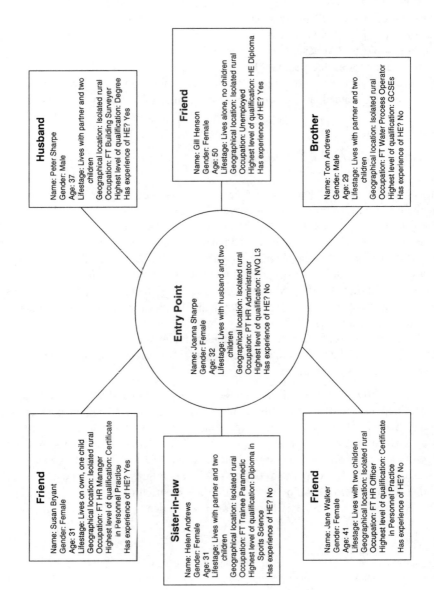

indicator reveals that two members can be located in class 2, two in class 3, one in class 5, one in class 6 and one in class 8.

- All but one member of the network (Joanna's brother) achieved some GCSEs at grades A* to C, and two females achieved A levels although only one proceeded to university (one year after leaving school). Four members of the network (all female) have achieved level 3 as their highest level of qualification.
- Most of the network members participated in initial post-compulsory education and have re-participated in vocational and work oriented opportunities during their adult lives.
- The network has experience of HE, with two members (one male and one female) having HE level qualifications (level 4 or above). The higher level qualifications achieved in the network are vocationally oriented. One female member is currently pursuing a level 4 qualification related to her career.
- There is a mix of life-stages including: four members who are partnered with dependent children (i.e. two mixed sex couples), two (currently not 'partnered') females with dependent children and one single female with no children.
- The employment status of the network members is mixed: four are in full-time employment. Of these, two are the male partners with dependent children and two are the 'unpartnered' female parents. Two members, the two female partners with children, are in part-time employment. One female is long-term unemployed due to chronic ill-heath. All those in employment are located in organisations in the public sector.

Our interviews with network members have generated a range of biographical accounts relating to the spheres of family, education and work, and which provide insights into network norms and discourses. As the analysis below will indicate, there is evidence that the network has generated a dynamic set of inter-personal ties, the nature of which helps explain educational decision-making within the group as well as for Joanna herself.

Analysis

For the purposes of this chapter, the analysis of the network data is organised around two sub-sections: initial post-compulsory education, and subsequent LLL. As the discussion will indicate, this distinction is associated with broader social and institutional changes, which are reflected in the way interviewees make sense of their educational and career biographies. The focus on initial post-compulsory educational experiences reveals similarities between the interviewees and the tendency to a 'joint network' account based around the theme of 'standardised biographies'. The focus on LLL also provides some evidence of collective attitudes and shared experiences, including between males and females. The collection of network rather than solely individual evidence reveals the relevance of gendered standpoints to understanding decision-making. In particular, the ambivalence towards educational participation that features in Joanna's narrative is linked to her network's expectations of her as a wife and mother and how these roles are relevant to perceptions about the timeliness of any future educational and career decisions.

Initial Post-compulsory Education

All members of the network come from similar socio-economic backgrounds and none of them had parents with degrees. Most of the parents had left school at the earliest opportunity. The majority of network members spoke about their families' relatively low expectations regarding attainment during the compulsory schooling phase and aspirations regarding their initial post-compulsory transitions. For example, Joanna and her brother both talk about their parents as 'good hard working people', but they did not promote the importance of education, associate educational success with their children or raise their educational aspirations:

> ...I know they wanted me to do well and be happy but they certainly didn't think, they never gave the impression I could do much more than you know...never ever discussed the possibility of A levels or university. (Joanna, entry point)

> ...if you did your best that was good enough. (Tom, brother)

This experience was quite common across the men, women and families represented in the network:

> They [his parents] didn't actually discourage me from education but they weren't encouraging so consequently I drifted along. (Peter, husband)

> There was no pressure to achieve anything, there was also no accolade when you did. (Gill, friend)

Turning to post-16 transitions, most interviewees progressed to some form of education or training. Two of Joanna's friends stayed on to take A levels before entering the labour market. After a year, one of them, Gill, started full-time training as a speech therapist. Following their GCSEs two members of the network, Joanna and her future husband, moved on to Further Education (FE) College to pursue vocational qualifications, a third member (sister-in-law) stayed on at school for a year to do GCSE retakes and then entered FE also to study a vocational course. A fourth (brother) joined a Youth Training Scheme in the retail sector and another entered employment.

Generally, the interviewees spoke about a lack of 'formal' advice, guidance and support in relation to their post-16 decisions. This is a common theme across members and is emerging across several of our other networks. Joanna regrets that she was not made aware of a fuller range of careers while she was at school and college. To explain her views about the lack of careers guidance available in the past, she contrasted the sort of provision that is currently available and that she has a role in disseminating with her early experiences:

> As part of my job I do now I go to schools and I do careers fairs…and I'm like what do you want to do…have a leaflet, because we've got all that stuff about all the different jobs you can do. And I think if somebody had, had inspired me…it could have changed the whole course of what you could have done, had someone just given me a few ideas you know. (Joanna)

The patterning of the network's initial post-compulsory transitions is reflective of an opportunity structure in which university participation was still very much a minority option (approximately 15% of 18 and 19 year olds in 1986). The following quotation is illustrative:

> …my parents didn't really want me to go on into sixth form or go to university and I think at that time, when I was leaving school, university and that…was more for what you considered to be the really, really bright students and my parents, you know, they were more gently persuading me to go out to work…it was quite easy to get a job at 16. (Jane, friend)

The network evidence is in keeping with findings that indicate the importance of factors such as family background and experience of school to explaining patterns of participation in initial post-compulsory and entrance to HE between the ages of 18 and 21 (see for example Gorard and Rees 2002; Feinstein et al. 2004). The emerging analysis of the data collected in this case study resonates strongly with Feinstein et al.'s (2004) conclusion that parents' educational background has a strong influence on children's educational participation and achievement. We would argue interviewees' experience of post-16 transition is indicative of 'normal' or standardised biographies (Du Bois-Reymond 1998) for people from their social background, gender and generation, and this helps explain the convergence of their accounts. Gender expectations can be seen in terms of the subject areas undertaken by the young women, who all entered courses and jobs typically associated with their own sex. The following quotation indicates that such normative influences started early and reflect inter-generational influences, or to use the terminology of life-course theorists, 'linked lives' (Giele and Elder 1998).

> My mum worked in secretarial, sort of similar to me…they bought me a typewriter when I was about nine or ten and I think there were times they would say 'oh you know, we think you'd be good at this as well.' So I think there was a fair amount of influence there. (Jane)

Lifelong Learning

It is striking to note the extent to which members of this network have participated in education and training since their post-16 transitions and initial post-compulsory studies. There is a strong link between their involvement in 'LLL', associated awards, vocational development and employment. In general, members view qualifications as important for instrumental reasons, for example, in terms of gaining more financial security, improving employment prospects and accessing more satisfying careers, rather than 'for their own sake'. In this regard, there was an alignment between the discourse of the network (strong vocational rationale in educational decision-making) and the national policy discourse around the value of and reasons for LLL. A utilitarian discourse around the purposes of education is illustrated in the following observation:

> I tend to be sceptical of academic type courses, history and that kind of thing because I can't necessarily see there's a need to study it. Practical things that serve a purpose like science. Maths, I can see…. My view is if you learn something and it's useful to the community and society as a whole then it's worth doing, but I find subjects like English language or literature pointless because it doesn't serve a great deal of purpose. (Peter, Joanna's husband)

Joanna gained a range of secretarial skills and diplomas at college before joining the Community Health Authority (later the hospital health authority where she still works in the Human Resources (HR) department). Since working in HR she has gained an NVQ level 3 in Business Administration. Part of her job involves providing administrative support for employees following a range of courses. This experience has helped to 'open her eyes' to the variety of careers that are available in the health service, particularly in the allied medical field (e.g. nursing, dietician, speech therapy, and so on), and the diverse backgrounds of those pursuing qualifications and new careers in mid-life. To put it another way, her employment situation has given her access to bridging and linking forms of social capital that are challenging her to extend her sense of personal identity, or sense of belonging, by seeking membership (potentially) of a new social group. Joanna finds the successful progression of some work colleagues inspiring:

> …I meet amazing people in my job now and I think wow. I mean we've got nurses qualifying all the time and they're in their fifties and things.

Joanna's husband Peter envisaged that his National Diploma in Business Studies would lead him into office-based employment. However, he ended up doing bar work and studying part-time for an Accounting Technician award (level 3) but did not complete the course through lack of interest. He then had a variety of jobs, 'looking for something interesting' including financial advisor, store-man, and insurance broker. It was while working in a timber yard that Peter realised that he was interested in building design and construction and contacted Learn Direct for advice on courses. He was also influenced by his male friends who supported the formal advice he was being given. As a result, he undertook (while still working) a variety of distance learning modules with the College of Estate Management and eventually attained a degree in surveying. He currently has a permanent post as a building surveyor with a large public sector employer. Peter's ability to access resources through his interaction with Learn Direct provides a good example of the 'linking social capital' available in this network.

Peter made the distinction between 'career' (interest, skilled, long-term, progressive, higher status) and 'job' (short-term, for the money, less skilled, lower status). He is happy now that he has a career and can progress:

> It's nice having skills that not everybody has, like a doctor or somebody like that…that's a good feeling, curing a problem or curing someone's illness…. (Peter, husband)

The possibility of sharing an identity with those perceived to have careers as opposed to jobs was an important thread running through the interviews with Peter, his wife and the wider network. As Joanna remarked, 'he's got a career now'.

There are other similar accounts of 'LLL' in the network, characterised by positive outcomes in terms of achievement, enjoyment, improved self-confidence, career progression and mutual support. For example, although Joanna's friend Jane left school at 16, she has pursued several courses over the years, including an A level in Psychology, training as a massage therapist and fitness instructor and through her current job in HR, a certificate in Personnel Practice. She is also about to start the Diploma in Personnel Practice which is a two year degree level course. As the following quotation indicates, and like many adults making the transition to HE in mid-life, her motives are instrumentally and expressively oriented (Fuller 2007):

> I need to have some good solid qualifications to put myself in a better position and have more earning potential...it's my dream to be at a graduation ceremony and be the one who has achieved. (Jane, friend and work colleague)

Peter commented on the encouragement he has received from family and friends on his achievements as a mature student:

> They're really happy and pleased...they're impressed as well, they think I've done really well.

The strength of the interpersonal ties in this network, as manifested by indicators such as density (extent to which members know each other), emotional intensity and reciprocation, was evident in relation to interviewees' engagement in LLL. For example, Peter comments on the encouragement he has received from his wife, friends and other family members, and Susan (friend) talked about the support she had given Peter and the reciprocal and emotional nature of her tie with Joanna:

> I have supported him loads and loads and loads, and Joanna has brilliantly supporting [sic] Peter for four years.... Everything is about a team effort you know, if you think you can just do everything in your life without accepting any help from anyone else, then you are a fool...my friendship with Joanna has been her supporting me in times of need, and me supporting her in times of need. (Susan)

Such bonding resources were helping members to overcome a legacy of weak self-belief and confidence in their abilities and provide a reminder that bonding social capital should not automatically be associated with the creation of constraining behavioural and attitudinal norms (Thomas and Quinn 2007).

The Relevance of Gendered Standpoints

Following Henwood et al. (1998), Jane Ribbens McCarthy and her colleagues define standpoints as, 'concrete, materially grounded or shared experiences, socially defined group identities, or collectively articulated political viewpoints' (Ribbens McCarthy et al. 2003, p. 4). In speaking about her current life, Joanna identifies and positions herself as a mother with dependent children and it is clear that this 'standpoint' is relevant to the understandings she and network members have about her recent and potential 'choices'. Joanna's adoption of the maternal standpoint (foregrounding the relevance of the issues she shares with other mothers of young children), and the identity assumptions inherent in this standpoint that are shared within the network (and sections of society more widely) appear highly relevant to understanding her decision-making and her 'horizons for action' (Hodkinson et al. 1996). This is illustrated in the following quotation when Joanna's brother normalises her primary responsibility as carer and its link to her existing level of educational attainment:

> Joanna's very clever, she could do more but obviously she's limited by, because of [son's name] she can't, she had to commit a lot of time to him. (Tom, brother)

The traditional 'fixed' gender perspective on parental roles is reinforced by Joanna, when talking about school choice she uses the plural pronoun 'we' (referring to herself and her husband), but when referring to the associated caring duties she uses the first person singular pronoun 'I':

> ...we need to determine where, which school he's going to...and how I'm going to juggle.

Since the birth of their children both Peter and Joanna, following periods of maternity leave, have continued in employment, with him maintaining full-time and her changing to part-time work. Similarly, Tom and Helen (Joanna's brother and sister-in-law), also operate on the full-time male and part-time female earner model. Helen stresses that working part-time enables her to fulfil the family's needs: 'I get to spend more time with the children and I get to spend more time at home and do things at home.'

Hakim (1996, 1998) has shown that post-children employment behaviour within couples is related to gender, class and prior educational attainment and differences in social values between groups. Data from the 2001 census indicate the association between social class and gender, the higher the social class of male and female partners, the more likely women are to be in full-time employment: women in mid-range social class positions and without HE are likely to maintain part-time employment; those in relationships with males occupying lower social class positions are likely to have the most interrupted employment trajectories (Bonney 2007). Furthermore, survey data indicate that female graduates are more likely than their less highly qualified peers to access high status professional careers and to continue in full-time employment following the birth of children (ibid). The pattern of employment associated with Joanna and Peter, and with Tom and Helen, appears rather typical for their class and educational backgrounds and the way this plays out between male and female partners, and maternal and paternal standpoints. Following Bott (1957), it also indicates the worth of contextualising educational and career decision-making within conjugal roles and the values existing in households, 'networks of intimacy', as well as the wider social groupings with which their identities are located. It is interesting to note that within this network, there was no perspective that diverged from standardardised expectations of maternal and paternal divisions of labour and responsibilities within heterosexual, two parent households.

An analysis of Joanna's interview reveals the sort of weighing up of the possible courses of action that she might embark on to further her education and career. In this regard, it seems to reveal the sort of sociological ambivalence that Connidis and

McMullin (2002) associate with role conflict between male and female partners in relation to caring and work spheres and which our data suggest encompasses LLL too. Joanna concludes that she would like to develop her career and recognises that this would probably involve HE but is uncertain about when, in terms of life-course and life-stage, this will be possible or 'appropriate'. One of her concerns revolves around whether she would be able to study part-time at an institution to which she could travel relatively easily. Given that the family lives in an isolated area where there are limited options: 'I've looked into things like that but they're full-time courses and there's only a limited erm…, colleges in the UK, so you know it would mean moving…and I can't do that with young children.' Ambivalence is captured in her follow up observation, 'you know maybe in time I would' [undertake professional training].

Her husband, Peter, believes that Joanna could develop her career and attributes her relative lack of progress to low self-confidence and lack of parental encouragement. However, the following comment indicates that the gendered and normalised nature of the couple's decisions is also a relevant factor, whilst at the same time hinting that there is the potential for change: 'she could do more with education but now she's focused on the children…[she could do more qualifications]…in time, yes.'

The influence of gender and life-stage and the maternal and female partner standpoints are strongly evident in this network. For example, Jane, Joanna's close friend and work colleague, and mother of two teenagers aged 16 and 18, talked about her shifting educational and career aspirations. She is currently about to start a Diploma in Personnel Practice and in the following quotation links her changed marital status and personal circumstances to wider social trends:

> I think I had different aspirations then. I wasn't thinking much beyond getting married and having children because when my generation, that was how we saw our lives, that we'd go and get ourselves a nice little job and then we would get married. I was married at 19…had my first child when I was 22 and that was all I was aspiring to do. So it's changed…I'm divorced and the children are growing up.

The mothers in Joanna's network are all in employment and keen to progress their careers through the pursuit of higher level education. Consequently, they have many issues in common. However, in contrast to Joanna and Helen, Jane and Susan (Joanna's friends) are both divorced, have older children and are in full-time work. They foreground the links between their partner status, developing their careers, increasing their income and gaining some financial security. Jane's comment is illustrative:

> I'm a single mother, I need to be supporting…I think because I'm 41 now and I feel I need to…have some good solid qualifications and put myself in a better position for more earning potential.

The above analysis has indicated that a key theme in this network revolves around educational and career decision-making from the maternal point of view and the gendered and classed identities and expectations that persist in relation to this standpoint. Joanna's 'horizons for action' have expanded in adulthood via the bonding social capital she has developed through her marriage and adult friendships as well as the bridging social capital she has acquired by means of the 'weak ties' available in her employment. Joanna is aware of examples of working mothers who have become professionals and who she is beginning to view as a group to which, in time, she could imagine belonging:

> I've seen a number of, loads of nurses that have been like NA's, nursing auxiliaries for years and they're going to, 'oh, I'm going to do it…train to be a nurse'…and off they go and three years later they're a nurse…I just really admire them. They both had children and…you know…they do it, and I just think I really like that.

Concluding Remarks

This chapter has exposed some of the ways in which educational and career decision-making is embedded in, and can be understood in terms of the relationships that constitute a network of intimacy. The empirical discussion has used one of our project's networks as an illustrative lens through which to focus on gendered aspects of personal and collective decision-making. The evidence suggests that Joanna's and other members of the network's earlier standardised biographies, characterised by tacit decision-making based on gender and class expectations, have begun to loosen up as awareness of possible employment and lifestyle options grows. For example, two of Joanna's friends (Jane and Susan), both of whom she met through work, are both employed full-time and are seeking higher level qualifications. The network discourses around lifelong and vocational learning, working hard, and the growing importance of having a career are also pushing Joanna towards engaging in higher level education and training. In this regard, she can be seen, through her inter-personal ties to be accumulating 'bridging' and 'linking' social capital, as well as 'imagined' social capital which is moving her towards new forms of participation and belonging. On the other hand, the collection of network data has exposed the normative expectations around gender roles and responsibilities between male and female partners. These expectations can be interpreted as constraining factors, and suggest that, to some degree at least, Joanna's current life-stage can be characterised in terms of 'getting by' rather than 'getting ahead'. One of the interesting aspects of the analysis has been to notice the ways in which gender continues to have an influence on 'choice'. However, this effect is manifested quite subtly as members of the social network do not express overtly stereotypical attitudes about male and female roles. In this regard, they tend to indicate that their own views are more liberal and fluid than those they experienced while growing up.

The extent to which the ambivalence associated with competing expectations and identities will continue to feature in Joanna's (and similar women's) educational and career decisions is interesting: when (in relation to paternal and maternal standpoints) will it be (if at all) the 'right time' for her to pursue higher level qualifications, work full-time and develop a career; how old (independent) will her children need to be before it is appropriate for her to pursue educational and career progression, what kinds of emotional and practical support would facilitate her transition?

In order to help us make sense of the network data, we are drawing on a range of rich conceptual resources and writers who have grappled with how to analyse social networks and interview material collected from people with inter-personal ties. In this regard, we have found the literature on social capital helpful, particularly in terms of distinguishing between different types and their relevance to understanding educational decision-making. We envisage that our ongoing analysis of this and the other networks will enable us to contribute to the relevant theoretical debates, particularly in relation to notions associating different types of social capital with positive and negative values (Schuller et al. 2000) and the extent to which the different types of capital are revealed as distinctive.

From the perspective of our project, the overarching task is to try to understand the extent to which network data can help explain educational decision-making. To do this, we are trying to characterise the nature of our networks in terms of indicators of the strength of interpersonal ties such as density, mutual confiding and reciprocal services. Applying these to Joanna's network reveals that this is indeed a closely knit group that has a tendency to generate joint accounts in relation to the value of LLL as well as in terms of what types of behaviour, in relation to education, work and family, are expected from differently positioned members of the network. We suggest that the emerging analysis points to the potential of the network approach to contribute to understandings of the social and relational nature of decision making and, in the case of Joanna, is helping to illuminate the role of gender and identity issues in explaining why she has not, so far, participated in HE. As our analysis of the other networks develops, we will be able to explore how the influence of gender plays out differentially for male and female network entry points.

References

Archer, L., & Hutchings, M. (2000). Bettering yourself?: Discourses of risk, cost and benefit in ethnically diverse, young working class non-participants' constructions of Higher Education. *British Journal of Sociology of Education, 21*(4), 555–574.

Archer, L., Hutchings, M., & Ross, A (2003). *Higher Education and social class: Issues of exclusion and inclusion*. London: Routledge Falmer.

Ball, S. J., Maguire, M., & Macrae, S. (2000). *Choice, pathways and transitions post-16: New youth, new economies in the global city*. London: Falmer.

Beck, U. (1992). *Risk society: Towards a new modernity*. Newbury Park: Sage.

Beck, U., Giddens, A., & Lash, S. (1994). *Reflexive modernisation: Politics, tradition and aesthetics in the modern social order*. Oxford: Polity.

Bonney, N. (2007). Gender, employment and social class. *Work, Employment and Society, 21*(1), 142–156.

Bott, E. (1957). *Family and social network*. London: Tavistock.

Bourdieu, P. (1984). *Distinction*. London: Routledge & Kogan Paul.

Bourdieu, P. (1986). The forms of capital. In J. G. Robinson (Ed.), *Handbook of theory and research for the sociology of education*. New York: Greenwood.

Bourdieu, P., & Passeron, L. (1977). *Reproduction in education, society and culture.* Chicago: University of Chicago Press.

Bradley, H. (1997). *Fractured identities: Changing patterns of inequality.* Cambridge: Polity.

Brine, J. (1999). *Under educating women: Globalising inequality.* Buckingham: Open University Press.

Brooks, R. (2005). *Friendship and educational choice.* Basingstoke: Palgrave Macmillan.

Burke, P., & Jackson, S. (2007). *Reconceptualising lifelong learning: Feminist interventions.* London: Routledge.

Coleman, J. (1994). *Foundations of social theory.* Cambridge: Belknap.

Connidis, L., & McMullin, J. A. (2002). Sociological ambivalence and family ties: A critical perspective. *Journal of Marriage and the Family, 64*(3), 558–567.

Crompton, R., & Mann, M. (1986). *Gender and social stratification.* Cambridge: Polity.

David, M. (2007). Equity and diversity: Towards a sociology of higher education for the twenty-first century? *British Journal of Sociology of Education, 28*(5), 675–690.

De Souza Briggs, X. (1998). Doing democracy up close: Culture, power and communication in community building. *Journal of Planning Education and Research, 18,* 1–13.

Department for Education and Employment. (1998). *The learning age: A renaissance for a new Britain.* London: Stationery Office.

Du Bois-Reymond, M. (1998). 'I don't want to commit myself yet': Young people's life concepts. *Journal of Youth Studies, 1*(1), 63–79.

Feinstein, L., Duckworth, K., & Sabates, R. (2004). *A model of intergenerational effects of parental education.* Research Brief RCB01-04. Nottingham: Department for Education and Skills.

Field, J. (2000). *Lifelong learning and the new educational order.* Stoke-on-Trent: Trentham.

Forsyth, A., & Furlong, A. (2003). *Losing out? Socioeconomic disadvantage and experience in further and higher education,* Bristol: Policy Press, pp. 1–69.

Foskett, N., & Hemsley Brown, J. (2001). *Choosing futures: Young people's decision-making in education, training and careers markets.* London: Routledge Falmer.

Foskett, N., Dyke, M., & Maringe, F. (2004). *The influence of the school in the decision to participate in learning post-16.* Research Report RR538. Nottingham: Department for Education and Skills.

Fuller, A. (2007). Mid-life transitions to HE: Developing a multi-level explanation of increasing participation. *Studies in the Education of Adults, 39*(2), 217–235.

Fuller, A., & Paton, K. (2008). Widening participation in Higher Education: Mapping and investigating the stakeholder landscape. *Journal of Access, Policy and Practice, 6*(1), 4–20.

Fuller, A., Beck, V., & Unwin, L. (2005). The gendered nature of apprenticeship: Employers' and young people's perspectives. *Education and Training, 47*(4/5), 298–311.

Fuller, A., Johnston, B., & Heath, S. (Eds.), (2011). *Rethinking widening participation in higher education: The role of social networks.* London: Routledge.

Gambetta, D. (1996). *Were they pushed or did they jump? Individual decision mechanisms in education.* Oxford: Westview.

Giddens, A. (1990). *The consequences of modernity.* Cambridge: Polity.

Giddens, A. (1991). *Modernity and self-identity: Self and society in the late modern age.* Cambridge: Polity.

Giele, J. Z., & Elder, G. (Eds.). (1998). *Methods of life course research: Qualitative and quantitative approaches.* Thousand Oaks: Sage.

Gilchrist, R., Phillips, D., & Ross, A. (2003). Participation and potential participation in UK Higher Education. In L. Archer, M. Hutchings, & A. Ross (Eds.), *Higher Education and social class: Issues of exclusion and inclusion.* London: Routledge Falmer.

Gorard, S., & Rees, G. (2002). *Creating a learning society?* Bristol: Policy.

Granovetter, M. (1973). The strength of weak ties. *American Journal of Sociology, 78*(4), 1350–1380.

Hakim, C. (1996). *Key issues in women's work.* London: Athlone.

Hakim, C. (1998). *Social change and innovation in the labour market.* Oxford: Oxford University Press.

Halford, S., & Leonard, P. (2006). Negotiating gendered identities at work: Place, space and time. Basingstoke: Palgrave.

Heath, S., & Cleaver, E. (2003). *Young, free and single: Twenty-somethings and household change.* Basingstoke: Palgrave.

Heath, S., & Johnston, B. (2006). *Decision-making about employment and education pathways as an embedded social practice: Methodological challenges.* Non-participation in HE Working Paper Series, No.1, School of Education, University of Southampton.

Heath, S., Fuller, A., & Paton, K. (2008). *Network-based ambivalence and educational decision-making: A case study of 'non-participation' in higher education.* Research Papers in Education, *23*(2), 219–229.

HEFCE. (2004/34). *HEFCE widening participation and fair access research strategy.* Bristol: HEFCE.

Henwood, K., Griffin, C., & Phoenix, A. (1998). Introduction, In K. Henwood, C. Griffin, & A. Phoenix, (Eds.), *Standpoints and differences: Essays in the practice of feminist psychology.* London: Sage.

Hodkinson, P., Sparkes, A., & Hodkinson, H. (1996). *Triumphs and tears: Young people, markets and the transition from school to work.* London: Fulton.

Jackson, S. (2007). *In search of lifelong learning: Politics, power and pedagogic challenges.* Inaugural lecture, Birkbeck, University of London.

Johnston, B. (2006). *Methodological Review: Mapping the literature in relation to the challenges for the non-participation project.* Non-participation in HE Working Paper Series, No. 4, School of Education, University of Southampton.

Johnston, B., & Heath, S. (2007). *Educational decision-making as an embedded social practice: Methodological challenges and ways forward.* Non-participation in HE Working Paper Series, No. 7, School of Education, University of Southampton.

Jones, R., & Thomas, L. (2005). The 2003 UK Government Higher Education White Paper: A critical assessment of its implications for the access and widening participation agenda. *Journal of Education Policy, 20*(5): 615–630.

Keep, E., Mayhew, K., & Payne, J. (2006). From skills revolution to productivity miracle—not as easy as it sounds? *Oxford Review of Economic Policy, 22*(4), 539–559.

Leathwood, C., & Francis, B. (Eds.). (2006). *Gender and lifelong learning: Critical feminist engagements.* London: Routledge.

Luscher, K. (1999). Ambivalence: A key concept for the study of intergenerational relations. In S. Trnka (Ed.), *Family issues between gender and generations. Seminar report.* Vienna: European Commission, Directorate-General for Employment and Social Affairs.

Macleod, F., & Lambe, P. (2007). Patterns and trends in part-time adult education participation in relation to UK nation, class, place of participation, gender, age and disability, 1998–2003. *International Journal of Lifelong Education, 26*(4), 399–418.

Maringe, F., & Fuller, A. (2006). *Widening participation in UK Higher Education: A policy overview. Non-participation in HE.* Working Paper Series, No. 3, School of Education, University of Southampton.

Morris, M. (2004). Key questions—the NFER report on careers education and guidance. In B. Campbell (Ed.), *Careers education advice and guidance in sheffield.* Sheffield: Sheffield City Council.

Olsen, W., & Walby, S. (2004). *Modelling the gender pay gap.* Working Paper Series No. 17. Manchester: Equal Opportunities Commission.

Peter, K., & Horn, L. (2005). *Gender differences in participation and completion of undergraduate education and how they have changed over time.* Washington: National Center for Education Statistics (AWP215).

Pugsley, L. (1998). 'Throwing your brains at it': Higher Education, markets and choice. *International Studies in Sociology of Education, 8*(1), 71–92.

Putnam, R. (1996). Who killed civic America? *Prospect, 1996*(March), 66–72.

Putnam, R. (2000). *Bowling alone: The collapse of and revival of community.* New York: Schuster.

Quinn, J. (2005). Belonging in a learning community: The re-imagined university and imagined social capital. *Studies in the Education of Adults, 37*(1), 4–18.

Reay, D. (2003). A risky business? Mature working class women students and access to higher education. *Gender and Education, 15*(3), 301–317.

Reay, D., David, M., & Ball, S. (2005). *Degree of choice: Social class, race and gender in Higher Education.* Stoke on Trent: Trentham.

Ribbens McCarthy, J., Holland, J., & Gillies, V. (2003). Multiple perspectives on the 'family' lives of young people: Methodological and theoretical issues in each case study research. *International Journal of Social Research Methodology, 6*(1), 1–23.

Roberts, K. (1984). *School leavers and their prospects: Youth in the labour market in the 1980s.* Milton Keynes: Open University Press.

Ryrie, A. C. (1981). *Routes and results: A study of the later years of schooling.* Sevenoaks: Hodder & Stoughton.

Schuller, T., Baron, S., & Field, J. (Eds.). (2000). *Social capital: Critical perspectives.* Oxford: Oxford University Press.

Staetsky, L. (2008). *Participation in Higher Education: A review of quantitative literature.* Non-participation in HE working paper. School of Education, University of Southampton.

Thomas, L., & Quinn, J. (2007). *First generation entry into Higher Education: An international study.* Maidenhead: SRHE and Open University Press.

Webb, S., & Warren, S. (2007). *Public issues and private troubles—adult learners, 'responsible learners' and the new FE.* Paper presented at British Educational Research Association annual conference, Institute of Education, London, September.

Woolcock, M. (1998). Social capital and economic development: Toward a theoretical synthesis and policy framework. *Theory and Society, 27*(1), 151–208.

Chapter 17
Power, Resistance, and Informal pathways: Lifelong Learning in Feminist Nonprofit Organisations

Leona M. English

Introduction

Although lifelong learning has become a catchphrase for government bureaucrats and policy makers in Canada and elsewhere (see Boshier 1998), their funding priorities continue to be restricted to institutions of higher education and ad hoc literacy programmes. The informal learning sphere has been both underfunded and neglected, despite the fact that most adults 'are active learners, and very little of this learning is registered through specific education and training courses' (Livingstone 1999, p. 68). Women, for instance, have traditionally pursued learning through craft organisations, suffrage and temperance movements, cooperative ventures, and libraries, along with state-sanctioned higher education[1]. Informal routes continue to attract them, even though the types of learning venues may have changed. In recent times feminist nonprofit organisations have become popular public learning spaces for women. In order to document some of this informal learning, this chapter focuses directly on a qualitative study of 16 female employees and board members of such nonprofit organisations to explore how they have learned about feminist pedagogical practices, funding opportunities, grassroots organising, and leadership, and how to actively pursue a social change agenda.

Increasingly feminist nonprofit organisations, like the ones to which the 16 women in this study were connected, are alternatives to the traditionally male and gendered institutions of higher education, yet they are often ignored by governments, adult educators and gender researchers who have been more interested in how women enter or are excluded from the halls of academe (see Benseman 2005). For working class, low literate, and vulnerable populations of women, feminist nonprofit centres may provide a sustainable and safe lifelong learning pathway. This

---

[1] 'Higher education' is the term used in Canada to denote much post-compulsory education, including trades college, university, community college, nurses' training etc.

L. M. English (✉)
Department of Adult Education, St. Francis Xavier University, Antigonish, NS, Canada
e-mail: lenglish@stfx.ca

S. Jackson et al. (eds.), *Gendered Choices,* Lifelong Learning Book Series 15,
DOI 10.1007/978-94-007-0647-7_17, © Springer Science+Business Media B.V. 2011

chapter proposes that we look more closely at such informal venues which often help women make the transition to schools, enter the workforce, or become more active citizens. Here, I explore these sites of learning as both complex and contradictory, yet highly effective in facilitating informal learning at the community level.

Some cautions are in order. To begin with, it would be simplistic to read all feminist organisations as holding similar views and practices of feminism, given that feminism has many forms (see Code 2000). What these feminist organisations do share is a concern to improve the lives of women through political and social change, although how they do this varies with the institution and its members. It would be simplistic, too, to do a reading of nonprofit organisations as good and caring, and higher education as bad and rigid; or to paint informal learning as good and formal learning as awful. Instead, a Foucauldian poststructural lens (Foucault 1977, 1980) is used to shine light on the intersection of power, knowledge, and discourse within feminist nonprofit organisations in order to further understand how women learn and lead, as well as work for and against government, within these organisations (see also Brookfield 2005; Chapman 2003; Dreyfus and Rabinow 1982; English 2006). Foucault allows us to look at women's so-called preferences and choices more critically and to view them for the complex and multilayered events they really are (see Hakim 2003 for support of women's free choices). As Michel Foucault's theory suggests, even benevolent organisations such as feminist nonprofit organisations are sites of power, knowledge, and resistance. It is precisely within this context that significant learning occurs, often because of the complexity.

Theoretical Underpinning

Several bodies of theory are helpful to this discussion. The first is Foucault's (1977, 1978) poststructural theory of power and knowledge which is used to analyse the learning content, strategies, and resistances (Hughes 2000) that are part and parcel of this informal learning. Poststructuralism, or at least the Foucauldian approach to it, allows me to look at the intersection of power and knowledge in women's learning, especially as it relates to their interpersonal relationships with colleagues and board members, as well as to their external dealings with the bureaucracies of government and the community. Michel Foucault draws attention to the ubiquity of power and its refusal to be located only in recognised and hierarchical structures such as government, the divinity, or the presidency. In particular, he acknowledges the pathways of power that flow capillary-like through all our relationships, and through our bodies, as well as the resistances that always seem to accompany that power. He wants us to attend to the particularities of the familiar and how this minutia is imbricated in each moment and interaction. It is within this minutia that learning occurs.

Foucault's (1980) interest is in the less overt and more political ways that power is exercised (used, not owned); in this case it would apply to how women are created as learning, activist and feminist subjects in the process. According to Foucault, power is not a commodity we possess; it is relational and exercised between us at all times. Power is effected through practices, techniques, and procedures—what he calls technologies or practices of power—all of which we use constantly. According to Foucault, every time power is effected, there is a resistance; when closely examined, this site of resistance reveals the intricacies of power and its effects. Part of the learning and the creation of knowledge within feminist organisations is bound in this network of using power and resisting.

Foucault proposes a pastoral power, in lieu of sovereign power, to explain the seemingly benign exercises of power by groups such as government. Applied to government, pastoral power is exercised through the provision of money to care for women, such as providing housing and income support, introducing supportive policies around schooling and employment. The government becomes a socialist presence, ensuring care for everyone, even taking criticism for not caring enough. In so doing, governments oversee how women conduct themselves (see Dreyfus and Rabinow 1982, pp. 208–226). Yet, the pastoral power is productive in that it avoids punishment and 'encourages' individuals to choose or to desire conditions that lead to their improvement. Women on social assistance benefits, for instance, may take the training course in hair styling that is offered, in order to appear willing and able to work, even if they have no transportation and child care money. Yet, these same women may resist by finding creative ways to have expenses reimbursed, while earning their diplomas and becoming self-reliant.

Pastoral power is also confessional. In turn for the care, women must confess or bare their souls by filling out means tests, which require them to reveal the most intimate details of their lives. The hallmarks of this pastoral power, exercised by both the feminist organisers and the state, include intrusion into the private life of the individual through these various confessional practices, or micropractices and technologies of power (see Howley and Hartnett 1992). Through micropractices and techniques, feminist organisations and their members and directors are subjected—and subject themselves—to self-discipline (see Foucault 1980), that is, in fear of who is watching them, they check their anger at government and poverty, in order to appear docile and compliant, that is, deserving of funds. The strength in this theory is that it allows for some degree of choice and pushing back on the part of women.

A related body of theory here is on women and learning, which has been developing steadily since *In a Different Voice* (Gilligan 1982) and *Women's Ways of Knowing* (Belenky et al. 1986) pointed to some of the unique aspects of women's learning in the last quarter of the twentieth century. It became *au courant* to speak of women's learning as caring and connected, and to separate this from men's ways of knowing which are seen to be more logical and impartial. What ensued from these publications was a large body of responsive and supportive literature that addressed some of the dangers of a stereotypic and essentialist readings of women as unique and precious (e.g., Goldberger et al. 1996). Yet, some stereotypes of women being relational (Fletcher 1998), caring and connected (Belenky et al. 1986), and inclusive (MacKeracher 2004) remain. Admittedly, within adult education itself, later literature tended to be somewhat critical, and to be open to multiple positions and actors within feminism (Hayes and Flannery 2000). Little, however, was done to focus on women outside the official educational sphere especially in the nonprofit sector where women are notably great in number. There has been some attention to informal learning among women in technology (e.g., Butterwick and Jubas 2006) and some on learning in nonprofit organisations generally (Sousa and Quarter 2003) but none specifically on women's learning in nonprofit organisations. This chapter helps fill the gap.

Given that there are multiple forms of feminism—radical, liberal, critical, to name a few (see Code, 2000)—it makes sense that not all feminists or feminist writers have welcomed poststructural/postmodern theoretical frameworks. Marxist feminists such as Mojab (1998) protest that in focusing on nonunitary subjectivity and fluidity, postfoundational theories undo the achievements of modernity for women in addressing patriarchal systems that oppress them. Other critics charge postfoundational feminists of stripping away notions of agency and unitary subjectivity, of playing with women's lives and negating material bodies, all of which have been important to feminist's struggle to unite against patriarchal institutions (see also Butler 1994, 1999). Poststructural feminists such as Bronwyn Davies and Susan Gannon (2005) take on the detractors, pointing out that feminist poststructuralism is not about taking away agency for women or denying that institutions exist:

> The *agency* that feminist poststructuralism opens up does not presume freedom from discursive constitution and regulation of self (Davies, 2000a). Rather it is the capacity to recognize that constitution as historically specific and socially regulated, and thus as able to be called into question. (Davies and Gannon 2005, p. 318)

It is precisely in the attention to the ways that women are regulated and discursively produced that Davies and Gannon think women and feminism can be reconstituted. This chapter draws heavily on Davies' substantive work of negotiating the tensions of feminism and Foucault. Like Davies, I am concerned with acknowledging the ways in which women are produced as subjects and how they can effect change of that production, so that they are not determined as subjects. I am concerned with how they can create their own identity(ies) as knowing subjects, who are indeed agentic.

A third body of theory that is of use here is informal and incidental learning theory (e.g., Watkins and Marsick 1992). A prime example is the extensive national analysis of the incidence of informal learning in Canada, done by David Livingstone at the University of Toronto. Building in part on the tradition of Malcolm Knowles who studied informal learning in the 1950s, and Alan Tough who quantified informal learning in the 1970s, Livingstone's (1999) research shows that 90% of adults are involved in informal learning for work or for general interest, and that the average amount of time they spend on such learning is 15 hours per week. This is an increase from Tough's (1979) finding that 70% of the 66 adults studied had been involved in a learning project that they had developed themselves. According to Livingstone, such untapped learning is problematic for those who lack credentials or who have perceived barriers to learning. In particular, he found that 'those with self-rated poor reading skills tend to spend considerably more time in informal learning activities than those with greater reading facility' (p. 69). For Livingstone, and for all with an interest in lifelong learning, inattention to this group of informal learners is very problematic. He notes that 'the collective recognition of this informal learning and its occurrence across the life course can lead to people more fully valuing both their own learning capacities and those of other social groups' (Livingstone 1999, p. 68). It can also provide higher education and government with more accurate information with which to design learning programmes, as well as to meet the needs of those who already posses considerable skills and knowledge. Livingstone's findings have particular relevance for low-literate and socially disadvantaged women, which the organisations in this study typically serve.

Methodology and Data Collection

Many women are involved in nonprofit organisations as clients, employees or staff, directors, occasional visitors, and board members. Some of them may have held various identities over time (e.g., clients who became board members or directors, or board members who became directors). This research uses a purposeful sample (Marshall and Rossman 2006) comprised of board members and directors to explore their learning within the organisation. These participants were chosen because they were accessible for research given their regularised contact with the organisation for work and meetings. As well, they were most likely to be knowledgeable about the inner workings and offerings of the organisation, and to provide the most meaningful data. Of the 16 women interviewed using a semi-structured protocol, 8 were directors and assistant directors (minimally paid) and 8 were board members (volunteers). The participants range in age from 25 to 60 and have been involved from a minimum of 1 year to a maximum of 25 years (the median length of involvement was 5 years). Four of the board members are no longer serving on the board but are still attached to the organisation. Of the 16 interviews, 4 were done by email, 4 in person, and 8 by telephone. The data are analysed with particular attention to strategies around relationships, dealing with conflict and feminist practice. Questions centred on how these women learned about feminism, how they worked with/ against government and each other to negotiate power in the organisation, and how they learned from each other.

Typical of the nonprofit centres discussed here are local women's centres, transition or safe houses for women who are victims of abuse, and counselling centres for women. In addition to the nonprofit organisations that offer shelter are those that offer programming including preemployment training, literacy instruction, and personal development courses. Located in rural and economically disadvantaged areas of Atlantic Canada, they also offer psychosocial support for women through a drop-in centre, while others have lending libraries. The organisational structure (and particular feminist orientation) varies from organisation to organisation, yet they are all for women by women, and they have a political agenda to forward the cause of women. The general structure consists of a paid director, one or two paid staff members, and a volunteer board of about 10 members. In almost all cases the organisation relies on government funding as well as contributions from the community.

Context of the Study

The interviews highlight the participants' increasing knowledge of how they are affected by geography, economic conditions, and social class. And, as Michel Foucault notes, it is the differentiation of the legal, traditional, and economic conditions which enable or bring power relations into play (Foucault 1980; Marshall 1990). In becoming part of a community unit, the feminist nonprofit organisation, these women learned informally how a collective voice could be more effective in achieving justice. Whereas individually some faced unemployment, or were underpaid and underemployed, coming together in this local collection was a learning experience. The organisation is a place for them to take stock of their own circumstances and their shared plight. The nonhierarchical environment, participation in board decision making, and engagement in feminist activism often provided the impetus for learning skills that might not have been otherwise available given their social and economic location. Factors such as illiteracy, lack of employment, class difference, and access to higher education play into their narratives. They also affect their key areas of learning: learning to use resistance, silence, subversion and strategy to create themselves as feminist actors and knowers.

Technologies of Power and Resistances

Although half of the 16 women interviewed have university degrees, most indicated that their learning about feminism and feminist organisations occurred informally and incidentally through participation in the local organisation. They learned by observing the daily operations, talking to more experienced members, participating in board meetings, and organising commemorations and events for women. They learned about feminist participatory practices such as sharing in circles during board meetings, using consensus to come to decisions, and participating in committees. The regime of truth in these organisations is that these feminist practices are best practices, helping to further the notion of women as collaborative. Feminist procedures such as circles and talking things through are technologies of power that produce effects; they produce power that is not negative—it is in effect, very creative (Foucault 1977, p. 194).

Learning Through Participation

One of the key areas here is with regard to the ways in which women's organisations operate. For instance, on the surface they function in ways that are democratic and participatory. For instance, the directors encouraged a participatory structure where routine meetings are informal, often involving food and chat, and where leadership is shared. Common is the use of a living room type setting where participants sit in a circle intended to encourage conversation and sharing. Intentional learning activities are structured into these meetings and in the overall operations of the board. Attempting to practice or enact equality, the directors want to help board members learn about or be introduced to the ways of the organisation: how to chair a meeting, how to apply for funding, how to organise a women's event (e.g., anti-violence protest or International Women's Day celebrations). Given the particular structure of endorsing informal learning and inclusion, talking about issues of power and conflict in this research was difficult for both board members and directors/leaders.

For many of the board members feminist practices were new. In traditional community groups there is indeed sharing and cooperation but what was new was the intentional effort to increase skills in self-reflection and organisation. Some had never chaired a meeting or taken minutes before. An experienced director pointed out the span of her learning: 'I have been involved since '84, kind of working on projects... the learning experience is everything from learning how to engage with government to understanding women's oppression.' As one director noted, we 'come to decisions though collaboration and negotiation'. Another pointed out they were able to work through the issues because 'it was all women on the board; women are less inclined to grandstand or to engage in impression management'. Yet, for some of board members these feminist participatory practices were not without their effects. While directors were inclined to use the discourse of negotiation and consensual decision making, some of the board members experienced this discourse as a technology of power that suggested 'top down' and 'patriarchal' ways of being. One woman explained why she left after 5 years serving on the board. She noted that she just gave up since 'We had become like a men's organisation.' The woman who left felt the power of seniority and position of the designated leader's voice and the undue influence of more senior board members (in some cases founders of the organisation). The feminist pedagogical practices of group sharing and consensus, not to mention collegiality, furthered and helped to reproduce the regime of truth that women work together well. It also produced a parallel, albeit minor, discourse of resistance among the leavers. As Michel Foucault (1980) notes, 'Each society has its regime of truth...that is, the types of discourse which it accepts and makes function as true' (p. 133). This regime of truth allows the nonprofit organisation to run smoothly and produce educational and other opportunities for women. It also produces resistances when women leave who do not feel they have been heard. Feminism is a contradictory and complicated frame and only in being involved do the women learn this. Women who are active in the organisations learn to negotiate the contradictions, allowing care and conflict to operate as parallel regimes of truth.

For rural and socially disadvantaged women, one key aspect of learning is about effective ways to be an advocate for oneself and others through lobbying government (activism). The 'effective ways' constitute a different kind of activism than the public feminist activism of the 1960s (first and second wave feminism) which most often involved marches and protests. For 21st century women in a grassroots nonprofit organisation, the activism often consists of silent, subversive, and strategic approaches, reminiscent of James Joyce's (1968) 'silence, exile and cunning'

(p. 251). The nonprofit organisations being studied here were 'tasked' to care for, advance and defend the rights of women, especially through promoting education and literacy training. To support this work, the organisations needed to engage creatively with government funders. The women were learning that a simplistic view of activism as only visible protest, and of voice as only talking, is naive: Like Alecia Jackson (2004), they 'rely more on my actions and daily practices to disrupt the category of…woman' (p. 688, note 6). And, many feminists are like Jackson—they are less concerned with making their voices heard in traditional ways and more focused on accomplishing the work of the Movement in strategic and subversive ways through their actions and their daily practices. They also work to enable women to learn and exercise voice. Yet, this does not negate the fact that some women do visible protest—the point here is that the women in this study learned that these are not the only forms of resistance.

Resistance Through Silence

Much of the time in board meeting and in the regular running of these feminist organisations is taken up with funding:learning how to access it and learning how to retain it. When viewed through the lens of Foucauldian poststructuralism (1980), silence becomes a micropractice of resistance to the funder's (government) exercises of power. The government exercises power by holding and controlling the funds and dictating public policy around how the funds can, or will, be shared with feminist organisations. The first specific technology of government power is in its categories of funding. Government typically allocates funding to women's organisations through two main envelopes: 'core' funding for the regular running of the organisations and 'project' funding for specific activities that must be applied for, like preventing date rape and reducing teenage pregnancy. Government keeps core funding to a minimum, which produces the effect of the organisation constantly having to devise ways to get more, or even to keep what it has. If it really wants to provide education to women for literacy purposes, it may have to strategise to attain a long-term or sustained programme.

The opportunity to apply for project funding for special causes such as AIDS and crime awareness, or LBGTQ safety training, is made available to nonprofit organisations by government (e.g., Marple and Latchmore 2006). Feminist organisations apply for these funds complying with the rules of full disclosure of funds on hand, and needs in their organisation. In bearing all in this confessional practice, they appear to be meeting the government's demands. Their written proposals mirror the government discourse of management, executive directors and boards of directors, a hierarchical discourse that they claim not to use in the routine running of the feminist organisation. The power of government seeps into the feminist's proposal prose, yet they get the money and are, as one board member said, 'creative with how they use it'. Women learn to subvert these infralaws of the state (not actual legislation but policies determined by efficiency-seeking bureaucrats) by using the money for other purposes. As one director explained, 'We have no choice but to apply for what's on the go. We spend a lot of time filling out forms for projects but at least they keep us afloat.' In learning to keep quiet, feminist organisers can become effective challengers of government, using project funds to cover core costs or to engage in projects they believe worthwhile for women. They learn through networking that this strategy of silent resistance is utilised by feminists in other jurisdictions (see Fuller and Meiners 2005, p. 170) and it expands the definition of 'what counts as resistance' (Thomas and Davies 2005, p. 718). Silence, however, is one of many strategies they learn to use.

Using Strategy to Resist

Another technology of power exercised in feminist nonprofit organisations is strategising. Women directors and board members learn quickly and often incidentally that they need to be strategic in what they ask for and how.

In response to the government discourse of inquiries, hearings, and other bureaucracies, the women in this study strategically and routinely comply with their own discourse that at times mocks the government. The women in this study note that they do the expected public protests before government inquiries, and supplement it with their own strategies. They resist the government structures with the use of 'hidden transcripts' (Scott 1990, p. 4), private discussion and decision-making, as opposed to public expositions. They resist by fostering their commitment to egalitarianism, through the use of consensus, circles, and shared decision making. In essence, they are learning how to be strategically democratic and active in their own future. One experienced board member in her mid-40s explained what she had learned: 'In terms of practical skills I have had both formal and informal learning. I have learned to lobby government, to be diplomatic, as well as to find strategies to try to work with government. It is no easier these days than yesteryear to do that and to secure funding.'

Such exercises of power render the feminist organisers postactivist and postheroic (see Ford 2006, p. 84). They learn to be activists of a new era, who sometimes uses public displays of protest (e.g., one woman in the study talked about Take Back the Night marches) and sometimes a subversive and quiet form. They learn to use a 'subtle, routine, low level form of struggle and challenge' (Thomas and Davies 2005, p. 720) that may not take down a government but it will produce effects. Their resistance is built from within the system to some degree, which is not without its effects on the feminist organisation. More importantly, though, these women are learning to be 21st century agents of change and are doing so from within the grassroots. These postactivists still use the visual rhetoric of posters and marches, but have learned that they can be even more effective by adding to their repertoire the sophisticated strategies of silence, subversion and strategy. Their power is exercised through each of these technologies.

The 16 women in this study are learning to be an integral part of the feminist movement, that in its very existence is a resistance to bureaucracy, a way of disrupting smooth readings of organisations and those who work in them. The nonprofit feminist organisation exists as a public resistance to state control over women's bodies—their wellbeing, economic security, and self-image. The organisation pushes into the public sphere the discourse of woman, sexuality, and feminism. In studying these feminists through power theory we see how they lend a gendered and contextualised view to Foucault's theories of power (see English 2006). They not only perform resistance in observable acts and behaviours but also in their multiple subject positions. And through participation and informal learning, the women in this study became seasoned actors and protestors.

Using Subversion to Resist Government Discourse

Government-speak is managerial and businesslike, as represented in the discourse of agendas, proposals, deliverables, funding envelopes, directors, and boards of directors, and fiscal restraint. This official discourse can have the effect of deflecting attention from the actual intent of government actions, pronouncements, or policies. Some of these participants report being 'initially overwhelmed by the sheer volume of the paperwork and the bureaucracy' which arguably is government's intent. Women in this study report performing resistance to this totalising bio-power (control over women's bodies) by the use of their own technologies of power. One subversive way is forming alliances with other groups (see Butler 1999). Here is how one organisational director, who describes herself as very political, talks about the response to funding cuts in her province. 'It's been very convenient for politicians, and media and some bureaucrats to foster that. To paint us all as being a bunch of whacko, militant, man hating, blah, blah, blah, to dismiss us.' Their reverse discourse is postheroic and postactivist, in that it uses quiet, forceful and nonpublic means to effect change (see Ford 2006, p. 84). And, at times it is non-cosy, subversive and creative or as one woman described it, 'sometimes we pretend to be agreeable and ladylike'. What is interesting here is that groups of women within these organisations learn to work together to effect change, publicly or privately. The importance of women's collective action has not changed, though these women are learning to use it for their advantage.

The creation of the resistant and subversive subject is one of the effects of this government exercise of power. Yet, it is also true that governments' objectives and the feminists' are very different. Michel Foucault's attention to the 'types of objectives pursued intentionally by those who act upon the actions of others' (Marshall 1990, p. 24) is helpful. The feminists within the nonprofit organisations learn to subvert government technologies of power by collaborating with other similar organisations and working with them to lobby government. Their resistance is a unified voice, which has the effect of making government listen. One director described an instance of how she did this: 'All the women's centres, all the transition houses and all the men's programs, we all got together and formed a loose coalition to address these funding cuts which at this point they have, they've stopped.' Subversion becomes a technology of power that is an alternative to public protest. Feminists learn informally and incidentally how to be most effective in dealing with funders.

As feminists they resist the identity that is ascribed to them (e.g., 'militant, crazy activist') and they engage in a project of identity re-construction. Whereas the narrative of subservience runs through the feminist organisations (one board member said, 'We take what we can get from government' and another 'we spend all our time trying to find out where the money is'), there is a counter narrative also at work there. These feminists have created yet another subject position: that of effective and caring worker, subversive feminist and community developer. One director described her leadership as 'trying to do what she can for and with the women in the community' and helping 'women on social assistance get the most they can from this system'. The latter is in sharp contrast to the government labelling of women's organisations as deviant social organisations. Traced all through the interviews with these feminists was a reflexive construction of themselves as leaders and resistance fighters, who, as one executive director put it, really 'showed government bureaucrats a thing or two'. And, for most of these women, learning a new way of being had occurred gradually through active participation and not through courses or direct instruction.

The visual rhetoric of marches and banners, which characterised early versions of feminism, have been supplemented by a postheroic and postactivist stance which is sometimes less visible, operating beneath the surface and coursing through the veins of these feminist organisations. This is a feminist activism that resists the government expectation of constant confrontation or simplistic compliance with the policies of the state. In taking the masculinist government technologies of power (inquiries, grants, competitions, etc.) and subverting them these women have become postheroic and postactivist; they do not conform to the essentialist expectations of heroes (often military, male, and macho) or of activists (often loud, abrasive, and confrontational). Theirs is an activism and heroism of cooperation, linkages, and support (see also Thomas and Davies 2005), one which is a longstanding dimension of feminist activities. One only has to think of Rosa Parks who quietly refused to give up her seat, and of women's groups such as the suffragists and temperance activists who knew the importance of forming alliances long before it was considered heroic (McCammon and Campbell 2002). This contemporary enactment of feminism has been learned through trial and error and everyday struggle.

And, working in silence, as with most of these analyses of power, there is the resultant spate of overlapping and competing discourses that these women have learned to negotiate (see also Ford 2006). This study revealed a number of them: inventors, creators, victims, militant warriors, subversives, and shrewd negotiators. Here is how one veteran director described herself:

> You learn…all on your feet. There was no manual to pick up. I mean even with our re-entry program here, which we started about two and a half years ago, maybe three years ago. When we started we had bits and pieces of information…. We had to invent that ourselves. We learned together.

These discourses work simultaneously, sometimes pitted against each other, to create subjects who are at times divided about the worth and integrity of dealing with government in these ways. Yet, these discourses also work to create subjects who are postactivist, who carefully negotiate a fluid identity to support their beliefs, their organisations, and their causes. They have developed the capacity to entwine discursive knowledge with financial resources, and the ability to decide how these resources can be apportioned. Their ultimate technology of power is knowing intuitively and otherwise that the capillary power of government is embedded in the daily practices and decision making of their feminist organisations, yet they can and will resist alignment with the state. Their resistance does indeed count as a source of social change and becomes a useful life skill for them. The supportive structure of the organisation allows them a safe place to sort out and live these contradictions.

Discussion of the Findings

It would seem that feminist nonprofit organisations not only have a role in keeping feminism as a movement alive (see Ferree and Martin 1995), but they also have a huge role in supporting and facilitating women's learning. Yet, this learning is largely undocumented and unacknowledged.

One of the key areas of learning that surfaced in this study is in how to exercise power. Borrowing from Lesley Treleaven (2004) who has applied Foucault to organisational learning, I note four particular ways that these 16 participants have learned to exercise power and in so doing become effective, knowledgeable, and skilled in practice. Power is exercised *productively* by them in the creation of circles, as well as democratic and inclusive spaces for women from all social economic strata. Power is exercised productively in creatively drawing on the available funding to increase access to employment, further their literacy levels, and develop personally. Power is exercised *relationally* in the way the directors and board members work with each other to develop relationships and create lifelong learning spaces. Power is exercised *discursively* through the organising and dialoguing that makes the lines of power with government visible. Yet power is also exercised *coercively* by government in its troubling of funding guidelines and practices; and within the nonprofit organisations by feminist practices such as circles and coerced sharing.

These 16 participants are complicated multidimensional subjects, a view that a feminist-Foucauldian lens makes possible. Operating here are power, resistance, caring, and complicity, possibly all at once because of the women's willingness to deal with contradictions and to learn on their feet. As learning theorists such as MacKeracher (2004) note, they learn through experience and from the everyday. Consistent with the early learning literature (e.g., MacKeracher 2004) which characterised women's learning as caring, people centred, and connected, these women do and did seem to learn in relationship. And they learn from that relationship that not all women are caring and connected. In these sites of learning, they negotiate the politics of their situation, not only with respect to government but among themselves, which is a dimension of learning not well developed in much of the women's learning literature such as Hayes and Flannery (2000). The capillary power of 'feminism' affects them as does the operational power of senior members and of colleagues. The women learn to push back, resisting control and enacting agency, in short they exercise power and resistance, which are at the heart of Foucauldian analysis. In a challenge to detractors of poststructuralism (e.g., Mojab 1998), these feminists are actually able to see how they have been constituted by social and political factors, and to reconstitute themselves as knowing subjects.

Yet, like the people in David Livingstone's (1999) study, as well as in Watkins and Marsick's (1992), the women's learning is largely undocumented and unacknowledged. Through technologies of power—silence, strategy, subversion—they have resisted the regime of truth produced by government and perpetuated by higher education officials and faculty that only higher education can educate. Through their resistances they produce the truth effect that learning can indeed occur in the community and that it can be valuable. Their varied micropractice draw attention to the many women in the community who do not have access to credentials and yet who have experienced lifelong learning in a very real and effective way. Learning can indeed happen within a nonprofit organisation: studies such as this one open the possibility that this informal learning can be documented and recognised in some way.

These participants have a great deal to teach higher education about what counts as learning. Not only are women learning in these nonprofit organisations but their very presence and influence in them serves to change traditional notions of bona fide learning communities as well as government policies on fundable learning providers. Some of the women who are active in women's centres, for instance, have been excluded from traditional places of learning because of illiteracy, financial exigency and social class, factors that Benseman (2005) and McGivney (1993) have highlighted. Community based nonprofit centres for women provide an alternative education as well as a rallying point for activism around funding policies for areas such as literacy and preemployment training. In lobbying for change, women in these centres provide social and political support for other women. They gain confidence and skills that help them can potentially help them cross the class divide into higher education (McGivney 1990, 2001). For those who already have a postsecondary education, their new learning can help them assist other women, increase their own job opportunities, and advance the cause of women generally.

Given the uniquely feminist orientation of each of the nonprofit organisations from which these women come, they are forced to deal with issues of power and resistance. By their very mandate of addressing political issues that affect women, these nonprofit organisations are in a unique position to foster learning in challenging areas that other community based organisations such as the Red Cross or craft associations might not have to grapple with in a direct way. A stated feminist perspective means that their learning has indeed been challenging and has forced introspection and critique, and increased the participants' ability to be active participants in civil society. This is a unique contribution that these organisations make to learning.

In some cases these women will pursue higher education, and if not them, then the clients that they are serving through the nonprofit organisation. Women in their literacy programmes for instance, might register for community college or employment training. Even with a PLAR (prior learning assessment and recognition) process in place, though, much of their experiential learning about power, bureaucracy and feminism will not be valued, further enforcing the patriarchal nature of higher education and the discourse of government which sanctions only formal learning. Studies such as this one challenge such a narrow view. Educators can look to what happened here to see how these women defy stereotypes of female learners, how they challenge the norms of caring and connected knowers yet at the same time value a generally noncompetitive space to work out their differences. This study suggests that it is precisely because they are female knowers who value community and emotionally supportive environments, lauded by feminist learning theorists such as MacKeracher (2004) and Belenky et al. (1986), that they manage to learn all they do. In the absence of the bottom-line agenda that drives commercial organisations, they have safe spaces within which to practice strategies of resistance and to try out new ideas.

The data here may also be helpful in changing how government funders might see feminist nonprofit organisations. The feminist nonprofit organisations may indeed be useful conversational partners in the funding and education drama and may be sites for more training programmes and preemployment initiatives. Government and higher education might become more open to recognise women's informal acquisition of skills and knowledge such as community building, organisational skills, activist skills, funding strategies, feminism, conflict, power, and negotiation. Perhaps more threatening for government might be the women's learned expertise in resistance to funder pressures, their strategic forms of protest, and in the ability to negotiate conflict and to exercise their own power.

The women in this study have moved outside the homeplace and have chosen the in-between informal venue of women's organisations as their learning space. Nowhere is this activism more apparent than in attempts to garner and protect educational and training funding for women's education programmes, whether oriented to literacy, anti-violence education or positive space training. Yet, for all the heroic celebration of these women's lives and learning, I would hasten to add a caution. Although they resist, these women are not always in a place of full choice or control. As Davies and Gannon (2005) point out, their agency is not in protesting evil institutions or standing outside them. Their strength and agency are in recognising how they are affected and effected as subjects through their encounters. So Catherine Hakim's (2003) notion of the independent women making clear-cut decisions on careers or employment (preferences, in her terms) apart from their 'discursive regimes and regulatory frameworks' (Davies and Gannon 2005, p. 318) does not necessarily apply here. This study shows that women's choices are affected by the interplay of power, discourse, and resistance among the various actors in the nonprofit sphere. It is within the nonprofit organisation with multiple competing discourses that they are constituted as knowing subjects capable of being and acting. The lines of power make choices and resistances far more complex and difficult to trace than merely saying yes or no to an array of options. Yet, within this situation they engage in multiple forms of learning that contribute to feminist activism and agency.

Given the data gathering technique of semi-structured interviews it would be difficult to quantify the informal learning, much less to assess it directly for credit or PLAR recognition. Yet, this study offers an initial insight into how learning occurs in the feminist nonprofit sector. As with most qualitative work, this study provides the groundwork from which other studies may be generated.

Conclusion

This chapter has looked at some of the ways in which feminist nonprofit organisations serve to nurture informal learning for women They appear to provide spaces where women can be initiated into funding and negotiating strategies, learn from each other, and become more aware of the political dimensions of caring for women. These nonprofit centres function as incubators of new ways of being feminist and of actively creating one's own subject position(s).

This chapter attempts to further the development of a more critical body of literature on women and informal learning, by using the insights of poststructuralism and gender and learning. By focusing on specific informal sites and instances in which women gather to learn we can uncover women's everyday learning practices, and critically reflect on them. This enables us to know better how we can support women and encourage their learning processes inside and outside official institutions.

In the spirit of Alecia Jackson (2004), this chapter has disrupted categories of totalitarian government bureaucracy and powerless and victimised women, and shown how feminist's daily practices work to interrupt labels and essentialist views of learning as occurring only in formal postcompulsory education.

Acknowledgement The author would like to acknowledge the research assistance of Nicole Woodman Harvey in carrying out this study. This study was supported by a Social Science and Humanities Research Council grant.

References

Belenky, M. F., Clinchy, B., Goldberger, N., & Tarule, J. (1986). *Women's ways of knowing.* New York: Basic Books.
Benseman, J. (2005). Participation. In L. M. English (Ed.), *International encyclopedia of adult education.* New York: Palgrave.
Boshier, R. W. (1998). The Faure report: Down but not out. In P. S. Jarvis, J. Holford, & C. Griffin (Eds.), *Lifelong learning in the learning society* (pp. 3–20). London: Kogan Page.
Brookfield, S. D. (2005). *The power of critical theory: Liberating adult learning and teaching.* San Francisco: Jossey-Bass.
Butler, J. (1994). Contingent foundations: Feminism and the question of 'postmodernism'. In S. Seidman (Ed.), *The postmodern turn: New perspectives on social theory* (pp. 153–170). Cambridge: Cambridge University Press.
Butler, J. (1999). *Gender trouble: Feminism and the subversion of identity* (2nd ed.). New York: Routledge.

Butterwick, S., & Jubas, K. (2006). *The organic and accidental IT worker: Women's on-the-job teaching and learning experiences.* Proceedings of the National Conference of the Canadian Association for the Study of Adult Education. York University, Toronto, Canada. http://www.oise.utoronto.ca/CASAE/cnf2006/2006onlineProceedings/CAS20062%0Cover%20&%20TOC/Proceedings%20of%20CASAE%202006-TOC.html. Accessed 5 May 2009.

Chapman, V. L. (2003). On "knowing one's self" selfwriting, power, and ethical practice: Reflections from an adult educator." *Studies in the Education of Adults, 35*(1), 35–53.

Code, L. (Ed.). (2000). *Encyclopedia of feminist theories* (pp. 318–325). London: Routledge.

Davies, B., & Gannon, S. (2005). Feminism/post-structuralism. In Bridget Somekh and Cathy Lewin (Eds.), *Research methods in the social sciences.* Thousand Oaks: Sage.

Dreyfus, H., & Rabinow, P. (1982). *Michel Foucault: Beyond structuralism and hermeneutics. With an afterword by Michel Foucault.* Chicago: University of Chicago Press.

English, L. M. (2006). A Foucauldian reading of learning in feminist nonprofit organizations. *Adult Education Quarterly, 56*(2), 85–101.

Ferree, M. M., & Martin, P. Y. (1995). Doing the work of the movement: Feminist organizations. In M. M. Ferree & P. Y. Martin (Eds.), *Feminist Organizations: Harvest of the new women's movement* (pp. 3–23). Philadelphia: Temple University Press.

Fletcher, J. K. (1998). Relational practice: A feminist reconstruction of work. *Journal of Management Inquiry, 7*(2), 163–186.

Ford, J. (2006). Discourses of leadership: Gender, identity, and contradiction in a UK public sector organisation. *Leadership, 2*(1), 77–99.

Foucault, M. (1977). *Discipline and punish: The birth of the prison* (trans: A. Sheridan). New York: Vintage.

Foucault, M. (1978). *The history of sexuality: An introduction* (Vol. 1). Harmondsworth: Penguin.

Foucault, M. (1980). *Power/knowledge: Selected interviews and other writings 1972–1977* (trans: R. Hurley). New York: Pantheon.

Fuller, L., & Meiners, E. (2005). Reflection: Empowering women, technology and (feminist) institutional change. *Frontiers: A Journal of Women's Studies, 26*(1), 168–180.

Gilligan, C. (1982). *In a different voice.* Cambridge: Harvard University Press.

Goldberger, N., Tarule, J., Clinchy, B., & Belenky, M. (Eds.). (1996). *Knowledge, difference and power: Essays inspired by women's ways of knowing.* New York: Basic Books.

Hakim, C. (2003). *Models of the family in modern society.* Aldershot: Ashgate.

Hayes, E., & Flannery, D. (2000). *Women as learners.* San Francisco: Jossey-Bass.

Howley, A., & Hartnett, R. (1992). Pastoral power and the contemporary university: A Foucauldian analysis. *Educational Theory, 42*(3), 271–283.

Hughes, C. (2000). Resistant adult learners: A contradiction in feminist terms? *Studies in the Education of Adults, 32*(1), 51–62.

Jackson, A. Y. (2004). Performativity identified. *Qualitative Inquiry, 10*(5), 673–690.

Joyce, J. (1968). *A portrait of the artist as a young man. With six drawings by Robin Jacques.* London: Jonathan Cape (First published 1916).

Livingstone, D. W. (1999). Exploring the icebergs of adult learning: Findings of the first Canadian survey of informal learning. *Canadian Journal for the Study of Adult Education, 13*(2), 49–72.

MacKeracher, D. (2004). *Making sense of adult learning* (2nd ed.). Toronto: University of Toronto Press.

Marple, L., & Latchmore, V. (2006). LGBTQ activism: Small town social change. *Canadian Woman Studies, 24*(4), 55–58.

Marshall, J. D. (1990). Foucault and educational research. In Stephen J. Ball (Ed.), *Foucault and education: Disciplines and knowledge* (pp. 11–28). New York: Routledge.

Marshall, C., & Rossman, G. B. (2006). *Designing qualitative research* (4th ed.). Thousand Oaks: Sage.

McCammon, H. J., & Campbell, K. E. (2002). Allies on the road to victory: Coalition formation between the suffragists and the Woman's Christian Temperance Union. *Mobilization: An International Journal, 7*(3), 231–251.

McGivney, V. (1990). *Education for other people: Access to education for non-participant adults: A research report.* Leicester: National Institute of Adult Continuing Education.

McGivney, V. (1993). *Women, Education and Training. Barriers to access, informal starting points and progression routes.* Leicester: National Institute of Adult Continuing Education.

McGivney, V. (2001). *Fixing or changing the pattern? Reflections on widening adult participation in learning.* Leicester: NIACE.

Mojab, S. (1998). Muslim women and Western feminists: The debate on particulars and universals. *Monthly Review, 50*(7), 19–30.

Scott, J. C. (1990). *Domination and the arts of resistance: Hidden transcripts.* New Haven: Yale University Press.

Sousa, J., & Quarter, J. (2003). Informal and non-formal learning in nonprofit organizations. Nall Working paper, #72. http://www.oise.utoronto.ca/depts/sese/csew/nall/res/index.htm. Accessed 23 August 2007.

Thomas, R., & Davies, A. (2005). What have the feminists done for us? Feminist theory and organizational resistance. *Organization, 12*(5), 711–740.

Tough, A. (1979). *Adult's learning projects* (rev. ed.). Toronto: Ontario Institute for Studies in Education.

Treleaven, L. (2004). A knowledge-sharing approach to organizational change: A critical discourse analysis. In H. Tsoukas & N. Mylonopoulos (Eds.), *Organizations as knowledge systems: Knowledge, learning and dynamic capabilities* (pp. 154–180). New York: Palgrave Macmillan.

Watkins, K. E., & Marsick, V. J. (1992). Towards a theory of informal and incidental learning. *International Journal of Lifelong Education, 2*(4), 287–300.

Chapter 18
Lifelong Learning in Later Years: Choices and Constraints for Older Women

Jan Etienne and Sue Jackson

Introduction

In this chapter we examine some of the choices and constraints for older women in accessing learning in later years. We illustrate the types of learning with which older women participate as well as the choices open to them, although we also question the reality of 'choice', even for a group of seemingly more privileged women, as we discuss below. The chapter explores something of the aspirations of older women learners through drawing on key findings of a research project which examined lifelong learning and the Women's Institutes in England and Wales[1] (see below), although we show implications for older women learners that move beyond specific institutions and national boundaries.

The research was conducted with members of the National Federation of Women's Institutes (NFWI) in England and Wales. The NFWI is the largest organisation for women in the UK with a membership of over 200,000, and is largely although not entirely located in rural areas. Its mission is to educate women to enable them to provide an effective role in the community and to expand their horizons so that they are able to develop and pass on important skills. The majority of its members are over the age of 50. The NFWI is organised through a network of regional Federations with local Institutes which enable informal learning opportunities to take place. In addition, a wide variety of courses are delivered at Denman (the NFWI's residential college) where women participate in a range of learning activities.

The research methods used in the study were largely qualitative with the use of focus groups and one to one interviews. A total of 11 interviews were conducted with NFWI officers (including at Denman College) and Women's Institutes Advis-

[1] ESRC RES-000-22-1441 (2005). Learning citizenship: lifelong learning, community and the Women's Institutes.

J. Etienne (✉)
School for Policy Studies, University of Bristol, Bristol, UK

Department for Social Policy and Education, Birkbeck, University of London, London, UK
e-mail: j.etienne@bbk.ac.uk

ers, and 15 focus groups were held involving members from 24 local Women's Institutes (WI). We transcribed and analysed all tape-recorded interviews. The various quotations which feature throughout this chapter are samples from across a total of 26 of the transcripts. The local institutes were selected from five NFWI Federations from a cross section of rural and urban areas of England and Wales:

- The largest Federation, with 248 institutes and 9,500 members, covering a large geographical area from the industrial south-east of England to rural villages
- A Federation in a sparsely populated region, mainly consisting of rural farmlands and market towns, although it includes an affluent spa town and has a total of 101 institutes
- One of the smallest Federations, with 33 institutes, covering a largely urban area, including institutes in socially and ethnically diverse communities
- A Federation with 45 institutes in ethnically diverse towns and a range of villages in the North of England
- A Federation in Wales with 95 institutes and almost 4,000 members, covering a diverse geographical area, from a major city of Cardiff to the rural Welsh valleys

Drawing on the data collected and analysed, the chapter begins by considering the repercussions of discourses and policies which describe lifelong learning as a social and/or individual responsibility, exploring the connections between lifelong learning and active citizenship. It moves on to outline issues of identity, learning and community for older women. The chapter considers the wider consequences of women only learning environments and the implications of funding cuts in a climate of financial insecurity and within an increasingly ageing society. The interview data demonstrates the hurdles and obstacles to learning faced by women at a particular stage in the life course: older age[2]. Although the women in this study are in the main privileged, white, educated and middle class[3], the paper concludes that very little learning choices exist for them, demonstrating that opportunities for 'lifelong' learning severely decrease for older people.

Lifelong Learning and Active Citizenship

Lifelong learning policies have risen to prominence in recent years, and are high on the educational, economic and social agendas of many governments (including in the UK, elsewhere in Europe, North America and Australia) as well as of international organisations such as the OECD, UNESCO and the World Bank. Current discourses and policies show two major and sometimes conflicting messages.

---

[2] We recognise that in many ways 'older age' is a meaningless term covering a wide range across the lifecourse. A little over 75% of the women in this study were aged 65 and over.

[3] Whilst we recognise that both 'race' and 'social class' are contested categories, this was defined either by the women themselves, who were asked to state their ethnicity and social class, or (where social class was not stated) in relation to educational backgrounds and occupations.

Lifelong learning is seen as a key to self-improvement *and* as contributing to societal good. To engage in lifelong learning is seen as being socially responsible, with an onus placed on the individual in order to benefit the wider community. As the UK's then shadow minister for lifelong learning, further and higher education explained:

> I crave social justice; a cohesive society in which each plays a part and all feel valued, a Britain without barriers to self-improvement, without limits on opportunity. I desire this not just because I believe in the virtue of individual worth, but also because I know that when people feel valued the common good is fed. (Hayes 2008, p. 2)

On the one hand, therefore, lifelong learning has become the responsibility of all individuals, on whom it is incumbent to engage in learning throughout their (working) lives. It is for us all to grasp opportunities offered and to continue to improve ourselves. On the other hand, learning—including learning for work and to ensure social cohesion—is too important to be left to individuals, and requires state intervention. However, where there are no concerns about learning for work or about learning for social cohesion—as is the case with regard to older women—then the state no longer feels a need to explicitly intervene. Nevertheless, as we will go on to show, intervention takes many forms and cuts in funding for some types of learning, including the informal learning with which many older women engage, is another type of intervention. Although rarely explicit 'policies and practices of lifelong learning, in very different contexts and with different groups of learners, are gendered in their construction and effects' (Leathwood and Francis 2006, p. 2).

Although there has been much evidence (see, e.g. the work of the Centre for the Wider Benefits of Learning[4]) that learning brings better health and an increased sense of wellbeing for older learners, these groups are not seen as a priority. Neither is there recognition that older citizens can and do remain active and can positively contribute to the social wellbeing of a nation. Whilst a lifelong learning agenda should impact on all individuals throughout their lives, the reality is that it is increasingly geared towards employment and vocational learning for those between 18 and 30. Kamler (2006) argues that the current emphasis on people learning 'throughout their lives' clearly appears to mean 'working lives', whilst Jackson (2005) demonstrates that even if older learners are included in the rhetoric of lifelong learning they are not always part of the reality.

What counts as learning is highly contested (Burke and Jackson 2007) and the (mainly) informal learning undertaken by older learners is rarely acknowledged and almost never supported by governments, including those in Europe, North America and Australia. In her work on older learners and lifelong learning, Barbara Kamler asks how we use the knowledge accumulated over a lifetime in ways that benefit not only the learner—the older person—but the society in which they have lived (Kamler 2006, p. 162). Informal learning in particular acknowledges and values the extensive life experiences that older individuals have to offer both with regard to

---

[4] See http://www.learningbenefits.net/.

their own quality of life and for the benefits of the wider community. For example, Adshead and Jamieson (2001) have shown that older women who learn together retain important friendships that foster good relations whilst working with others in the local community. The learning that takes place within informal and community settings can play a pivotal role in helping to improve confidence and quality of life. We argue that this type of learning also has capabilities beyond individual personal achievement and towards a collective agenda of social responsibility. Widening and adapting the type of informal learning practiced successfully by organisations such as the NFWI can serve to foster good relations across communities, as we go on to show below.

Lifelong learning takes place in many different ways and in an endless variety of settings and may emerge through activities such as volunteering and community participation (Schuller and Field 1998; Jackson 2002). Informal and community lifelong learning dominates the learning that older people undertake, including members of the WI (Jackson 2006). Women are a significant proportion of the older population in the developed world and it is becoming clearer that policy makers (see, e.g. National Institute for Adult and Continuing Education 1999; Better Government for Older People 2000; Department for Works and Pensions 2005) can learn from hitherto hidden examples of approaches to informal learning in which many women engage (see, e.g. Jackson 2002, 2006).

There has been increasing national and global political interest in the ideas of learning societies and learning organisations which seek to reflect a commitment to encouraging and celebrating learning (Field 2000), although understandings of learning organisations do not always include groups such as the NFWI. However, we argue here that this is a mistake as participating in informal learning, including through the activities that membership of such organisations can offer, has been linked to increased levels of practical community involvement through voluntary activities, positively encouraging active 'citizenship' (Crick Report 2000). This in turn can lead to greater involvement in aspects of social life such as political awareness and a heightened sense of social responsibility. Given the increased interest in lifelong and informal learning it is not surprising to find that it is explicitly linked at policy level to other community/social initiatives in the UK such as neighbourhood renewal. All these different strands of policy are designed to involve specific groups of people such as parents, volunteers and tenants with a range of educational providers and community based agencies in an interconnected network of and for lifelong learning.

Hammond (2002) and Schuller et al. (2004) illustrate the extent to which people who are engaged in learning are more likely to be active citizens. Civic responsibility and active citizenship has been described as one of the most powerful modes of adult learning, providing opportunities for motivation, achievement and self-esteem (Schuller 2001). Active citizenship can involve regularly participating in the life of local communities through a range of activities, and the research demonstrated the wide variety of ways in which the members of the WI engage. Many of the women surveyed had an involvement in other organisations in the community around them, usually as a result of their involvement with the WI. Sixty percent of Federation

Chairmen[5] and seventy percent of women interviewed were involved in voluntary activities in their local area, including working as parish councillors, magistrates, school governors and church wardens. Others volunteered with charity shops, hospitals and hospices, and schools. As one respondent explained:

> Quite a few are involved in the churches. The church plays a big part in their lives. Many are involved in mothers' groups; scrabble clubs; book clubs: we have some local parish councillors; some JPs as well as some school governors. Some members are volunteers at the local hospital—helping in the book library, hospital visiting schemes. I myself teach basic skills at the local prison. *Mary, Institute I*[6]

In addition to local community work, many WI members are involved in national and international campaigns. These have included saving rural post offices, preventing local hospital closures, campaigns *for* adult education and care of the environment, and *against* supermarket packaging. Members have campaigned on issues such as care of the environment, GM foods, children's diet, renewable energy, human trafficking and world poverty. As one member said 'The WIs are the best lobbyists in the country!' (*Jenny, Institute U*).

Gendered Constructions of Family Life

Despite their political lives and campaigns, many of the WI members continue to be constrained by the gendered constructions of wives and mothers that defined them when they were younger. For older women in particular, it is likely that they would have lived their younger lives embedded within traditionally gendered family values (Thorne and Yalom 1982; Stacey 1996), with little opportunity to develop identities outside of the roles of wife, mother or ever daughter-in-law. Apparent family support could also be used to ensure that women stayed within the gendered constructions of family roles:

> My husband is the only child and his mother thought that you shouldn't want anything else other than your home, bringing up your children and your family and women that went out working were the causes of all the problems with the young people. *Margaret, Institute E*

> When I got the chance to get out…I was terrified of what my mother-in-law was going to say—and I really do mean terrified. *Liz, Institute V*

Others found that possibilities were severely curtailed by prevailing policies and ideologies of the time:

> As a young woman I worked in the civil service and those days when you are married you have to leave the civil service. It was the old fashioned idea that a married women didn't work anyway. If your husband couldn't afford to keep you that was that. *Mary, Institute I*

---

[5] The NFWI refers to 'Chairman/men' and the members we interviewed had little or no interest in discussing the gendered implications of this.

[6] Pseudonyms are used throughout.

Throughout the study there were numerous examples of women caring for family members with no choice or opportunities to explore their own much yearned for learning and social options:

> Before joining the WI, I was at home bringing up my family, my two sons. I started back to work when my youngest son was 11 years old, working for a GP part-time. I haven't worked then for 14 years which seemed a bit strange going back into the workplace at that time. But I did that until 1994 when I was caring for my in-laws who were both in and out of hospital for a period of time. So I had to give up my part-time work. *Judith, Institute O*

The majority of women interviewed in the study (80% of case study respondents) came from largely rural areas of the UK. Those living in rural areas revealed how isolated they felt when relocating to new areas, particularly when following their husbands for new employment opportunities. In such cases the women had little say over where, when and how they lived. Many women interviewed had given up their careers to support their husbands and raise their children. For the women, membership of the WI was one way of coping with new surroundings and a way of improving the quality of their lives, including training for work and acquiring new skills. As one WI member explained:

> I did a secretarial course when I left school, didn't like it very much, married young, had a couple of children. My husband was transferred to Germany; we spent 10 years living abroad and decided that our children were becoming too German. He got a job here and my neighbour encouraged me to join the WI. *Chris, Institute B*

Becoming involved informally with flower arranging led to her training as a florist and then working doing wedding flowers.

Other women showed how important the WI has been to them in moving beyond or through gendered constructions of family life and the constraints these can bring:

> I was a secretary after school and then I got married quite young and we had 4 children. My husband was at sea almost all of the time. And suddenly my husband got relocated so we left. My life was totally different. But then I got to know someone who belongs to the WI and now it's been terribly busy since! *Delia, Institute S*

> I had 34 years working in the same company after leaving school and I took early retirement to become a full time carer. When my caring duties ceased I was totally out of local activities and I was invited to attend a WI meeting and the rest, as they say, is history. *Deborah, Institute M*

> Then I had 3 children and I was caring for my mother-in-law at the early years of my married life so that kept me quite busy and then my mother-in-law died and very shortly after that, my mother as well. The WI turned up just at the right moment. *Annie, Institute D*

> We have notices generally around the area that there was going to be a WI opening in the local church hall which is next to where I live. I have got an elderly mother who does live with me and I can't go too far and it's absolutely beautiful to be right next door. So I said 'Okay I will go and have a look'. *Delia, Institute S*

In some ways, the women-centred support of the WI has taken the place of family support that would have previously existed. Vera noted that this was especially important for younger women, who may not have the family support that older women had enjoyed:

> They moved away from the family and they seem to get lost on the way. They haven't got any backup, they haven't mother-in-law, mother near by when they need help. *Vera, Institute R*

The WI enables women to support and work with each other in ways which allows them both to draw on gendered constructions and definitions and also to transcend them, finding ways to re/construct expectations of and identities for older women within the family.

'Suddenly I was somebody!' Re/developing Identities

Developing confidence and re-thinking what it means to be an older woman were key issues for many of the women in the research. Over 75% of the women in this study were aged over 65 and, despite coming from largely 'educated' backgrounds (some with undergraduate and postgraduate degrees and other qualifications, and often from professional backgrounds such as teaching, the health service and the civil service) many described a loss of identity as they left paid work or no longer felt that their traditional roles in the home were relevant. It is common for people to feel a loss of identity following retirement, which can also include the loss of social contacts, especially when encountering gendered stereotypes during retirement (Price 2000). There is a clear indication that older women suffer a loss of identity due to changing roles in the family, retirement and to societal perceptions of older women (MacRae 1990). Older women are often rendered invisible in a gendered society that also values youth over age.

One way to claim back an identity is through informal involvements and social network ties (MacRae 1990). A role in the WI gave some of the women a sense of identity that was missing elsewhere:

> I was now the President and on my first day out in the village.... 'Hello Vera'; 'How are you Vera?'; 'Nice to see you Vera'—Suddenly I was somebody *Vera, Institute R*

One of the most frequently given reasons for joining the WI was 'to meet new friends' and 'for enjoyment and friendship'. When asked about the benefits of membership responses included 'a sense of belonging and increased confidence', and women felt positively about being part of a large organisation that they described as helping to improve their lives. One way in which this happened is finding that others recognised that older women still have skills on which they can draw, including traditional skills of homemaking. The WI offers informal learning through a range of activities that are traditionally associated with homemaking, and which are highly valued by some of the members. Such activities include, for example, cake baking, jam making, needlecraft and flower-arranging. There was a high proportion of learning taking place that is more traditionally associated with older women's groups, including cookery, craft, flower arranging, garden produce and preserve making. Some respondents saw the development of these skills as adding value to their retirement, and others as reviving a 'dying art' of benefit to the wider community. Both of these elements were important aspects of the wider benefits of informal learning (and teaching skills to others). As Meridith (Institute R) said, 'We come from a generation that have been taught a little bit of these skills right from an early age.' It was important to her to be able to continue to develop such skills, as well as pass them on to others.

Learning involves the construction of identities, the project of becoming (Burke and Jackson 2007) and the impact of developing confidence is considerable for some women. The women interviewed spoke positively about retirement and the activities they were now enjoying and, once they joined the WI, they appeared to be motivated to learn, although this was often not initially the prime reason for membership. Other informal learning in the WI takes place through activities such as the regular local WI meetings, where members listen to invited speakers (35% of the women interviewed said they were learning through those talks); and activities such as organised walks, visits and exercise classes. As Joan said,

> From a personal point of view…I haven't got many opportunities to use my brain very much and I felt this was somewhere I could do something. Use my general intelligence if you like. *Joan, Institute L*

New opportunities can be developed through the learning that is offered through their organisation, including the ways in which members engage with the range of speakers that attend the local institute meetings. For example, in questionnaire responses, members stated:

- I have a greater variety of subjects to discuss mainly arising from speakers.
- I believe it makes me a more interesting person and therefore able to interact with other people.
- It makes me a more rounded person, broadening my horizons and encouraging me to try new things.

More formally, learning also takes place where knowledge is gained through WI roles such as that of Chairman, Treasurer or Secretary or WI Adviser. Members who hold more formal roles within the WI receive a package of training, which

> gives them the confidence to do the other things. We put on training classes here in January for the presidents, the secretaries, the treasurers and the press and publicist officers so that those people come here to be trained to do a better deliver within the WI and of course that gives them the confidence to then if they are invited to join some other organisations or gives them the confidence to apply to become a parish councillor or whatever. *Liz, Institute L*

Training for the role of WI Adviser, for example, includes sessions on public speaking which helps enhance positive identities:

> We also do public speaking courses. We have one of the national tutors as a member of our federation. All WI Advisers have to have public speaking, two sessions of that. That is very popular. That is something that the members do enjoy. And it does give you confidence and it's all learning. *Joan, Institute Y*

The WIs give

> opportunities to learn; wider knowledge of interesting subjects; opportunities to learn new skills; a sense of belonging; sense of community; appreciation of others; increase in confidence; awareness of the world around me. *Christine, Institute B*

For one member at least, joining the WI provided a chance to study for a higher education programme for the first time. Here the respondent shows the importance of this for her identity, including the way she is seen by others, in words that echo those of Vera, above:

> Membership of the WI gave me the confidence to study for a degree— after gaining a BA in Psychology—at home I'm suddenly somebody! *Annie, Institute D*

However, most members stay within the WI to develop their learning and skills, and the variety of roles within the WI also provide additional opportunities for learning:

> Well starting in my own WI level, I have been Secretary and President. I have served on all the committees. I have been chairman of home economics and the arts and then I have been vice-chairman of the federation and subsequently the chairman of the federation. And I am a WI adviser. *Maureen, Institute T*

WI members also learn in other ways through their involvement with the WI, such as conducting the research necessary to develop resolutions for Annual General Meetings. As Shirley explained:

> I have been to attend the meeting which is held where the speakers come along to give us information. And then I have to prepare the resolution to present to all the members. Bear in mind that we have 100s of members. It is pretty daunting because I hadn't ever done public speaking before and I have now presented 3 resolutions. *Shirley, Institute G*

Wider learning occurs when the women are able to pass on the knowledge accumulated to others, and to recognise and have recognised the links between learning and active citizenship. The connections between learning and active citizenship have been well documented (see section above) and, as Mehdizadeh and Scott's chapter in Part II of this volume shows, there are strong links between education and economic participation as essential elements of women's citizenship. However, less has been written about ways in which learning for active citizenship enhance identities for otherwise marginalised individuals, such as older women:

> I think it's very important because if we are to remain the biggest women's organisation which we are at the moment and represent the women's point of view we must not let it shrink to the point that people say 'Oh the WI is a handful of people'. It must be a good proportion of the population representing the female point of view which is one of the reasons we started out—women—from just housewives to something more important for the country. *Maureen, Institute T*

Not just to be, but to be seen to be, an active member of society was important to the majority of members. The women were asked how they benefited from informal learning in the WI and the three most popular responses were 'enjoyment'; 'better health and keeping active' and 'being seen as a valuable member of society'. Although ageing can bring a reduction in the number of activities with which a person engages (Atchley 1993), the continuation and development of some activities has important benefits, including a sense of shared social responsibility. As we go on to show below, for some respondents re/developing identities through a shared sense of community best happens in women-only spaces.

Women-Only Spaces

In moving on to discuss women-only spaces, we not suggesting that women are a homogenous group, and are very aware that the particular women-only space and shared sense of community of the WI is one that is a classed, racialised and sexualised (as well as aged) space. Nevertheless, a woman-centred focus is impor- tant to the women of the WI. In considering women-only spaces, we are mainly considering emotional and learning spaces rather than the physical spaces where women can re/develop their identities, although these do of course interact and are interdependent. The use and allocation of physical space can be a strong visual reminder of gendered power relations, and women can be literally side-lined in shared physical space (see Jackson 2004). The WIs are clearly important physical women-only spaces that are highly valued by the members, enabling the develop- ment of emotional and learning spaces for women, and giving women the ability to resist power relations elsewhere.

Since joining the WI many members spoke of their aspirations and increased confidence which mitigated against previous lack of identity and low self esteem. When asked about the benefits of the WI, Irene stated:

> Until I joined the WI I was always apprehensive about asking my husband if I could do this or do that, or go here and go there. Now I just say to him, I am going out tomorrow afternoon. *Irene, Institute H*

As part of the research the women were asked '*What are the most important benefits of membership of the WI?*' Nearly 50% said '*working with other women*'. Support for each other was highly valued:

> Being there for each other I think WI is giving me confidence and once you become sec- retary and president I think you gain confidence. I think as I was secretary for some time they ring me for things, for chatting and they feel that somebody is there that would listen. I think that is important that women are there for each other for all sorts of things, education, or just listening, a cup of tea and a shoulder. *Margaret, Institute E*

In particular, a safe and 'secure' woman-only environment was valued (for further discussion, see Jackson 2004, 2006). As one member said:

> They can go to Denman, they don't have to take a course, they could just do walking and singing and that would give them an opportunity to have a little holiday, branching out by themselves, knowing that they were going to be in a secure environment with other women.

The women-only space of their local Institutes gave the women the confidence to move into public spaces. They were more able to engage in community activities if they knew that other members of the WI would also be present, creating a women- only space within wider social spaces. Women felt they had something in common with each other, especially as members of the WI:

> I could go on that because I would go with my friends or at least I would know there will be all WI ladies there and therefore I would have something in common and I wouldn't be isolated. *Shirley, Institute G*

The lack of isolation was particularly important at moments of transition. The women described a range of support from fellow WI members particularly when going through separation, loss and bereavement and described how membership of the WI helped them cope at a time when they were frightened and alone, and to move on to develop new ways of being. For example, one woman talked of support following divorce.

> I went through a rather nasty divorce and if it hadn't been for the WI and the fact that I had friends and the support network that I needed…. Really it taught me that if you make friends what you put into it sometimes is what you get out again. *Ruth, Institute R*

Women-only spaces were particularly important for many of the women at times of bereavement.

> The friendship you make as a member of the WI is just amazing. The support members give to each other when they are going through bereavement is very special indeed. Many women who are not so active in the WI…when their husbands die they return to the WI and become alive again! *Myrtle, Institute E*

> After the death of my husband I don't know where I would be if it hadn't been for the support from the WI. *Sylvia, Institute C*

> I am a recent widow too. The friendship and the support from the WI have been immense and without that I would have been in a much worse condition. And also the confidence that I could do things on my own, it wasn't with the family all the time, I was doing something for me, for myself. *Irene, Institute H*

Women-centred support was important, too, at other times of difficulties, as well as at times of celebration:

> If they have tragedies in their lives or there are special celebrations—everybody looks after everybody else. *Monica, Institute P*

For many women, the opportunity to develop, learn and socialise in women-only spaces was a central way in which their identities become (re-)affirmed. Nevertheless, the women surveyed were aware that the future existence of the women-only spaces of the WI may well be under threat because of changes in the world around them:

> A lot of people now are forced to become introverted, they are afraid to go out, they don't join things…I don't really know what is causing it but the newspapers are frightening people, they don't go out at night. *June, Institute F*

This is particularly true of women living in rural areas, as is the case with the majority of women interviewed. There is a rural/urban divide in access to learning and social activities (Tuckett and McCauley 2005). In rural areas, where most of the women in this research are located, a severe lack of public transport prevents older women from attending education centres, and the older women are the more likely they are to be dependent on public transport (Jackson 2005). There is also a perceived risk about being out in the dark, which in winter in England can mean from around 3.00 in the afternoon. Remoteness was threatening the future existence of some WIs.

> Many years ago when I was secretary I did write to the county because we were starting to organise our county style base because we just couldn't get our memberships into […]. It's too far. There it was difficult to park anyway. That was rather a shame for us. We have been rather isolated. *Patricia, Institute H*

One member observed:

> Now people have become isolated therefore the more isolated they become they are less likely to join. They become introverted and defensive. *Val, Institute P*

Venturing out at night was a real concern for older women learners, who tried to find other ways to access learning and social networking opportunities:

> But it is in the evenings and we are an afternoon club and that makes a difference because there are a lot of elderly and they are not working and they want an afternoon meeting, people don't want to go out in the evening. *Delia, Institute S*

An ageing membership presents further concerns.

> Well our members are slowly dwindling. Some institutes have very few members. That tends to be in areas where women are more elderly. If you are very much older there is a lot to do—the older you are the harder it is to keep up with activities and so the WI closes. *Meridith, Institute R*

Of real concern to many members was the cut in funding for adult education that has been seen in the UK as well as in Europe, North America and Australia.

> We used to get a grant from […] County Council and our classes were grant aided so you could help, you would pay for the tutor. But of course they don't give us anything now so we now have decided that we will have workshops here to try to take the place of these of the granted classes. That is our big aim at the moment…. *Val, Institute P*

A lack of funding for non-accredited courses means that older women are denied opportunities that were also denied to them when younger (Jackson 2004). As one respondent explained, 'Some of us missed out on education when we were young, there weren't the opportunities', and there were real concerns by officers and members of the NFWI that the opportunities may be continuing to be denied. The less likely people are to have continued education whilst young, the less likely they are to participate when they are older (Sargeant et al. 1997; Schuller 2002), leaving older women doubly disadvantaged. The research has shown that women-only spaces are particularly important in helping overcome such disadvantage, and such spaces need to be developed through community and voluntary groups and organisations.

An officer at Denman College stated that far from women having less need for learning as they grow older:

> I think (lifelong learning) is actually more important…. The speed of changes in community, society, technology, these are all having an impact on individuals and families and I think it's crucial that people keep up to date because if they don't they would be out of step with society. Also I think…to keep people engaged in society, to keep people engaged with other people, learning brings people together…I think that it's absolutely crucial. What worries me now is that funding has been cut for a lot of these lifelong learning opportunities locally…. So I think in the future it is going to be very much down to community groups and voluntary organisations…

Yet the women-only spaces provided through such groups and community organisations are dwindling, especially spaces for older women. Like other providers of adult and continuing education, the NFWI have had problems with public funding, especially with regard to non-accredited courses, which the government will no longer fund. The NFWI has an active campaign to lobby Government on widening participation within a lifelong learning agenda, as these issues have potentially serious implications for older learners.

Conclusions

Even in retirement, choices that exist for the WI members are largely influenced by family responsibilities, money, networks of support as well as the expectations of the wider community. Listening to the voices of older women participating in the study has demonstrated the hurdles and obstacles to learning faced by a particular group of women at a critical stage in the life course. On the one hand the research shows the women in this project to be largely privileged, white, heterosexual, educated, middle class, confident and strong willed, living mainly in rural areas and in control of their learning lives. On the other, it shows that they are still constructed through dominant discourses about older women, embedded in the social construction of gendered roles within the family. Most significantly, the study has considered the reality of 'choice' for a seemingly privileged group of women and has demonstrated the many facets to learning and participation in later years.

Through informal learning, members of the WI are able to improve the quality of their lives and those of the community around them. Responses show that the key benefits of membership of the WI include the ability to develop positive identities which leave older women feeling that they can play an active and useful role outside of family responsibilities, and engage with their wider communities.

We argue that in an ageing society organisations like the WI can be an effective tool in promoting integration and community cohesion at a time when the numbers of elders from a range of cross-cultural backgrounds are increasing in significant numbers. Community cohesion policies suggest that all groups in society should strive for shared values, behaviour patterns and knowledge to allow all groups to feel that they are in some sense part of the whole. Adult education, whether delivered in further education colleges, universities, or in adult or community centres, has been one of the greatest building blocks of community cohesion. However cuts in funding has meant that older learners are increasingly not included as part of a strategy to help promote community relations and we have argued here that this has a particularly severe effect on women.

With cuts in funding and with the gendered constructions and identities for older learners, we have argued that very little choice exists for older women to participate in lifelong learning in order to broaden their horizons and benefit the wider community. The NFWI is one means whereby older women can continue to make societal contributions and continue to engage in their own lifelong learning. Finally, we have argued that safeguarding women-only learning environments for improving quality of life for older women learners in a climate of renewed government priorities for vocational learning is of significant importance.

References

Adshead, L., & Jamieson. (2001). *Education and the adult years: A study of students of the Faculty of Continuing Education*. Birkbeck: University of London.

Atchley, R. C. (1993). Continuity theory and the evolution of activity in later adulthood. In J. R. Kelly (Ed.), *Activity and ageing*. New York: Stage.

Better Government for Older People. (2000). All our futures. http://archive.cabinetoffice.gov.uk/service first/1998/op/newop.htm. Accessed 13 Dec 2008.

Burke, P., & Jackson, S. (2007). *Reconceptualising lifelong learning: Feminist interventions*. London: Routledge.

Crick, B. (2000). Essays on citizenship, London, Continuum.

Department for Work and Pensions. (2005). Opportunity Age: Meeting the challenges of ageing in the 21st century, London: Department for Work and Pensions.

Field, J. (2000). *Lifelong learning and the new educational order*. Staffs: Trentham.

Hammond, C. (2002). *Learning to be healthy: Centre for Research on the wider benefits of learning*. London: Institute of Education.

Hayes, J. (2008). *From social engineering to social aspiration: Strategies to broaden access to higher education*. London: Universities Association for Lifelong Learning, Birkbeck, University of London.

Jackson, S. (2002). Widening participation for women in lifelong learning and citizenship. *Widening Participation and Lifelong Learning, 4*(1), 5–13.

Jackson, S. (2004). *Differently academic? Developing lifelong learning for women in higher education*. Dordrecht: Kluwer.

Jackson, S. (2005). When learning comes of age. Continuing education into later life. *Journal of Adult and Continuing Education, 11*(2), 188–199.

Jackson, S. (2006). Jam. Jerusalem and calendar girls. *Studies in the Education of Adults, 38*(1), 74–90.

Kamler, B. (2006). Older women as lifelong learners. In C. Leathwood & B. Francis (Eds.), *Gender and lifelong learning: Critical feminist engagements*. London: Routledge.

Leathwood, C., & Francis, B. (Eds.) (2006). *Gender and lifelong learning: Critical feminist engagements*. London: Routledge.

MacRae, H. (1990). Older women and identity maintenance in later life. *Canadian Journal on Ageing, 9*(3), 248–267.

National Institute for Adult and Continuing Education. (1999). *Meeting the needs of older learners*. Leicester: NIACE.

Price, C. (2000). Women and retirement: Relinquishing professional identity. *Journal of Ageing Studies, 14*(1), 81–101.

Sargeant, N., Field, J., Francis, H., Schuller, T., & Tuckett, A. (1997). *The learning divide: A study of participation in adult learning in the United Kingdom*. Leicester: NIACE.

Schuller, T. (2002). *Age, equality and education, IPPR seminar series on age and equality*. London: Routledge.

Schuller, T., & Field, J. (1998). Social capital, human capital and the learning society. In R. Edwards, N. Miller, N. Small, & A. Tait (Eds.), *Supporting lifelong learning* (Vol. 3) *Making policy work*. Bucks: Open University Press.

Schuller, T., Bynner, J., Green. A., Blackwell, L., Hammond, C., Preston, J., & Gough, M. (2001). *Modelling and measuring the wider benefits of learning: A synthesis*. London: Institute of Education.

Schuller, T., Preston, N., Hammond, C., Brasset-Grundy, A., & Brynner, J. (2004). *The benefits of learning, the impact of education on health, family life and social capital.* London: RoutledgeFalmer.

Stacey, J. (1996). *In the name of the family: Re-thinking family values in a postmodern age.* Boston: Beacon.

Thorne, B., & Yalom, M. (1982). *Rethinking the family: Some feminist questions.* New York: Longman.

Tuckett, A., & McCauley, A. (2005). *Demography and older learners: Approaches to a new policy challenge.* Leicester: NIACE.

Chapter 19
Part III: Conclusion

Sue Jackson, Irene Malcolm and Kate Thomas

It is clear from the chapters in this section that women-only or women-centred sites of learning are important in developing safe spaces where women can resist the gendered, classed, racialised and ageist constructions of their identities. This includes, for example, vocational learning which recognises and values women's multiple experiences; networks of intimacy which enable educational and career choices to be made; feminist organisations; and women's social spaces. Although much of the policy and practice concerned with vocational education and training fails to recognise the value of different types of skills for the economy, including the key transferable skills that are developed by women's roles in the home, as Cable and Goodliff have shown, some vocational learning can enable women to develop professional identities which increase confidence in the workplace and beyond, and opens possibilities for women to redefine what 'professionalism' means.

As Alison Fuller, Ros Foskett, Brenda Johnson and Karen Paton show, however, learner and worker identities and the choices that are made are developed in sites other than education and the workplace. Choice is never just an individual process but comes about through the networks of intimacy and interpersonal ties between family and friends, and never in isolation from gender, social class or 'race'. There are competing and ambivalent expectations which continue to feature in education and career decisions and choices. Such choices can be aided and developed within women-centred spaces which enable resistance to existing power structures to be played out, and new subject positionings to be created.

However, with the cuts in funding for lifelong learning that are currently occurring across Europe, North America and Australia, and with the focus on a particular type of vocational education and training linked to the knowledge economy and to globalisation, such spaces are rare indeed. As this section has shown, with the

S. Jackson (✉)
Birkbeck Institute for Lifelong Learning, Birkbeck University of London,
26 Russell Square, WC1B 5DQ London, UK
e-mail: s.jackson@bbk.ac.uk

S. Jackson et al. (eds.), *Gendered Choices,* Lifelong Learning Book Series 15,
DOI 10.1007/978-94-007-0647-7_19, © Springer Science+Business Media B.V. 2011

gendered constructions and identities for learners in formal, workplace and informal sites, often very little choice exists for women to participate in lifelong learning in ways which helps construct and reconstruct positive identities. Nevertheless, some spaces can be opened out which enable women's everyday learning practices to be uncovered and de/re/constructed.

Chapter 20
Policy Challenges: New Spaces for Women's Lifelong Learning

Irene Malcolm, Sue Jackson and Kate Thomas

Introduction

This book is written at a transitional moment in women's lives at the beginning of the second decade of the 21st century. Authored by women who are practitioners, policy advisers and academics, the work draws on a view of feminism as the pursuit of an agenda for social change that aims to improve the position of women, furthering their influence and benefiting society overall by enhancing their contributions. The chapter authors make a distinctive contribution to lifelong learning research by specifically questioning the gendered assumptions that surround choice. While choice has been the mantra of neo-liberal politics in education (Apple 2001), the present volume adds to critical voices that highlight the bounded nature of choice. The authors critique gendered choices that constrain women and limit their access to certain types of learning and careers. Women's gendered pathways are influenced by assumptions about innate qualities of women and men. These assumptions inform education policies and broad cultural expectations of women. The choices available to them, for example, to enter male-dominated areas of employment, are reduced, and it is suggested that women's natures predispose them to certain roles in life such as caring for others. In challenging these assumptions, the authors in this volume highlight the potential for expanding women's contributions in the areas of learning, work and community. Against the backdrop of a political and economic environment where lifelong learning is gendered, racialised and classed, the potential of women's contributions in configuring alternative possibilities resonates throughout this volume.

The present work reflects the richness of writing on gender and lifelong learning. The book represents the authors' engagement with the themes of learning, work and identity which are linked critically, as gendered learning in each area reinforces gendered experience in the others, affecting the choices that are available. While the book title may suggest a linearity—that gendered learning leads to gendered

I. Malcolm (✉)
School of Education, University of Dundee, Dundee, UK
e-mail: i.z.malcolm@dundee.ac.uk

S. Jackson et al. (eds.), *Gendered Choices,* Lifelong Learning Book Series 15,
DOI 10.1007/978-94-007-0647-7_20, © Springer Science+Business Media B.V. 2011

work and then to gendered identities—it is important to emphasise the inter-relations among these themes and the porous nature of the boundaries that are sometimes drawn around them in policies and practices. In examining gendered choices in the context of these themes, we seek to challenge tendencies to conceptualise boundaries as fixed and portrayals of individual identities as uni-dimensional and static. Drawing on the work of Doreen Massey we could think about the interaction of influences that results from these porous boundaries as a form of "articulation" (Massey 1995, p. 345) which takes place among class, gender, social relations, economics and space, affecting gendered choices. The notion of articulation can support an analysis of gendered learning pathways through, for example, juxtaposing critiques of policies such as widening participation and the skills agenda with considerations of women's experiences. This makes it possible to emphasise complex inter-relations, and to disrupt normative assumptions about the influences on lifelong learning.

In drawing a conclusion to the foregoing discussions we offer a critical review of issues that they suggest, considering some implications for the field of gender and lifelong learning. The chapter begins with a critical reflection on inherent challenges in policy and in feminist positioning. We then consider policies of widening participation and the skills agenda as far-reaching influences on women's learning and work roles; next we examine the idea of women-only spaces, and lastly we reflect on the role of the imagined domain in forging new identities.

Policy Critique and Critical Positioning

In discussing policy influences in lifelong learning, we acknowledge policy's potential flux and instability as a technology that affects experiences of lifelong learning. In the UK, for example, its influence has sometimes been contradictory (see Burke, this volume) and this feature of the policy landscape in lifelong learning is likely to be compounded by new political and economic difficulties, due to the financial crisis in the west. In countries where new governments have been recently elected (e.g. Greece and the UK), fresh economic pressures are being exercised on citizens, challenging the nature of civic life to which adults' learning has traditionally belonged. Feminist critiques of lifelong learning, offering new horizons, may be difficult to produce in these circumstances. However, this is compounded by the position from which all of the authors in this book write. A significant paradox that emerges in the chapters above is the way that the authors, all of whom are involved in feminist praxis, work within and, at the same time, try to resist constraining policy frameworks and meta discourses. While they problematise policy discourses, suggesting alternative visions, there remain challenges in considering how these can be realised. The question that this raises for the future of feminism in lifelong learning is in what ways discussions such as those initiated in this volume can contribute to formulating new choices in learning, work and identity. This begins, perhaps, when women in lifelong learning challenge their own positioning and the ways that theory and praxis are developed, in order to find new ways of knowing.

Widening Participation Policy and Valuing Skills in Learning/Work

The book is interested in ways in which broadening of choice can widen participation in several arena, including in learning, in the workplace and in communities. Although, in the main, the chapters in this book are concerned with women's gendered choices, the authors also discuss choices which are located in constructions of masculinities, aspirations and decision-making processes. While widening participation is a central concern in lifelong learning policies and practices, choices are fashioned through the complexities of identities and identifications, through current discourses of transformation and social justice within widening participation debates. It has been argued that debates about widening participation make simplistic assumptions about targeting particular students, and about the benefits of participation (Thomas 2001). We raise a concern that debates do not explicitly address gender as an issue, and there is little recognition in discussions of widening participation in work-based learning, for example, of the difficulties faced in a gendered (and classed) workplace for women with children. Women make up the majority of part-time workers and the lack of choices that there are for women in balancing work and childcare cause particular disadvantages. Women's representation in employment has continued to increase in a number of western countries. However, women are still underrepresented internationally, particularly in positions of power and in specific sectors, such as technology (Faulkner 2004). This means that women's contributions are at the periphery of new areas of work in the knowledge economy and the digital economy. Their contributions are hidden and contested, as is women's complicity in some of the adverse effects of new economy developments.

The book highlights the gendering of skills and women's exclusion, critiquing the link between gendered choices and the skills agenda. Despite current discourses, we argue that learning for community development does not detract from the case for a skilled economy. However, this case is often presented in a way that neglects the complexities of the skills agenda and policies that promote it. For example, the nature of skills is contested, there are tensions around what types of skills are needed and whether new approaches to work represent de-skilling or up-skilling: there is some evidence that both happen to different groups in the same workplace (Munro and Rainbird 2002), having differential effects on women. Furthermore, due to the dynamic nature of work and the impact of changing technology, new skills quickly become outmoded. At the same time, instrumental and skills-based learning are also seen to have some beneficial effects on women's confidence and work efficacy (Hyde, this volume). However, the book highlights the paradoxical aspect of the skills agenda as authors critique the gendered nature of skills which essentialise women as being more suited to certain types of work, such as caring. The resulting tension casts doubt on the wider benefits of confining lifelong learning to developing skills, pointing to the relevance of a broader, more durable education for women's inclusion and career progress. Another problem suggested in the present volume is the way that a focus on a skills-based economy excludes not only women with caring responsibilities, but also other groups including older women. These women are not in the labour market and are constructed through dominant discourses, embedded in the social construction of gendered roles within the family. Nevertheless, women's community participation and active citizenship can be widened through informal learning and women's networks, benefiting the community and broadening the choices available to women in older age. For this reason, we argue that those working in the field of lifelong learning should continue to critique the gendered nature of learning dominated by skills development. Gender and citizenship is a critical issue for women, and one way to increase choices for women is to widen opportunities for community participation. This emphasises the importance of learning that is life-wide and, while it encompasses the benefits of having skills, it moves beyond these to embrace political and community dimensions. These dimensions are threatened by the depoliticisation of learning and work that is strongly focussed on skills to the exclusion of other aspects.

Space for Women: Contested and Women-Centred Spaces

The book demonstrates how spaces that women occupy are made up of a range of relations at different sites, from the public spheres of work, to the household (which may also be a place of work). The idea that women occupy spaces in a way that is related to gender roles has been developed in discussions of women's work (Fenwick 2006, 2008). Relating women's learning, work and identities to space allows us to highlight the way that diverse influences articulate in gendered choices. This view can disrupt some received notions of the relations between private and public, local and global and women's identification with private and local spaces.

One way to develop resistances to constructions of gender, to find new ways of knowing, is through women-centred spaces. It can be extremely beneficial for women to have a community of other women around them in order to contest gendered, classed and racialised spaces (Bloom 2009). Lifelong learning itself is a contested space, and a critique of the concept points to it as an ideological distraction that shifts the burden of increasing adaptability onto the worker. Some of the authors clearly demonstrate the enforced gender segregation that takes place in learning spaces and in the workplace. Indeed, it emerges that women-only spaces offer vital support for women and for the development of women's solidarity.

The book explores such issues in depth, demonstrating that although women only spaces are sites of power as well as resistances, significant and complex learning can and does take place. Learning through participation in women-centred spaces enables resistance through subversive strategies, including resistance to ascribed identities and the re-construction of new ones. Women-centred spaces enable the re-development of identities previously located through the gendered constructions of family life for older women, leading to the development of greater participation in learning and within communities.

Authors in the present volume show how globalisation and the neo-liberal economics of competition challenge women's positions and the social fabric of communities. A critical perspective on women's learning, work and identity emphasises their roles as actors at informal sites of globalisation, including seemingly neglected sites such as "households and communities" (Nagar et al. 2002, p. 260). While the discourse of lifelong learning suggests the need for high-skilled workers, taking an international perspective, many women are in peripheral positions in low-paid areas such as domestic work, catering and caring. Here, feminist and emancipatory discourses have been challenged by complicity when women's learning and (low paid) work in such informal spheres underwrites and actively constitutes public spheres of policies such as globalisation. This affects women's attempts to develop non-gendered identities in their positions as workers and learners. The problem is compounded by the fact that these influences on gendered work, learning and identity remain unrecognised. This problem underlines the importance of analysis and critical reflexivity (Burman 2006) in women's lifelong learning, to encompass the processes that contribute to gendered choices, as well as complicities with and resistances to these.

Women-only spaces are important for strengthening collective voices, and for supporting women in developing their visions, imagining new horizons and strengthening their influence in areas of work and learning where they are currently marginalised. However, while the book shows the benefits of women-only spaces, arguments to support these are also open to critique. We are aware that creating spaces for women does not guarantee that the forms of power exercised at such sites will necessarily be in the interests of all women. Such spaces also represent an exclusionary practice in themselves which, in principle, the advocates of women only spaces would, in other circumstances, reject.

Imagined Domains

The writing in the above chapters demonstrates that disrupting gendered choices has far-reaching implications for learning, work and identity. While women-only spaces and the support of these are important, a problem which seems particularly relevant for the future is how women are to increase their representation in other spaces, and what stance they should adopt there.

In order to realise some of the new possibilities discussed in the chapters above, women have to be able to imagine new spaces of representation and new identity possibilities. They need to envision new forms of learning and new roles that challenge the way diverse influences inform gendered choices. The interrelation of the book's themes points to imagined domains that connect them; however, the impact of imagined domains on women's gendered learning and its link to the forms of capital that women sustain have received little attention in education discourses. In other areas of social science, the connection between social capital theory and imagination is not new (Almond and Verba 1963; cited in Hooghe and Stolle 2003, p. 69). However, with the exception of Quinn's work on imagined social capital, it has not been taken up in education discourses (Quinn 2005).

Drawing on the imagined domain to analyse lifelong learning presents a number of theoretical and practical challenges. We expect learning to have tangible benefits that can be studied to enhance future practice. The ways in which the realm of the imagination contributes to women's learning, work and identity are inherently difficult to quantify, although some research points to its significance for the empowerment of women learners (Quinn 2003). It may be risky to raise the question of imagined domains in science, given that they appear antithetical to the foundation of rational thought. In the middle of the 20th century (and more recently) imagined domains have been exploited by political regimes that pursued oppressive policies and committed war crimes. In the 21st century they are recruited in marketing commodities, selling TV talent shows and in disseminating an extreme view of how women should look. Perhaps as a result of the contested nature of imagined domains, there has been little discussion of the struggles in imagination, or of the potentially contested nature of imagined capital that is influenced, for example, by neo-liberalism. The lack of debate on the role of imagined domains presents a further challenge for feminist writing in lifelong learning that seeks to develop new visions of women's participation. Arguably, new roles and new identities have to be imagined before they can be realised.

Conclusion

The book presents a case in favour of lifelong learning that eschews gendered choices and is able to respond to the challenge of social cohesion under the pressure of global competition. By linking learning, work and identity at a range of sites including the home, women's networks and the shop floor, the book addresses some of the normative assumptions about women's positions. It encourages critique of representations of widening participation and the skills agenda that deny their complex implications. Among the challenges related to this is the continuing depoliticisation of women's learning drawn from a narrowed concept of lifelong learning that focuses predominantly on skills. We argue in favour of feminist scholarship in lifelong learning that develops further the politicisation of women's work (Devos 2002) and relates it to women's learning.

The need to reconceptualise global and local, core and periphery, highlights the roles that women play in global economics, sometimes marginalised by techno-muscular capitalism, and in other ways complicit. The lack of feminist attention to neglected sites of women's learning and work that contribute to globalisation can be linked to concerns raised about the western and Anglophone domination of the field of gender and education (Öhrn and Weiner 2009): to address both of these problems an international perspective is needed. This requires engagement with the broad impact of gendered choices, considering these from a position that highlights the inter-relatedness of women's experiences in different countries (Gillard et al. 2007).

New feminist directions in lifelong learning must begin by looking at women's roles in spaces that are not yet imagined and begin to envision women's presence at new sites of learning and work, opening up new identity possibilities. Women's progress in schooling and in higher education is due to the expectations of women themselves: increased gender consciousness in being able to imagine equal participation shows that women's expectations have been a force for social change. In this way, choice could be reclaimed from its neo-liberal configuration. This may open up further possibilities to challenge the political agendas that underpin lifelong learning policies.

Theoretical developments might support such a reconfiguration of choice through further work on the role of imagined domains and how women can contribute to and influence new knowledges (Jensen 2007) that are developed across the areas of articulation discussed above. In this way, new "imaginative geographies" (Massey 1994, p. 2) of lifelong learning may be created. The book makes a case in favour of continued involvement by feminist educationalists with policy to support learning that is life wide, and not job narrow. This means advocating learning programmes that are based on ideas of social justice and on continued engagement with some of the complexities of gendered choices that are highlighted in this book.

References

Apple, M. (2001). Comparing neo-liberal politics and inequality in education. *Comparative Education, 37*(4), 409–423.

Bloom, L. (2009). 'When one person makes it, we all make it': A study of Beyond Welfare, a women-centered community-based organization that helps low-income mothers achieve personal and academic success. *International Journal of Qualitative Studies in Education, 22*(4), 485–503.

Burman, E. (2006). Emotions and reflexivity in feminised education action research. *Educational Action Research, 14,* 315–332.

Devos, A. (2002). Gender, work and workplace learning. In F. Reeve, M. Cartwright, & R. Edwards (Eds.), *Supporting lifelong learning: Vol. 2. Organizing learning* (pp. 51–63). Suffolk: Open University Press.

Faulkner, W. (2004). *Strategies of inclusion: Gender and the Information Society.* European Commission, 5th Framework, Information Society Technologies (IST) Programme, SIGIS, Edinburgh.

Fenwick, T. (2006). Contradictions in portfolio careers: Work design and client relations. *Career Development International, 11*(1), 65–79.

Fenwick, T. (2008). Women's learning in contract work: Practicing contradictions in boundaryless conditions. *Vocations and Learning, 1*(1), 11–26.

Gillard, H., Howcroft, D., Mitev, N., & Richardson, H. (2007). *Missing women: Gender, ICTs and the shaping of the global economy.* CRESC (Centre for Research on Socio-Cultural Change) Working Paper No. 29, CRESC, University of Manchester, Manchester.

Hooghe, M., & Stolle, D. (2003). *Generating social capital: Civil society and institutions in comparative perspective.* Basingstoke: Palgrave McMillan.

Jensen, K. (2007). The desire to learn: An analysis of knowledge-seeking practices among professionals. *Oxford Review of Education, 33*(4), 489–502.

Massey, D. (1994). *Space, place and gender.* Cambridge: Polity.

Massey, D. (1995). *Spatial divisions of labour. Social structures and the geography of production* (2nd ed.). London: MacMillan.

Munro, A., & Rainbird, H. (2002). Job change and workplace learning in the public sector: The significance of new technology for unskilled work. *New Technology, Work and Employment, 17*(3), 224–234.

Nagar, R., Lawson, V., McDowell, L., & Hanson, S. (2002). Locating globalization: Feminist (re) readings of the subjects and spaces of globalization. *Economic Geography, 78,* 257–284.

Öhrn, E., & Weiner, G. (2009). The sound of silence! Reflections on inclusion and exclusion in the field of education and gender. *Gender and Education, 21*(4), 423–430.

Quinn, J. (2003). *Powerful subjects.* Stoke-on-Trent: Trentham.

Quinn, J. (2005). Belonging in a learning community: The reimagined university and imagined social capital. *Studies in the Education of Adults, 37*(1), 4–17.

Thomas, L. (2001). Power, assumptions and prescriptions: A critique of widening participation policy-making. *Higher Education Policy, 14*(4), 361–376.

Index

CPSIA information can be obtained at www.ICGtesting.com

234843LV00004B/6/P